Latin America

Latin America

The Allure and Power of an Idea

MAURICIO TENORIO-TRILLO

The University of Chicago Press
Chicago and London

The University of Chicago Press, Chicago 60637
The University of Chicago Press, Ltd., London
© 2017 by The University of Chicago
Published 2017.
Printed in the United States of America

26 25 24 23 22 21 20 19 18 17   1 2 3 4 5

ISBN-13: 978-0-226-44306-5 (cloth)
ISBN-13: 978-0-226-44323-2 (e-book)

DOI: 10.7208/chicago/9780226443232.001.0001

Library of Congress Cataloging-in-Publication Data

Names: Tenorio-Trillo, Mauricio, 1962– author.
Title: Latin America : the allure and power of an idea / Mauricio
    Tenorio-Trillo.
Description: Chicago : The University of Chicago Press, 2017. | Includes
    bibliographical references and index.
Identifiers: LCCN 2016033494 | ISBN 9780226443065 (cloth : alk. paper) |
    ISBN 9780226443232 (e-book)
Subjects: LCSH: Latin America. | Latin America—Name. | Latin
    America—Civilization.
Classification: LCC F1408 .T29 2017 | DDC 980—dc23 LC record available at
    https://lccn.loc.gov/2016033494

♾ This paper meets the requirements of ANSI/NISO Z39.48-1992
(Permanence of Paper).

This is for la meva Xaparreu, es clar; *and in memory of the late teachers whose voices tuned mine: Frederick P. Bowser, Francisco Galván, Charles A. Hale, Tulio Halperín, Friedrich Katz, Catherine Nelson, and José Luis Piñeyro. And for Ida, Enrique, and Valeria.*

CONTENTS

ACKNOWLEDGMENTS

This book owes a lot to the classroom. I thank the many students in Mexico City, Austin, Chicago, Jerusalem, and Barcelona who over the years assisted me with their inquiries and criticisms. As for books, they have been merely a vice; friends have been the guides in my immersions in many unprescribed stories: from Helena Bomeny and Lúcia Lippi, I learned Brazil; listening to Ana Sofía Cardenal, Núria Font, Mario Pérez Montoro, Víctor Farías Zurita, Josep María Fradera, Juango Romero, Anna Caballé, Apen Ruiz, and Marc Estiarte, I got to know Las Españas; Samuel Amaral, Jorge Myers, Ida Vitale, and Enrique Fierro taught me El Río de la Plata; my early approach to US history owes a lot to James Sidbury, Neil Kamil, Judith Coffin, William Forbath, William Tobin, and Sergio "Atila" Guerrero; and from Fernando Escalante, Jean Meyer, Beatriz Rojas, and Lucía, I learned the rest. Muzaffar Alam, Tomy Agostini, Emilio de Antuñano, Yuna Blajer, Dain Borges, Brodwyn Fischer, Laura Gandolfi, Amos Gewirtz, Luis Fernando Granados, Ramón Gutiérrez, Patrick Iber, Matico Josephson, Emilio Kourí, Tabea Linhard, Pablo Mijangos, Pablo Palomino, Erika Pani, Xavier Pla, Guillermo Rosas, Martha Lilia Tenorio Trillo, and Marco A. Torres assisted me in various and invaluable ways. They all, however, are not to be blamed. They did their best. *De tener, no tengo ni remedio; sí gratitud: mil gracias.*

In which the author briefly introduces the topic and current debates, or an explanation of a death foretold, which never came, as well as of the author's goals in once more returning to the topic

Somos víctimas de una verdadera e insensata obsesión y así de tan manoseada identidad se nos dice, ¡imagínense el disparate!, que es urgente defenderla, que se nos la quiere hurtar, pero sobre todo se nos dice, como si se tratara de un tesoro escondido, "que la gran tarea de politólogos, historiadores e intelectuales latinoamericanos de todos los plumajes consiste en entregarnos a la búsqueda de nuestra identidad". Y así se da el caso de que hasta el secretario de un municipio encaramado en una sierra anda al hallazgo de la identidad de "nuestra" América, porque, eso sí, nunca falta el bendito pronombre posesivo que inviste a quien lo usa de un inequívoco tinte de acendrado patriotismo latinoamericanista. Pero lo grave en esa grita y algaraza es que no sólo hay broma; hay el gato encerrado de un muy serio problema que, perentorio, reclama ahora nuestra atención.

—Edmundo O'Gorman, *"Latinoamérica: Así no,"* Nexos, no. 123 *(March 1988): 13*

The idea of "Latin America" ought to have vanished with the obsolescence of racial theory. Or so I thought years ago.[1] But it is not easy to declare something dead when it can hardly be said to have existed. Then again, neither God nor *égalité* ever truly existed. To be sure, "Latin America" has never designated a geographically or historically tangible reality—at least not with a minimum of empirical and conceptual rigor. Alas, the expression has worked as the title, as the generic name of a well-known plot that is both the autobiography of the term ("Latin America") and the story of a belief that has escaped extinction since its origins as an idea and a project in the 1850s. Nonetheless, as durable as the term has been, it has rarely been a matter of *vulgari eloquentia*. It certainly has undergone a barely endurable intellectual metempsychosis. For the adjective *Latin* in "Latin America" has stored a basic array of racial, historical, and cultural beliefs that have functioned as the elementary syntax with which long-lasting, if messy, *modern* yeses and nos have been phrased—progress and tradition; the machine and the *milpa*; empire and/or nation; *Gemeinschaft* and *Gesellschaft*; race and culture; alienation and authenticity; modern freedom through, or despite, history; identity as personal achievement, as ecstasy, or as a reluctant inevitability.

Thus, the idea of "Latin America" has been used during nearly two centuries to essay these basic yeses and nos in a variety of fashions: Latin, meaning French imperialism vis-à-vis US expansionism; Latin, meaning, in Spanish, an alternative ontology, neither Europe nor the US; Latin, meaning specific obstacles to industrialization or to democracy; Latin, meaning, in Spanish or in English, a Marxist modernizing revolution or an indigenous, post-Marxist, antimodernizing revolution. Leftovers from various explanatory feasts can still be felt in the term. But just as when we unwisely yield to the temptation to debate the existence of God, attempting to prove or disprove the existence of "Latin America" would already be to take part in the plot embodied in the term. But it has never been a real place, a clear civilization, or a well-demarcated and unique culture or group of cultures. Moreover, I believe the term has often obscured more than it has revealed. Throughout this book, therefore, the term Latin America should be taken with a grain of salt—regard it as being always surrounded with what are called "scare quotes."

Like the common Spanish surname Matamoros, which so starkly tells of tragedy, yet passes unnoticed in common Spanish parlance, Latin America is taken for granted, a form of common sense despite its nonexistence and its unpleasant historical connotations. Hence the concept deserves respect. It was capable of incarnating itself as the geographical and cultural assumption of post–World War II theories of modernization, which took for granted the existence of a Latin part of the Americas—traditional, Catholic, patrimonialist, backward, messy, violent—where a new social engineering could be applied. The power of the term lies precisely in its ability to be taken for granted—serving less the supposition of a place, a culture, and a people, and more the need of the other America for a mirror, like the one appealed to in the fairy tale: "Mirror, mirror on the wall, who is the fairest of them all?"

The concept also enchanted Marxist revolutionary utopias to the extent that by the 1970s *la revolución* and *Latinoamérica* were fully synonymous. Then, maybe for the first time, the term became widely used by more than just intellectuals and university students (see chapter 5). Moreover, the latest postcolonial, or "coloniality" approach, the recent liberation, trans, post, alternative modernity kinds of treatment of the term Latin America have been, as it were, a "más me quere [*sic*], más me pega" (The more he loves me, the more he hits me) for the very idea of Latin America. The concept's potential to designate a unique civilization, homogenous in its universal promiscuity and ontologically different from the assumed paradise of mechanism and power, has only been made more alluring by the neo-*indigenista*, postcolonial, alternative episteme kinds of critiques of the idea of Latin America.

Since it is so enduring, it would be foolish to dismiss the influence of the term Latin America as, in Nietzsche's terms, "second nature."[2] No. The term is here to stay, and it is important. What shall we do with it?

G3

The first thing to do is to expose, to enjoy, and to dwell on the irony of the history of the idea of Latin America. Rome was both the *imperium populi Romani*—the adoption of Roman laws and institutions—and the Roman Empire itself, formed by the often violent conquest of vast territories whose inhabitants sometimes resisted and sometimes demanded Latin *urbanitas* and all that Roman culture brought with it. "At the beginning of his fortune," wrote Leopold von Ranke in the 1820s, ". . . Ataüf, King of the Visigoths, conceived the idea of gothicising the Roman world, and making himself the Caesar of all; he would maintain the Roman laws. . . . He later despaired of being able to effect this. . . . Eventually the purple of a Caesar passed to the German houses in the person of Charlemagne. At length these likewise adopted the Roman law. In this combination six great nations were formed—three in which the Latin element predominated—viz., the French, the Spanish, and the Italian; and three in which the Teutonic element was conspicuous, viz., the German, the English, and the Scandinavian." Thus, here we have it, Rome and Latinity, dividing the world; this is an old story, one that was—in a way, still is—what Ranke believed: the division "of our nations into hostile camps upon which all modern history is based." The Crusades spirit "gave birth to colonization." The hate between "Teutonic" and "Latin" races included, according to Ranke, the fear of absorbing Jewish and Moorish features. This is hence the old master plot.[3]

The idea of a Latin part of America was somehow a modern twist on an old imperial idea—a twist that resulted from the clash of the modern nations and empires. The imperial and racial nature of the term has persistently charged it, to a degree that extends beyond the mere peccadillo of its uses during the French Second Empire's attempt to stop the "Anglo-Saxon races" in Mexico. In fact, it is nearly impossible not to voice imperial and racial connotations when articulating the concept of Latin America. To be sure, Napoleon III's *l'Amérique latine* in Mexico failed, but not that other *latinité*: the unification of the Latin people par excellence (Italy). The military alliance among all "Latin nations" of Europe failed, but the racial, cultural, and political assumptions that were embodied in the term *Latin* did not. Historiographically and philologically, Latin America still connotes not only an obvious and durable imperial anti-Anglo-Saxonism, but also echoes of many other cultural, racial, and political imperial projects.[4] There has never been a meaning for Latin America that did not involve conterminously Europe and the Americas. Indeed the opposition of Anglo vs. Latin in the Americas was a peculiar recasting of lasting European dichotomies.

Latin America, to be sure, has meant many things over the nearly two centuries of its odd existence. It has been used and abused culturally or racially by Jacobin liberals and by reactionary Catholics; by monarchists and by republicans; by populist regimes and by Marxist ideologues; by conservative US think tanks and by avant-garde US anthropologists. To extract from the concept's inherent anti-US nature a truly liberal, even liberating democratic and antiracist essence would be the same as to consider, say, Pan-Slavism a real democratic struggle just because it was defined against England and France. Of course, Latin America, like many other raciocultural nineteenth-century ideas, at times was used as a call for social inclusion. And yet, it was so used not as an antiracist but as a racial argument, claiming superiority over other "races," excluding certain groups and often maintaining a strong faith either in an enlightened oligarchy or in impossible forms of direct popular ruling with no need for the ugly games of electoral democracies. *Latin* has been charged with such strong utopian content (a continental union, a spiritual superiority) that when intellectuals and politicians used it, they rarely felt the need to speak of specifics (How can we achieve or improve Latin American democracy? How can we achieve Latin American equality?). Moreover, *Latin* meant always not barbarian, and thus often not black and not Oriental.

What the concept meant initially, for instance, among 1850s Chilean or Colombian intellectuals, varied depending on whether they were in Paris—as was often the case—or in Santiago or Bogota.[5] The 1850s meaning was marked, in America, by the Mexican-American War, and the 1856 US intervention in Nicaragua; in Europe, by the growth of Pan-Slavism, *iberismo*, and Latinism resulting from the post-1848 reconstruction of empires. Thus Latin America began then to be used as a form of antibarbarism (the barbarous being US individualism and materialism, or Eastern European Jewish and backward enclaves, or Russian-sponsored Pan-Slavism). The term also began to imply unity of a natural spirit (the Latin), that entelechy at times articulated with romantic eloquence and at times considered simply a racial (scientific) fact. Hence the idea of Latin America became a synthesis of enduring languages: that old one of civilization (Rome) vs. the rest; of Catholic Spain vs. its countless enemies; the one used in France to oppose Russian imperialism, defining Eastern Europeans as barbarians in need of civilization; and that of *iberismo*, understood as unity in diversity of peoples belonging to a common God and spirit—alas, with diverse sovereignties.

In 1850s Paris, one of the first proponents of the term Latin America, Chilean Francisco Bilbao (1823–1865), advanced the concept (mostly referring to South America) as a direct echo of French anti-Pan-Slavism. For Latin America, as an idea, was born simultaneously as an enchanting grand perspective but also as a challenging earthly reality whose specificity has been hard to demarcate. For Bilbao—a Mason, a radical exponent of a Catholic social agenda (friend, follower, and translator of the controversial French Catholic thinker and friend of Auguste Comte, H. F. R. de Lamennais)—the Mexican-American War and US intervention in Nicaragua made indispensable the need to contest "Yankee" individualism—which, he believed, had expanded in the same way that "Pan-Slavic servitude" had conquered Eastern Europe. From a clear-cut grand perspective, Russia appeared to Bilbao as "la barbarie absolutista" (absolutist barbarism), and the United States was "barbarie demagógica" (demagogic barbarism). In terms of specificity, however, the picture blurs. Bilbao's guide, Lamennais (1783–1854), had developed a democratic ecumenism by considering all religions equal but Christianity the universal tradition and the voice of the masses. Bilbao's ecumenism was as utopian but not as egalitarian. He was adamant about the exclusion of Brazil and Paraguay from his notion of Latin America. "We do not include Paraguay and Brazil," he argued sustaining unity for South America (*La América en peligro*, 1862), because "we don't deem them worthy to be part of the struggle's front line." After all, Brazil was then a slave society and an imperial monarchy: "An Empire rises and gets wealthier over tears," he said of Brazil.[6]

Therefore, the early proponents of the term Latin America, like Bilbao, had no clear geography for Latin America; it meant in fact South America but without Brazil and Paraguay. Not even Mexico was truly included in

Bilbao's early use of the term Latin America. For him, Mexico lacked a real republican consciousness, precisely because of its complicated relationship with the United States. In Mexico, he observed, "the opposition against the U.S. is a hate that also encompasses the republican spirit of its own neighbor, which in turn Mexico cannot understand, for Mexico comes from very different principles and antecedents. In the resulting confusion, we see doubt emerging out of lack of beliefs, caudillos resulting from the lack of principles, and hence overall selfishness. Where is unity in Mexico's nationality?"[7]

As a grand perspective, the original idea of Latin America could breath freely the oxygen of many large American and European debates. In specific terms, though, it always was an unresolved enigma. Therefore, when speaking in general terms, Latin America became, for Bilbao and other early advocates of the term, the incarnation of the durable nineteenth-century Romantic traditionalism that still resonates today: the Bilbao Law, as it were—we, the "Latins," said Bilbao summarily in the 1850s, though he could be speaking of Latin America today, "have not lost the tradition of human destiny's spirituality. We believe in, and love, everything that unites; we prefer the social over the individual, beauty over wealth, justice over power, art over commerce, poetry over industry, philosophy over texts, absolute spirit over calculations, duty over interest." If the name Latin America has had a lasting sense, this is it: the Bilbao Law.[8]

Indeed, Bilbao, the early proponent of Latin America, synthesized the clichés and truths that still resonate in the term. But he also, as did very few—maybe only the Cuban José Martí (1853–1895) in the late nineteenth century—distanced himself from what the term would overwhelmingly connote in the long run. For he advocated, on the basis of his radical version of social Catholicism, a kind of social inclusion that the term Latin America would only regain, at least ideally, in the second part of the twentieth century: "The Black, the Indians, the deprived, the hopeless, the weak, find in us the respect owed to the title and dignity of human being."[9]

This meaning was redefined by the momentous French intervention in Mexico in the 1860s. Then there were two Latin Americas: one sponsored by old republican champions of an anti-US Latin American unity (mostly meaning southern Spanish American, excluding Brazil), and the new Latin America championed by the monarchical and French-sponsored anti-Anglo-Saxonism centered in Mexico. The enemies of the latter were not only liberal republicans like Benito Juárez but also the Lincoln administration. Thus the Latin America of the old South American republicans became, if momentarily, supportive of the United States. In the 1862

Congress of the Sociedad de la Unión Americana, in Santiago, Chile, the 1850s proponents of Latin America rejected the French-sponsored Latin America by making their idea of Latin America akin to a sort of early Pan-Americanism. They even reevaluated the Monroe Doctrine as an American (Pan-American) defensive policy against European powers—as did such contemporary intellectuals as J. M. Torres Caicedo and Justo Arosemena, and such later figures as Brazilians Manuel de Oliveira Lima and J. M. Machado de Assis, although they rejected any sense of unity with Spanish America. Therefore, in the 1860s, Lincoln's United States was considered radically different from the pre–Civil War United States. The US envoy at the 1862 Santiago Congress, Mr. Mackie, was warmly welcomed, and his words directly addressed 1850s Latin Americanism by referring to the 1856 US involvement in Nicaragua as an action of the "wrong" United States: "Walker's filibusters, added Mr. Mackie, were the same who today are rebels [the Confederates]."[10] In turn, in the 1860s struggles of semantics over the expression Latin America, Brazil excluded itself ambivalently, supporting Maximilian but rejecting a French-led Latin America, and above all fearing the radical measures taken by the Lincoln administration over the course of the war regarding slavery and citizenship for former slaves. And the term kept changing.

Just after the defeat of Maximilian's empire in Mexico, a group of US and South American intellectuals launched, as it were, an anti–Latin American publication from New York: *Ambas Américas: Revista de educación, bibliografía y agricultura* (1867–68). Domingo Faustino Sarmiento, then one of the most prominent writers in Spanish of America, launched the publication. His travels in the United States and the context of educational and agricultural transformation during Reconstruction had convinced him of a less Latin and more *Ambas Américas* route for the continent. It was a journal intended as a forum where US and Spanish American intellectuals could interact, especially in terms of practical educational and agricultural ideas. The effort lasted for two years, translating and criticizing education policies throughout the continent. It was not an *iberista* or pro-*latinité* proposal, but it was rooted in a well-established South American liberalism and sponsored by progressive US educators and Hispanists. Sarmiento counted on the input of Mary Mann (Mary Tayler Peabody), the widow of the prominent Massachusetts politician and educator Horace Mann; she was the translator of Sarmiento's *Facundo* into English. Sarmiento also had the support of the Boston Hispanist elite (George Ticknor, especially).

The magazine did not refer to Latin America or to any notion of continental union or common spirit—neither was there mention of Pan-

Americanism. It was simply the recognition that the United States was the educational, industrial, and agricultural model to follow, which needed to be known in the rest of the continent. And it was also a call for the US intelligentsia to recognize the intelligence of the other America. It did not last, but it was one of the many projects in the midst of those advanced by Spanish American intellectuals in Paris and South America. In 1872, Ramón Páez—son of Venezuela's hero of independence and longtime caudillo, José Antonio Páez—continued this trend with *Ambas Américas: Contrastes* (1872). A writer and painter, Ramón Páez had been partly educated in England, and was then living in New York. He was a convinced believer in the US educational revolution, which was the path to follow by the "*morohispánica*" (not Latin) America, including such an un-Latin thing as women's education. All these efforts certainly sounded, both then and now, un–Latin American.[11]

But over the nineteenth and early twentieth centuries, other periodicals, in French and Spanish, supported one or another Latin Americanism through literary Hispanism or through senses of *iberismo*. For instance, there were the prominent philological journals, such as the *Revue Hispanique* (1894–1933) and the *Revue des Langues Romanes* (started in 1870), devoted to all the Iberian languages, which included a lot about the American world. There were also the *Revue de l'Amérique latine* (1922–1932), sustained by the prominent French Hispanist Ernest Martinenche; the *Bulletin de l'Amérique latine* (1911–1921), published by the Sorbonne; and *L'Amérique latine* (1923–1940s), a fusion of various journals devoted to America and Brazil. There were also the Argentinean periodical *Nuestra América* (1918–1926), edited by E. Stefanini, and the *Unión Ibero-Americana* (1885–1926), a successor to the *Revista de las Españas*, published in Madrid. In Brazil, the *Revista Americana* (1909–1919), a diplomatic endeavor launched by the Barão de Rio Branco, sought a certain cultural rapprochement with both the United States and South America. In such a way, by the mid-twentieth century the idea of Latin America had gained some institutional intellectual existence (see chapter 2).[12]

All in all, by the 1890s Latin America had lost its strong French connotations and had won emphatic senses of spiritual superiority through *hispanidad* or *iberismo*. By the early twentieth century, racial theory was more important to the concept than either any form of republicanism or the early twentieth-century philological and cultural arguments that sustained, for instance, *iberismo*. The violence consubstantial to the concept—as encounter of civilization vs. *barbarie*, spirit vs. matter, or as clashes of antagonist cultures, religions, and empires—also kept changing. As was the case with

Ranke, for Bilbao, both the Anglo-Saxons and the Latin Americans were in a state of perpetual violence with each other, upholding a cosmic order that could exist only by preserving the equilibrium: "America, in its two-fold nature as Saxon and Latin, witnesses not the contradictions of ideas, as in Europe, but the exclusivity of ideas. America has crippled harmony. Harmony is individualism and sociability. The North embodies individualism; the South, sociability. The Saxon-Yankee is Protestant and federal; the Spanish American is Catholic and a centralizer; . . . the Yankee is the centrifugal force; the American from the South is the centripetal force. Both are necessary for order to exist." By the 1970s, the idea of Latin America, still expressing its "spiritual" and racial connotations, had transformed the Bilbao-like violent equilibrium into a morally sanctioned call for revolution. Latin America was then, in the words of Eduardo Galeano, "the region of the open veins," which had been the eternal victim of Europe and the United States—the *"proxenetas de la desdicha"* (procurers of misery).[13]

The concept of Latin America, however, has been deeply rooted in profound European and American ways of knowing. Thus, once it was articulated, it kept reinforcing enduring social and intellectual explanations while gradually eliminating old connotations or adding new meanings. These added meanings lasted or not, depending both on specific circumstances and on their harmony or disharmony with the enduring commonplaces so eloquently evoked, as it were, by the Bilbao Law.

ଔ

Within its European roots, the idea of Latin America belonged to one of the many related cultural and political reformulations that since the late eighteenth century sought to redefine imperial contours. The simultaneity in the articulation and actions of these various reformulations made each one what it was or is—there were both large-scale projects (such as Pan-Slavism, Pan-Germanism, or *iberismo*) and smaller ones, such as the many forms of "imperial nationalisms" (Provençal, Catalan, Portuguese, Hispanic, Mexican, Brazilian, French, or Italian). In the 1860s French sense, *l'Amérique latine* meant anti-Anglo-Saxonism—and still does—after a racial fashion. But it also implied Catholic antimodernism, anti-Semitism, and anti-Protestantism—which were also somehow present in, say, early twentieth-century Mexican, Catalan, French, and Spanish nationalisms.

The United States, as the Comte de Gobineau maintained, was "infected by all the corrosive fruits of modernity." And all sorts of Latins echoed this basic notion, with or without reference to the United States (or England); with either self-pride in authentic Latin institutions and "spirit," or with self-critical revulsion at the historical burden of Latinity. Alfonso de Maia—the embodiment of Iberian values, a character in the late nineteenth-century Portuguese masterpiece *Os Maias* (J. M. Eça de Queirós)—phrased his simultaneous dislike of both US individualism and the modernizing attempts of the Portuguese Empire: "to politicians–'less liberalism and more character'; to men of letters–'less eloquence and more ideas'; to citizens at large–'less progress and more ethics.'" In the 1930s, in Argentina, the influential Spanish ideologue of *hispanidad*, Ramiro de Maeztu, defended not *liberté, égalité et fraternité* but *"servicio, jerarquía y hermandad"* (service, hierarchy, and brotherhood). In the same decade, an "oriental Latin," as he then called himself, Mircea Eliade, saw the Salazar regime in Portugal as the natural result of the exhaustion of nineteenth-century, non-Latin *"demoliberalismo."* For Eliade, António de Oliveira Salazar was the true spiritual renovation of *"latinidad."* And in the 1990s, in English, distinguished scholar Ilan Stavans unveiled, as if for the first time, the Quixote-like condition of Latinos in the United States: their inability to distinguish between reality and dreams.[14] Indeed, the adjective "Latin" has implied antimodernism, which in turn implied strong authority, distrust of full liberty, spirit over matter, subjectivity over objectivity, and distrust of individualism (corporate and spiritual goals over individual passions and interests)—that is, the Bilbao Law.

Throughout the nineteenth century, the meanings of Latin America were part of debates over *iberismo* and *latinité*. As an ingredient in these debates, Latin America was a conservative idea by birth, a dream not only of the unity of a supposed race, but also of all the enemies of individualism, democracy, and modernization. In Second Empire France, advocates of a Latin empire toyed with the idea of supporting the Confederate states in the US Civil War—emphasizing in *latinité* its love of order, of local autonomy and tradition (as in the defenses of *latinité* in the South of France in the 1850s). If, as John Phelan argued in the 1960s, Napoleon III's Saint-Simonian Minister, Michel Chevalier, was the mastermind of the idea of *l'Amérique latine* during the 1860s French intervention in Mexico, it was because Chevalier's 1830s trip to the United States had fostered in him both respect and fear for the United States through reactionary notions of *latinité*. In his report from his 1839 trip to the United States, he confirmed that France was better fitted than Austria, Prussia, England, or the United States to reestablish order in Spanish America. France "has a physiognomy more strongly marked, a mission more clearly defined, and above all, she has more of the social spirit. She is at the head of the Latin group; she is its protectress." For, "in the events which seem about to dawn upon us, France may, then, take a most important share. . . . She alone can save the whole [Latin] family from being swallowed up by a double flood of Slavonians and Germans." And yet, by the 1860s, *latinité* seemed to Chevalier to be compatible with France's recognition of the Confederate states. "The recognition of the Southern States will be the consequences of our intervention [in Mexico]," wrote Chevalier in 1861. The North planned to make, he argued, "the negro food for powder," but France's notion "of philanthropy and our moral sense alike revolt from these ferocious exaggerations of the love of liberty." Slavery was not a problem for recognition of the South: "France will use her influence to secure the gradual emancipation of the slaves without making slavery a ground for refusing recognition."[15]

In turn, Mexican liberals were allies of the "Black president," Abraham Lincoln against the Latin empire. And understandably so. For the antimoderns, the French Mexican adventure was the Crimean War all over again: the Russian role was played by the United States; the role of Turkey went to Mexico, which was to be defended from itself by a European Latin power, thus establishing a Latin kingdom. And yet, before, in the early 1850s, the idea of Latin America as a dream of unity in South America—in such thinkers as Colombian (Panamanian) Justo Arosemena or Bilbao—was a liberal reaction to US policies in Central America. But it was then also a statement against individualism, Protestantism, mechanization, and materialism. Moreover, this early use of the term also involved a sort of exorcism: Latin America meant the liberal un-Latinizing of illiberal Spanish America, the end of decades of unbound reactionary passions and *caudillismo*. In 1864 Lima, in another congress calling for the unity of Spanish America, Arosemena put it clearly: "If there are fraternity and love among the American peoples, the Congress is hardly necessary; if there are not, the Congress is hardly possible." And thus he pointed to the need to exorcize the idea of Latin America before the real Latin America could exist: "The Spanish race of America has the selfishness of the Conquistador, the distrust of the Indian, and the pride of the old Castilian. Thus its vices and some virtues."[16] By the mid-twentieth century, no one using the term Latin America dreamed of a Latin anti-Slavic kingdom or of exorcizing the vices of the Spanish American race from Latin America. But the term did mean a defense of tradition and some form of spiritual superiority over the materialistic Protestant world.

The history of the term's antidemocratic and antiliberal connotations is convoluted. To be sure, the term has always included a populist call for the authentic people—whether the Latin race; or the Portuguese- and Spanish-speaking peoples; or the proudly hybrid, mythological, Catholic race of America; or the anti-imperialist proletariat of the tropics—to unite, resist, or emerge. Moreover, Bilbao, in a way, could be considered the early promoter of the idea of Latin America as a democratic, all-inclusive polity, and José Martí as a late nineteenth-century example of the same. The problem is that Bilbao's idea of Latin America did not include what today is seen as Latin America—not Brazil, not Paraguay, and not really Mexico—and did not accept any sense of practicality in democratic representation. He rejected any form of parliamentary and delegated representation, and thus advocated a sort of direct and constant self-representation in a Catholic community (*El evanjelio americano*, 1864).[17]

Another early liberal advocator of a Latin American union, Justo Arosemena, supported full citizenship for all, regardless of race, in a hypothetical Latin American union, but he was clear that this was hardly attainable through democratic means: "A large nationality constituted by disperse elements, as homogenous as they might be, requires a very powerful domination, an irresistible imperative, so much so that, if not for Bolívar, San Martín, or Iturbide, I cannot see how that nationality could have existed. Those who dream of this gigantic construction [a South American union] think of treaties and pacts among peoples, and forget that such transactions are unknown in history because they go against the nature of things." For him, Rousseau's social contract had "*desbordado la democracia*" (overflowed democracy), and Hobbes had "*engreído el despotismo*" (made despotism conceited). For Arosemena, Anglo-Saxons were better than Latins, for in them the "*principio de razas*" (race principle; i.e., racial superiority) had "*cumplida aplicación*" (had been fully applied): "In the Anglo-Saxon race, passion does not prevail over reason, as it does in the Hispanic race." Anglo-Saxon America had the climate and the predisposition to attract European immigration, "whose mixture improves the original population in political, moral, and industrial respects."[18] Hence, Latin America, for these early proponents of the term, was far from a fully democratic and antiracist idea. For it was an idea of its times, no less, no more.

In turn, José Martí's democratic creed derived from his own experience of the United States—its Civil War, its large African American struggle, and its assimilation of immigrants, including Chinese.[19] But he did not live long enough for us to see what his democracy for Cuba would have entailed. Yet his 1877–78 support of Guatemalan dictator Justo Rufino Barrios cannot be read as a doctrine of democratic development for "Nuestra América." Martí lived in Guatemala during those years—the years of his love for María, "La niña de Guatemala" of his poem—and became close to Barrios and his intellectual allies, who supported a liberal authoritarian modernization of Guatemala. Barrios himself supported Cuban independence. But Martí's views of the Barrios modernization and of the vast Indian population in Guatemala are not very different from those expressed by "bad" liberals such as Justo Sierra or Barrios himself: Indians would overcome their atavism, laziness, and backwardness through education, becoming liberal citizens.[20] The truth is that Martí's "Latin America" was in fact something else: "Nuestra América," meaning a modern, liberal, if not fully democratic, modernizing utopia, including the US experience, which was Martí's.

I believe that in very few historical moments, and only very recently, has the term Latin America designated a struggle for liberal democracy—maybe only in the "Latin" undertones of the Portuguese and Spanish (and then Brazilian, Argentinean, Chilean, Uruguayan, and even Mexican) transitions to democracy, starting in 1974 with Portugal's Carnation Revolution. By the early twenty-first century, however, Latin America, spoken in English, has returned to populist ideas of indigenous power and spiritual and moral superiority vis-à-vis an imaginary West. In Spanish, the term regained its populist, antiliberal connotations in, for instance, the Venezuela-led "Bolivarian revolution" and among its admirers in the United States.

More irony: Washington Irving's views of Spain, together with European *iberismo* and *latinité*, were echoed by late nineteenth-century US *hispanismo*, only to later become the patrimony of precisely what US Hispanism was not supposed to be from the very beginning: "Latino Studies." That is, *l'Amérique latine* became the equally imperial but now US-based and lasting term "Latin America" (in English), which was articulated as the non–United States or as the United States that somehow was, and is, not really the United States—Latino, Latina: the racio-cultural cluster of things that were assumed to be the authentic realm of a large part of the US population. Now, in the twenty-first century, all of them, on either side of the southern US border, are Latins, as Napoleon III would have had it—millions of them US citizens but somehow exoticized as different, as belonging to another cultural ontology, mythically linked to a nonexistent Atlantis: "Latin America." The identity politics that has sanctioned Latinos in the United States electorally and commercially has not brought obsolescence to the term Latin America; rather, it has furnished the ethereal concept with a very material political and commercial market (see chapter 4).

CR

In terms of legal infrastructure, the expression Latin America has meant very little, despite either the various nineteenth-century legal unification attempts or the academic and diplomatic presence of the term in English or French. The few instances in which the region known as Latin America acquired as a whole some legal infrastructure were when it was included in the International Bureau of the American Republics, later the Pan-American Union, and later the Organization of American States. These organizations, however, were meant precisely to dissolve the "Latin" unity within a Western hemisphere unity commanded by the United States. They incorporated the US, English- and French-speaking Caribbean, and Canada. The lasting expression of this Pan-Americanism was its building (1911), designed by Albert Kelsey and French architect Paul P. Cret, and erected in Washington, DC, bordering the Washington Mall. The building embodied commercial and cultural features of decades of US attempts at hemispheric union: from Washington Irving–like views of Spain to US interests in the continent's natural resources; from fascination with Maya and Aztec archaeology to the stereotype of a patio inspired by Catalan and Mexican architectures. Two sculptural groups representing the North and South Americas, each composed of a maternal figure and a boy, still guard the entrance of the building. Their significance was explained in 1911 by the director of the Pan-American Union: "In the North American group the boy, strikingly alert in feature and action, expresses the more energetic spirit of the fully awakened North. The figure of 'South America,' while young and strong, has a softer and more sensuous quality, expressive of tropical ease and luxuriance. . . . [The boy] conveys a sense of great future possibilities of which he is not yet conscious." Good or bad, this is the history of the Latin regions acting institutionally together in world affairs, and the Pan-American view of the "luxuriance" of the South was not very different from that of twentieth-century Latin Americanism.[21]

The institution "Latin America," unlike the institution "Europe" in the last five decades, has meant very little compared with such powerful documents as Mexican, Brazilian, or Peruvian passports. To be sure, late eighteenth-century "criollo patriotisms" and early nineteenth-century "Americanisms" were important political and intellectual tools for imagining both a new world made of modern nation-states and a continental group of newcomers. The 1850s notions of Latin America included these connotations. Moreover, the term Latin America has acquired important symbolic connotations during the twentieth century, beyond those of intellectuals. But its political and economic importance pales vis-à-vis not only a national citizenship but also "natural" multi-citizenships: Mexican and American for Mexico; Italian, Spanish, and Israeli for Argentina and Uruguay; black, Portuguese, Italian, and Spanish for Brazil; black, French, Spanish, and English for many parts of the Caribbean.

Latin America thus connotes a feeling that is hard to measure and difficult to interpret. In the few recent surveys that actually ask about self-identification in different Spanish-speaking countries (with such options as Latin American, Caribbean, North American, South American, Central American, citizen of the world. . . .), the results show no Latin American pattern. Mexico, for instance, the only country for which data differentiate between the general population and the leaders, turns out to have more ordinary citizens than leaders who self-identified as Latin American. But the "popular" Latin American feeling seems to be in decline in Mexico: in 2006, 62% self-identified as Latin American, while 50% did so in 2012, and 43.5% in 2014. Mexico's leaders, however, felt less Latin American, but their feeling shows growth: in 2006, 49% of the sampled leaders self-identified as Latin American; in 2012, 51% did so. In Colombia, 43% self-identified as Latin American in 2008; 51% in 2012, and 59% in 2014. In Ecuador, 41% did so in 2010, 50% in 2012, and 53.4% in 2014; in Peru, 25% in 2008, 34% in 2010, and 38% in 2014; and in Chile, in 2008 only 31% self-identified as Latin American (almost equivalent to the 27% of Mexicans who in 2012 identified themselves as "citizens of the world"). Mexico has been at the core of the meaning of Latin America as it is projected to the world, mainly due to its long coexistence with the United States. Thus the Latin American identification seems important in Mexico, as if, being so close and so entangled with the United States, self-identifying as Latin American helps to maintain one's own Mexicanness. Brazil, on the other hand, is a very different story: in 2014 3.7% of interviewed Brazilians identified as Latin American, 13.5% as citizens of the world, and 79.4% as Brazilians. In any case the term clearly has some symbolic power in the region, but it can hardly be said to denote a real institution or a homogenous symbolic identity of the people south of Nogales, Sonora[22] (see chapter 6).

CR

Over the last decades, especially in Spanish and Portuguese, there have been several criticisms of the very utility of the term Latin America.[23] Prominent writers of my generation, such as Jorge Volpi, have appointed themselves the post–Latin American writers who do not deal with Latin

American landscapes: the first true cosmopolitans in our poor valleys of Comalas (Juan Rulfo), tropical Pasagardas (Manuel Bandeira), and Macondos (Gabriel García Márquez). Thus Volpi announced the end of Latin America, or at least of the Latin American writer, and unveiled the painful truth once again, as if for the first time: Latin America does not exist. Oh, really? What intellectual, writing in Spanish, or Portuguese, or Nahuatl in the nineteenth or twenty-first century, is not cosmopolitan, is not both more and less than Latin American? Another Mexican writer, Juan Villoro, as a young pupil in the 1960s at Mexico City's *Deutsche Schule*, discovered the advantages of satisfying his teachers' exoticist desires by assuming his own non-Westernness, his Latin Americanness. But as an accomplished writer in the twenty-first century, he saw it clearly: "La única patria verdadera se asume sin posar para la mirada ajena" (The only real fatherland is adopted without posing for the foreign gaze). And yet, the current success of writers like Volpi in the monopolistic, Spanish-speaking literary market is nothing more than the merchandizing of an old notion and a familiar position, that of the Latin American writer—a position that young writers assume profitably, if not happily, if they want to gain fame in Barcelona or New York.[24]

Moreover, in 2014 even the late Eduardo Galeano—the author of the old Latin Americanist manifesto (still a best seller in English translation), *The Open Veins of Latin America* (1971)—changed his mind. The "open veins," he said, were not a metaphor—it was suicide: "I wouldn't be capable of reading this book again," he said at a Brazilian book fair, "I'd keel over. For me, this prose of the traditional left is extremely leaden, and my physique can't tolerate it." But of course his American editor (at Monthly Review Press) disagreed. "Please! The book is an entity independent of the writer and anything he might think now," argued the editor of Galeano's best seller in English—though a Brazilian critic considered that Galeano "should feel really guilty for the damage he caused."[25]

The recent success of Roberto Bolaño's novels in English seems to have redefined the understanding of Latin American literature in the United States, beyond the so-called magical realism of the 1960s and 1970s boom. Bolaño was indeed a unique and complicated character, difficult to portray as an embodiment of Latin America. Yet the texture of language games that display the absurdity and irony of a Latin American identity in *Los detectives salvajes* (1998) is hard to translate into English. Who cares about this absurdity and irony in English? Instead, in English, Bolaño has been molded into a new figure of Latin America, the world of his works, as Sarah Pollack has argued, "recast this time in visceral realist but equally exotic terms as a space safeguarding the adolescent idealism of the 70s, ripe with sexy, savage, Che Guevara-esque adventurers of uncompromising artistic and existential rebellions, an argument since echoed by Horacio Castellanos Moya and Jorge Volpi, among others."[26] The question is, What is new about this? Success in English for a writer of Spanish in America still requires formatting by the lasting meanings of Latin America.

Also, it has become a cliché of certain conservative, Spanish-speaking intellectuals—from the 1976 liberal criticism by Carlos Rangel of the idea of Latin America to those by Álvaro Vargas Llosa—to mock the Latin American condition, which is a rather easy target. Yet the politics of some of these criticisms is so radically conservative that they have achieved little resonance in larger intellectual or academic circles, whether in Spanish or English. Besides, their own anti-Latinism backfires: some of them are the star Latino intellectuals of mainstream Miami or New York.[27]

More telling is the recent Brazilian anti–Latin Americanism that seeks to expose the nonsense of the term Latin America, as in Leandro Narloch and Duda Teixeira's *Guia politicamente incorreto da América Latina* (2011). To be sure, this is an old crusade, in which Brazil distinguishes itself from the rest of the continent—a task skillfully performed in the 1820s by José Bonifácio and by Joaquim Nabuco and Eduardo Prado in the 1890s (see chapter 3). Of course, there was also an eloquent, if small, Brazilian pro–Latin Americanism, more a form of self-criticism than of love for Latin America, better expressed in Sérgio Buarque de Holanda's self-criticism of the Portuguese colonization of Brazil vis-à-vis Spain's colonization of Mexico and Peru; or in Manuel Bandeira's ironic "Rondó dos cavalinhos" (1920s): "Os cavalinhos correndo,/ E nós, cavalões, comendo . . . / Alfonso Reyes partindo,/ E tanta gente ficando . . ." (The little horses running / and we, big horses, eating . . . / Alfonso Reyes is leaving / and so many others staying).[28] This is thus an old story. But Leandro Narloch and Duda Teixeira use humor to mock what they see as intrinsic to the idea of Latin America: constant lamentation, the making of all local expressions into a form of cultural resistance, the love of violence. They do this by addressing Latin American icons such as Che Guevara, Simón Bolívar, Francisco Villa, or Salvador Allende: "The more nonsense [*bobagens*] they [the heroes] talk, the more they sabotage their own countries, the more monuments and T-shirts will be produced to honor them."[29] But in fact Brazil's increasing global relevance is bringing about the obsolescence of the term Latin America much more effectively than any book or critic . . . at least for Brazil. Former Brazilian president Luiz Inácio Lula da Silva at times made geostrategic use of Latin America—showing solidarity with Evo Morales's Bolivia or Hugo Chávez's

Venezuela. But that was only one, and not the most important, geostrategy used by Lula; it paled vis-à-vis his playing the BRIC (Brazil, Russia, India, China) or the Luso-Africa-America cards.[30]

The best analysis in Spanish—and for that matter in any language—of the origins and challenges of the term Latin America is by Miguel Rojas Mix (1991).[31] This was indeed a full anatomy of the term, a serious criticism of its imperial and racial connotations. Rojas Mix's account included a robust reading of the early 1850s Chilean, Colombian, and Venezuelan advocators of a defensive union of republics (always excluding Brazil) against, first, the United States, and then Europe itself. Rojas Mix, moreover, covered with erudition and parsimony, as very few had done, the telling challenges to the idea of Latin America advanced by *indianismo* and Afro-Americanism. He showed that the former, in its post-1970s radical version (Fausto Reinaga, Guillermo Bonfil Batalla), if fully followed, would obliterate the idea of a Latin or any other America other than a pre-America—a region returned to indigenous people who would have remained, one might assume, immune to any change, endlessly the same.

On the other hand, Afro-Americanism, in Rojas Mix's view, was the confirmation of the anti-black consensus of most of the European and American sponsors of the idea of Latin America—with few exceptions. As Rojas Mix showed, from Torres Caicedo to Catholic José Vasconcelos or radical José Carlos Mariátegui, Latin meant not black. In Mariátegui's Inca socialism of the 1920s, blacks were still seen, as Rojas Mix showed, mostly as a source of "sensuality, superstition, and primitivism"—an "obstacle made of barbarism." In the same way, César Vallejo, the great Peruvian poet, while living in 1920s Paris, wondered and affirmed too much simultaneously: "Europe can ignore the Africans, the Australians, but us [Latin Americans]?"[32] Nevertheless, Afro-Americanism, Rojas Mix argued, was an important literary trend that began to radicalize in the 1970s through the influence of Franz Fanon's writings (and, one should add, of the African American civil rights struggle, and of the decolonization of Africa). Rojas Mix's account was conceived in the context of the bitter debates around the fifth centennial of Europe in America (1992). At that time, the literature on "Afro-Latin America" had not yet reached the productive stage of the last two decades. But "Afro-Latin America" is an idea that, as an academic trend and as a social movement, is also disintegrating the very concept of Latin America, either in the name of an Afro-American large experience (including above all the United States and Africa) or in the name of important national agendas: Afro-Colombian or Afro-Brazilian rights and struggles. The idea of Latin America is a rather odd complement to these struggles.

Rojas Mix, however, also made a strong defense of what he believed to be the "socialist and libertarian" connotations in the works of some early advocators of the idea of Latin America—especially Bilbao (1850s) and Martí (1890s). As he put it, somewhat bombastically, "Bilbao not only preceded other thinkers in the use of the term 'Latin America,' but he is also the precursor of the meaning the concept would later acquire in the Latin American lefts. In Bilbao, the concept is framed within an anticolonial and anti-imperial thought, within a project of a socialist society." Thus, not surprisingly, at the end Rojas Mix made a call to save the idea of Latin America; such a union was for him, in 1991, not utopia but urgency. But it was one based not on the archaeology of utopian versions of the term, but in an identity yet to be realized, inspired in the future. "Latin America," he argued, could not be a choice of the Hispanic, the Afro, the Indian, or the "usaica" identity; it would be a "we" still in the making that nevertheless— O magic of Latin America!—already included the we: "It is not through pike and hoe that we are to find it [Latin American identity]. It is a creative problem. . . . It is the materialization of a project that will go on selecting its own past. Latin American identity will be what we do with it, and that is why its roots are in the future."[33] I myself share and applaud the conclusion—identity as a constant making, finding roots in the future. Yet, I do not see why it has to be coped by such strong dictum as "Latin America."

◌ℜ

In Spanish and Portuguese, art historians and critics have done much to mock the "*neurosis identitaria*" (Gerardo Mosquera) implied in the concept of "Latin American art."[34] In the 1940s and 1950s what was known as the Mexican artistic renaissance was canonized as quintessential Latin American art by world collectors and critics—through various prominent exhibitions of Mexican art in the United States and Europe and, not least, through various US commissions granted to the holy trinity of Mexican painters (Rivera, Orozco, and Siqueiros). The customer is always right, and thus post-revolutionary Mexican regimes became the generous primary patron of this art, which was marketed as the final return to an authentic, popular, and ethnically proud Mexico. Hence, despite the artistic boom in Buenos Aires or São Paulo (starting in the 1920s), Latin American art in the world came to be seen mostly through Mexico-centric eyes. São Paulo's momentous artistic modernism and Buenos Aires's avant-gardism of the 1920s did not seek a Rivera-like ethnic and nationalist art. Of course, Mexican revolutionary art was somehow part of Paulista and Porteño experiments, as were the many world vanguards that fed both the Mexican artistic renaissance and São Paulo's modernism. São Paulo and Buenos Aires, however, did not have the appeal of a revolution in a revolutionary era; moreover, they could not count on a lasting connection to US cultural markets and desires that projected Mexican revolutionary art to the world. Brazilian modernism's accent was on radical avant-gardism; Rivera sought political radicalism by taming his own twenty years of Parisian artistic avant-gardism. Mexico was sexier for world artistic taste in the 1930s; it seemed too exotic and ethnically radical vis-à-vis the less exotic, though radical, vanguard experiments of either São Paulo or Buenos Aires. As the 1920s Peruvian intellectual Antenor Orrego put it, commenting on the possibility of a truly new American art, "Mexico represents Europe's lack of understanding of America, that is, of what is uniquely American. Argentina represents America's understanding of Europe, that is, of what is sublimely European."[35] Thus, if art had to "un-frog" itself from its European spell, Mexico was the elixir to drink.

Starting in the 1970s, the mere possibility of a Latin American art was deeply contested. Post-1945 Argentine, Mexican, or Brazilian artists often aggressively vetoed the idea of a Latin American art. In one of the various symposia on the matter from the 1960s to the 1990s, Argentinean painter Ernesto Deira maintained, "Latin America does not exist as such. . . . If Latin America does not exist as a concept, how could one ask for something characteristic of its art?" But US and European critics defended the existence of Latin American art—often with Mexico-centric eyes. And they did so at various points on the grounds of commonality in resistance and oppression, based on the suffering of the two conquests (Shifra M. Goldman)—the Spanish and the US conquests—or on the belief in a sublime collective and anti-individualist spiritualism. All of these arguments, to be sure, were mere echoes of the idea of Latin America. "The concern for human values constitutes perhaps the most cohesive force throughout Latin America," wrote the leading US art historian of Latin America, Jacqueline Barnitz, in the 1960s. "Because of it there exists a sort of ideological consistency far greater than among North American artists who are still trying to reconcile what little individuality remains with the overpowering spokes of the industrial wheel." This is Latin American business as usual.[36]

The debates over the possibilities of Latin American art in the 1960s and 1970s displayed a common dilemma in the arts and literature. On the one hand, there was the clear de-Latin-Americanizing aspiration of artists in Mexico City, São Paulo, and Buenos Aires, or of Argentinean, Mexican, and Brazilian artists living in Paris, New York, Barcelona, or Madrid (from José Luis Cuevas to the Brazilian concretists). On the other, there was the dogged fencing off of any artistic or literary expression of "Latin" people within the confines of the lasting meanings of Latin America by collectors, art critics, and scholars in New York, Paris, or Chicago. Mexican art critic Jorge Alberto Manrique lucidly captured this dilemma in the 1970s. Both the temptation of Europe, he argued, and that of non-Europe (the place defined as ontologically different from and alternative to what was believed to be European) were American (from all of America). For him, both in fact constitute what it means to be American. In a way, without the constant conflicts and chaotic struggles caused by both temptations, there was no possibility either of art in general or of Latin American art. When, as in the case of Mexico's post-revolutionary art, one of the temptations seems to have been absolutely victorious, artistic creation stagnates, and art becomes an ideological and stylistic cage: "The more successful the movements of the 1920s were as movements, not as the personal work of artists, the more they mortgaged their future in the long run."[37]

For Manrique, post-1945 artists in the Americas clearly opted to *"sentirse universales"* (to feel themselves to be universal). But in the 1970s, he wondered if that was the last of it: "Is this just another swing of the pendulum that makes us alternate between opening up to the outside and closing down on ourselves?" The doubt was there (would Latin America return to some form of identity nativism?); at the same time, it was not there (he used the "we," meaning Latin America). For as Manrique himself claimed, it was impossible to conceptualize Latin American art outside the confines of the concept of Latin America and all that it implied—Iberian conquest, mestizaje, "dependence, exploitation, neocolonialism, fictitious economics . . ." And yet every part of Latin America was different: "The desire to be the same, when indeed we are different, is an invention begun by Bolívar, Fray Servando Teresa de Mier, Talamantes, or Miranda, and many others. Perhaps it is a fiction: it was then and maybe—somehow—it is still." However, "this fiction has been created and maintained for so long that it has come to have the shape of reality. We have invented the concept of Latin America, and we have succeeded, in a curious way, in making reality look like the concept with which we describe it." And he believed that this had happened because, in a sense, the category of Latin America was seen as a way to gain citizenship in world art.[38]

Thus if there was and is a Latin American art, it would mean that the world had recognized an *"arte propio"* and yet *"universal."* Manrique believed that the Latin American artist would never have the peace of mind of a Frenchman to create and would always have to struggle with self-definition within the parameters of what Latin America meant. He believed that this constituted the possibility of Latin American art. And yet, ironically, to achieve a true world artistic citizenship would mean "that the concept of Latin America, of Latin American art, would disappear, and it would be replaced by something else." Hence, in Manrique we find a lucid analysis of how the category of Latin America could achieve timely and important artistic expression, only to disappear a moment later, like the maguey plant, which flowers and then dies.[39]

In the arts, in literature (e.g., Octavio Paz's *El laberinto de la soledad*, 1950), even in 1950s forms of philosophical and sociological *indigenismo* (e.g., Luis Villoro's *Los grandes momentos del indigenismo en México*, 1950), this enigma prevails: the hope that by being very, very local (native), art would finally reach universality. But then the problem becomes not that of a Mexican or Latin American identity, nor even that of being universal, but that of being accepted as such, as universal.

Even in very contemporary art criticism, the term Latin America has shown great survival skills. In a recent lucid, Aby Warburg–like essay, *Atlas portátil de América Latina* (2012), Graciela Speranza destroys and reconstructs the Latin Americanness of art in a single paragraph, as if the very hope (of newness, of being an alternative) implied in the term Latin America ought not to die. In one paragraph, Speranza first takes for granted the map of Latin America and then reveals its falseness, only to rescue the hope in the name of the lasting implications of the term Latin America: please include us, Latin Americans, as yours:

> I myself, who believe that artists and writers from Latin America neither have to show passports nor wave flags; [I who believe that] art has to speak in its own way without any sign of origins; . . . [I myself who] have come to wonder whether Latin American art or Latin America exists, am myself surprised when I consider the possibility that we ought to denaturalize these overused categories in order to reinvent them through other critical strategies and tools until the art of Latin America becomes part of the visible world, on the global map, which is being taken apart and put back together in the 21st century, this time around not so as to fulfill a condescending quota, not as the last fetish of the Others, but as art that reimagines . . . the world that it carries on and expands, without losing its singularity, [which is] the horizon of difference."[40]

In sum, in debates about the arts, Latin America seems to be an enigma that at times dissolves the term, at times recomposes it. Baltasar Gracián's old *Agudeza y arte del ingenio* (1648) seems to apply: "Poco es ya discurrir lo possible, sino se trasciende a lo impossible [*sic*]" (as things are, it is of little use to discuss the possible if the impossible is not overcome).

∾

In English, however, the idea of Latin America has not been much criticized, aside from the very historicizing of the old and new imperial connotations of the term and of the Cold War origins of Latin American Studies in the United States. Starting in the 1970s, an empirically solid and politically necessary criticism of the Cold War connotations of Latin American Studies emerged. This constituted an important intellectual and political terrain on which to base a non-imperial, more socially conscious, and even radical US Latin Americanism. Soon, other criticisms emerged about the lack of rigor and politicization of US Latin American Studies. Moreover, by the end of the Cold War, the distinguished US Latin Americanist Peter Smith wondered whether the 1990s world circumstances "presented an occasion to re-evaluate the entire concept of 'Latin America' and its practical significance." Thus, he clearly stated that "perhaps it was an outmoded construct, a romantic relic of an idealistic past." But then this expert in US-Latin America relations saved the term from extinction with more of the same: "Ironically these doubts were spreading just at the time when political and diplomatic coordination could provide Latin America's leaders with a potent and practical weapon for confronting and shaping global prospects in the century to come." I have my doubts whether the way to face twenty-first-century massive violence, total Mexican and Central American (human and economic) integration with the United States, the new US-Cuba relation, terrorism, and inequality is more Latin Amerianism. But the fact is that none of these criticisms was ever truly about the idea of Latin America and its deep-rooted cultural, racial, and linguistic innuendos.[41]

In the 1990s, as a result of post–Cold War scenarios, religious faith in globalization and hyper-specialization in various social sciences (especially economics, political science, and anthropology), US area studies, including Latin American Studies, were considered passé. So much talk about the post-this and post-that global world meant many challenges for the kind of US Latin Americanism that had boomed in the 1970s and 1980s. But the very idea of Latin America was never truly challenged. By 2011, three former presidents of the US Latin American Studies Association (LASA), Sonia Álvarez, Arturo Arias, and Charles R. Hale, articulated what was advanced as the alternative form of Latin Americanism for the twenty-first century, for a world that had lost all its innocence, especially its epistemological naïveté. They proposed a revisualizing and decentering of Latin American Studies: "We contend that LAS [Latin American Studies] has benefited enormously from deepened engagement with feminist theory, critical theories of race and ethnicity, various currents of inter- and postdisciplinary intellectual work associated with cultural studies, and with general epistemological scrutiny, starting with the very idea of 'Latin America.'"[42]

Hence the authors called for LASA's inclusion of Latin Americans, of oppressed people within Latin America, of the academic production by Latin Americans, and of Latin American epistemics, philosophy, and aesthetics. For, they argued, following Walter Mignolo, Latin America was "no longer a geographical entity to be studied," it was now "a reorientation of knowledge, an epistemology that looks at global concerns from a Latin American perspective." In other words, Latin America is no more, and yet there is a "Latin American perspective." In this way, the authors considered the idea of "Latin America" to have been criticized and redefined, and nonetheless to have survived all this, like a cat that always lands on its feet, no matter how far it falls. In fact, this serious criticism mentioned no doubts whatsoever about the very notion of Latin America. A Martian reader would understand that there had been many political, conceptual, and moral debates regarding Latin America, but would not learn exactly what a category such as Latin America was, or why it was needed.[43]

Thus the advantage of revisualizing Latin Americanism was simply more Latin America, assumed as an unquestioned automatism in English. Revisualizing Latin America would mean, the authors stated clearly, not questioning what Latin America means, but including more voices in the same meanings. Needless to say, this was no small feat in English, but it did not cast serious doubt on the category of Latin America.

A significant, relatively recent criticism of the idea of Latin America in English was Walter Mignolo's *The Idea of Latin America* (2005): "An excavation," he argues, "of the imperial/colonial foundation of the 'idea' of Latin America that will help us unravel the geo-politics of knowledge from the perspective of coloniality, the untold and unrecognized historical counterpart of modernity."[44] Indeed, this was a devastating criticism of the undeniable imperial DNA of the term, made in the name of a new perspective, that of "coloniality," which, Mignolo explains, "emerge[s] out of the condition of the 'colonial wound,' the feeling of inferiority imposed on human beings who do not fit the predetermined model in Euro-American narratives." As important as this criticism could be, I believe, it was not a doubting of but rather a strong reaffirmation of essential parts of what Latin America has meant for a long time: a real, racio-cultural, different, and alternative ontology (if now based not on racial and cultural mixture, not on French or Spanish versions of Latinity, but on the purity of its intrinsic indigenous component). Like the old *filosofía de lo latinoamericano*, Mignolo's work maintains the connotation of Latin America as a cultural place that naturally calls for utopias; as a constant peeling out of layers of inauthenticity in order to get to the real heart of the artichoke: an unspecified native soul formed either by reference to Nahuatl- or Quechua-speaking peoples, in sixteenth- or twenty-first-century Mexico or Peru, or to the so-called Latinos in the United States. Thus, as Mignolo argues, it is possible to affirm that "40 million Latino/as in the U.S. have already given themselves a shake and begun to brush the imperial memories out of their/our bodies." Don Santiago Ramón y Cajal—that wise, early twentieth-century Spanish (I guess "Latino") neuroscientist—would not only have marveled at the very possibility of forty million very different people having the same imperial memories; he would also have wondered what the other real memories in those Latin neurons might have been. All in all, I think Mignolo's criticism was not a questioning of Latin America, but a reaffirmation of Latin America as business as usual: it radicalized, and *comme il faut* in English and through an assumed radical alterity, the lasting and powerful ethno-cultural utopian implications of the term Latin America.[45]

Mignolo's coloniality partook of the larger "new" Latin Americanism that began to emerge in the literature departments of US universities in the 1990s. This trend was advanced, as it were, as an odd edict: "no longer there is either a reality or an epistemology to stand on and yet Latin America, the concept, we love you." This was a post-post-modernist disenchantment that once more proved that the poet's truth has no tense: "La decadencia añade verdad pero no halaga" (decadence adds truth but it does not cajole).[46] Through the 1960s and 1970s, for many US progressive students and scholars, Latin America meant either the Marxist or Maoist struggles in Cuba, Nicaragua, Peru, or Argentina or the vital US solidarity with people repressed by murderous dictatorships. During the 1980s and 1990s, however, too many things happened to their idea of Latin America—too many in the realm of academic concerns and theories, and too many in the world. Ugly democracies—there are no other kind—emerged all over the continent; revolutions in Cuba and Nicaragua lost their utopian and candid appeal; Marxism and "scientific materialism" became "passé" in academic forums full of "epistemological" daily revolutions; and then 1989 happened. Thus the revolt of epistemology—"the investigation of what distinguishes justified belief from opinion,"[47] which challenged the scientific and political conviction of the "Latin America" of revolutions, *dependencia* theory, and fixed political teleologies. US literature departments began to advance Latin Americanism in different and contentious combinations, as a self-assumed radical—in both theoretical and practical political terms—category in which no scientific or cultural assumption was left unchallenged—except for the very idea of Latin America.

Thus such literary scholars as Alberto Moreiras, Román de la Campa, Jon Beasley-Murray, and John Beverley have engaged in a sort of disciplinary soliloquy on the meaning of this radical option. Beyond theoretical nuances and grandiloquent assertions—difficult to follow for outsiders to the soliloquy like myself—it is hard to pinpoint a simple questioning of the use of the term Latin America. They indeed repackage the old connotations of the term with lots of new options for the US-centered academic left, meant to serve a post-1960s, post-1970s, and post–September 11 world. Moreiras, for instance, questions—or so I reckon—all epistemological assumptions that had justified romance philology or literary criticism, or history itself, but he has few doubts about the "civilizational" role that the very idea of Latin America still has to play in a supposed unseen "history threshold": "The Latin American civilizational crossroad [*El cruce civilizacional latinoamericano*] and its intermediate or vestibular [*sic*] position in relation to the macro-process associated with globalization, furnish today's Latin America with a crucial role in the crossroad [*encrucijada*] of history."[48] But, one wonders, when in the midst of a presumed new universe big bang would it make logical and practical sense to wonder about the role to be played by the earth's mythical Atlantis?

For his part, John Beverley, as a "*gringo bueno*" (his phrase), though not advocating violent struggle as the strategy to follow in today's Latin America, expressed nostalgia for the old revolutionary violence—thus, he disdained such intellectuals as Beatriz Sarlo, who have engaged in a serious self-criticism of the violent option. "Part of the originality and promise of the armed struggle in Latin America was embodied in the cultural superstructure," he argued. Hence Gabriel García Márquez or Julio Cortazar, he suggested, came from the "vanguard functions of the guerrilla focus." Still, one could be, as Joseph Roth or Stefan Zweig were, nostalgic for the Austro-Hungarian Empire, but neither they in the 1930s nor anyone today talks of reembodying the Austro-Hungarian Empire as civilization. And I do not really know whether Che Guevara, as Beverley argued, ought to be considered the cause of the 1970s Latin American literature; the human condition, however, is such that indeed great violence has produced indispensable artistic achievements that are valuable—unlike the idea of Latin America—as our species's reminders of evilness, not as nostalgia for violence or creativity.[49]

The revolt of epistemologists is sensitive to the criticism of engaging in jargon, and especially of being a US-centered academic trend that ultimately could be seen as imperial epistemology all over again. Beverley thus considers Argentineans or Mexicans who criticize the US revolt of epistemology as "neo-Arielistas"—old fashioned criollos or mestizos who grasp neither the authenticity of Latin America nor the worth of US-centered academic theories. So Mexican or Brazilian intellectuals who pursue old-fashioned philology or partake of the confines of their respective languages—those who write about, say, the problem of the very notion of Latin America and find tools more in Jorge Cuesta or Carlos Vaz Ferreira than in the last cultural studies reader (in English)—all would be, for Beverley, "neo-Arielistas" who have not overcome "a colonial genealogy." They represent neither their people nor any good social struggle but "the anxiety of intellectuals of bourgeois or middle-class background [that is, all intellectuals], generally ethnically European or mestizo [that is, everybody in the Latin confines of America], who are threatened with being pushed off the stage of history by, on the one hand, neoliberalism and globalization [Which one? Christendom, the Spanish and Portuguese languages? Modern times? The cosmopolitanism inherent in any kind of cultural production? Or the Internet?] and, on the other, by a heterogeneous and multiform proletarian/popular subject on whose behalf they had pretended to speak [Who pretends to speak for whom?]."[50]

In sum, the revolt of epistemologists, though hard to follow, is clear in its democratizing will—although expressed in a very elitist language and setting—in its anticapitalist but unclear political options, and in its dependence on the idea of Latin America. Beverley is adamant about his goal: "the affirmation of the distinctiveness of Latin America as a 'civilization' in the face of North American and European domination, without falling back on the exhausted formulas of complacent creole-mestizo nationalism." I myself consider the revolt of epistemologists less than a proof of the import of Latin America as a civilization and more as one more reason, if not the most important, to give up the very idea of Latin America. How would an epistemological revolt in US university literature departments look without recourse to Latin America?[51]

CR

In turn, historian Michel Gobat advanced, in English, a new and more nu-anced examination of the origins of the term Latin America. Unlike both Mignolo and the epistemologists, Gobat's account of the idea of Latin America fully includes the vast literature on the subject in languages other than English. Rather than emphasizing the input of the French Empire to the term, he rightly highlighted the impact of the 1856 regional protests against the William-Walker-filibustered regime established in Nicaragua. In fact, Gobat's is the first full-fledged account of the Nicaraguan affair and its multiple echoes among Spanish American intellectuals. Before the French-led invasion of Mexico, the Walker adventure in Nicaragua was *the* event that shocked many republics in the continent; it was a great stimulus for "unity" among the newly created republics against the imperial and filibuster policies of the United States. But Walker's was not the only fili-buster adventure launched from US territory after the Mexican-American War. There were many, begun not only by US citizens but, for instance, by the Cuban Narciso López, who attempted to invade Cuba. Walker himself had tried before to take over Baja California and Sonora. What is common in all these filibuster adventures is the support not of the entire United States but of US southern governments, often in opposition to the federal government (in 1848, López offered the direction of his Cuban adventure to Senator Jefferson Davis and to Robert E. Lee, who declined). Walker's Nicaraguan adventures say more about US internal contradictions than about all-powerful US imperialism; more about the origins of the US Civil War than of the post-1898 US empire. Walker ended his days with no sup-port from the US federal government and abandoned by his men who had been armed by southern states, shot by a Honduran firing squad in 1860. But Gobat derives from the reaction to Walker's Nicaraguan adventure an archaeology of hope in the term Latin America as a democratic, anti-imperialist, and antiracist idea.[52]

For Gobat, the early proponents of the term Latin America were liber-als, democrats, and antiracists who fought the imperial racist policies of the United States. Thus, regardless of the conspicuous racial, undemocratic, and elite connotations of the term, which Gobat acknowledges, he finds in the term a recessive gene of moral hope. Gobat is clear, or clearer than his 1850s historical characters: "Spanish American intellectuals, politi-cians, and diplomats increasingly viewed their relations with the United States in terms of a race war." For "strategic concerns alone did not push Spanish American elites to identify their societies with the Latin race.

They also adopted the concept to counter the racist views undergirding U.S. expansionism." Because racism was somehow alien to Latin America and had to be imported: "An influx of U.S. travelers during the California Gold Rush brought U.S. racism to the Southern Hemisphere in dramatic ways." Hence, following Miguel Rojas Mix but pushing the argument forward according to current race theory in US academe, Gobat highlights the interesting democratic contentions of such intellectuals and statesmen as Bilbao or Arosemena, making them soldiers in an antiracist army of nonstate popularizers of the idea of Latin America—though all of them were statesmen *tout court*, and though the term was never really popular in the nineteenth century. Hence Gobat's Latin Americanist conclusion:

> One way to decolonize Latin America might indeed be to erase the term from the global map. But it is also true that an anti-imperial and democratic ethos undergirded this geopolitical entity from the start. That this spirit is still alive is evident not just in the passionate latinoamericanismo of leftist leaders such as Venezuela's recently deceased Hugo Chávez, but also in the efforts of some Latina/o activists to remap the U.S.-Mexican borderlands— and perhaps the entire United States—as Latina/o America. . . . Given the vast movement of Latina/os and Latin Americans between North and South America, perhaps it is not preposterous to imagine, as the image created by Pedro Lasch suggests, that one day the entire Western Hemisphere may be remapped as Latina/o America.[53]

To each saint his *veladora*, and to each Latin Americanist her hope; but, since I do not see or feel the hope, the redeeming democratic aspects, in either the *latinoamericanismo* of the Hugo Chávez style, or in the genetics of Latinness, or in the *Begriffsgeschichte* of the term Latin America, I cannot say how beautiful or interesting it will be when the entire continent becomes Latino/a. What I can say is that among the earlier articulators of the idea of Latin America, there were indeed a few insightful characters who advanced ideas of equality and justice, at times beyond the strong, nineteenth-century racial lines—as when Bilbao opposed Chile's war against the Araucano Indians in the name of "the good news of fraternity supported in the respect of races' autonomy."[54] But that does not make Latin America— which is, after all, a racial term—a spring of profound antiracism in the language of twenty-first-century US identity politics.

Indeed, republican or liberal networks of nineteenth-century Spanish American intellectuals were of great symbolic magnitude, for these characters were at the core of the thinking and governing of their respective nations. They all wrote poems, history, essays, political plans, technocratic treaties, or travel books at the same time that they were senators or even presidents of their respective countries. But that does not make them popular messiahs of antiracist republicanism, as Gobat and, more recently, James E. Sanders have maintained. "It is Latin Americans," writes Sanders, commenting on mid-nineteenth-century Colombian and Mexican liberals, "who challenged the importance and meaning of race, posing universalism as a powerful opposing force."[55] Thus, Bilbao, and Giuseppe Garibaldi in Uruguay, become, for Sanders, "counter-mentalité" (vis-à-vis Europe and the United States), despite the fact that they and many others were at times more liberals than democrats, or the other way around; at times admirers and connoisseurs of the United States, at times critics; often Masons and Catholics; always Spanish and French speakers, always part and parcel of French, Spanish, US, and English discussions of constitutionalism, liberalism, republicanism, equality, freedom, and fraternity.

To be sure, in the 1880s Martí was what can be called a radical republican; but he was so because he was a Catholic, an admirer of Thoreau, obsessed with war and violence, and a follower of Henry George (socialist but racist)—"aquel mismo amor del Nazareno puesto en la lengua práctica de nuestros días" (that same love of the Nazarene articulated in the practical languages of our times), said Martí of George's *Progress and Poverty* (1877).[56]

Politically and intellectually, Bilbao, Arosemena, and Martí deserve the admiration displayed by Gobat—or Rojas Mix or Sanders. But, on one hand, a twenty-first-century believer of atomic theory can indeed find surprising and telling Lucretius's ideas about particles; but it would be unwise to call him Einstein. On the other, the best that can be said about them is not that they were sublime counter-mentalités, the true and only antiracists. No. The best homage to these and other Spanish American thinkers, yesterday or today, is to de-exoticize them, to consider them as skillful and unskillful as Tocqueville, as good and as bad.

That Latin America was originally an anti-imperialist concept was true to the extent that it was anti-US. But Latin America was and is an imperial concept. And yet, it would be as misleading to say that the use of the term Latin in Bilbao or among late nineteenth-century mulatto Cuban intellectuals in the United States was a full-fledged racial marker—meaning what "Latino" means in today's United States—as it would be to say that it was conclusively antiracist. In fact, 1850s articulations of Latin America were part of the secularization and modern translation of the Enlightenment and Catholic senses of brotherhood. Of course, before the "Latin" prefix even existed, "universal brotherhood" was part of modern political theology and of late eighteenth-cenury criollo patriotisms. The Americanism of the wars of independence often used *"fraternidad,"* though the term was then closer to its old Catholic roots than to the French revolutionary sense. Moreover, early versions of the concept of Latin America—articulated either by Bilbao or M. Chevalier—charged the term with a strong sense of fraternity derived from the many trends that fed the concept. Old Catholic, Iberian notions of *"fraternidades,"* together with French revolutionary notions of *fraternité,* as well as Masonic *fraternité* (many of the Spanish-speaking early sponsors of Latin America were Masons), Saint-Simonianism, nineteenth-century mutualism—all charged the term with a sense of fraternity.

This was a sense not free from contradictions, especially in view of the strong "universalism"—beyond the Latin command—implied by nineteenth-cenury notions of *fraternité.* Therefore, at times the *fraternidad* implied in the meaning of Latin America was a sense of racial *fraternidad,* at times a Catholic sense beyond race and Latinity, as when Bilbao affirmed, "Amar á tu prójimo" (Love thy neighbor): "Fraternity is both a principle and a feeling. It is a great refuge against life's sorrows and against frightening indifference. How could one not love one's own neighbor, one's own brother, that who recognizes in himself the omnipotence of liberty. My neighbor is another me; he is the depositary of my same spirituality; hence the embrace, the love within the community and identity of this great essence is necessary. Here lies the ineradicable fundament of democracy [Hé aquí el fundamento inexpugnable de la democracia]."[57]

Fraternidad was the keyword of nineteenth-century conservative Spanish thought. In the 1820s, the influential Catholic thinker and priest Francisco Alvarado asked Spanish liberals, "Charlatans without substance, from where have you taken if not from the Gospel those words Equality, Liberty, and Fraternity, . . . whose meaning you do not even understand?" The most influential nineteenth-century conservative thinker in the Spanish-speaking world, Juan Donoso Cortés, also argued that equality, freedom, and fraternity came not from the French revolution but from Calvary, and republican ideas had only made of them blasphemies: *"la república de las tres mentiras"* (the republic of the three lies). Bilbao appealed to the less reactionary, but not less Catholic, sense of fraternity, that of Lamennais, whose *"règne de la fraternité"* included modern liberal policies and economic reforms in order to allow people access to property, credit, and education.[58] This was indeed revolutionary in terms of nineteenth-century racial theory, but not in those of the twenty-first century.

During the nineteenth century, the idea of fraternity, like that of Latin

America, was racialized in, for instance, mutualistic societies in the United States. And yet, in the idea of Latin America there remains indeed a sense of quasi-Catholic fraternity, which has gained good and bad uses over time. Gobat identifies this fraternity and sees it as fully antiracist. I wish it had been that. For if indeed, as Gobat argues, early proponents of the idea of Latin America conceived their antagonism against the United States as a race war, the idea of Latin America was simply their racist weapon among the then-available racist arsenal. The concept has implied peculiar forms of racism that indeed cannot be necessarily equated to those of the United States. As much as I would like to share Gobat's philological and political optimism about the trajectory of the concept, I do not find any empirical or philosophical argument in the history and functioning of the term to be very optimistic about. But what is more telling in Gobat's recent account is in fact the enduring power of the term Latin America: it still stirs the alluring ideas of liberation and hope. Why the need to find in such a dubiously racial and ill-reputed term such interesting lessons for the present? Why not simply find them in redistribution, equality, or freedom of circulation in the continent? About Latin America, it seems, we can say what Bernard Williams said of religion: "It will be hard to give it up even if it is an illusion."[59]

⚕

What is in a name that makes it so eloquent and enduring? First, I will state some very basic connotations of the term in order to then say something more about the concept's roots in *iberismo* and *latinité*, which explain many of its lasting connotations. A note on Brazil and past and present anti–Latin Americanism, as well as a brief review of the impact of the term *Latinos* in the United States with regard to the current meaning of Latin America, will then be indispensable. Then I take a brief detour in order to test the actual presence of Latin America and its connotations in popular parlance. To be sure, this is a difficult field to explore; thus I construct, through memory, my memory, and through popular music, a window through which to examine the popular diffusion of the idea of "Latin America."

I do all this in order to submit a commentary on the most important twenty-first-century form in which the term has survived—namely, the US-centered textbook existence of Latin America. This is my own backdoor attempt, as a historian, at self-therapy. But let me be clear at once: there is plenty of extraordinary scholarship in English about Mexico, Brazil, and Colombia. But Latin America is another question entirely, and the problem is that this fine scholarship often feels the need to format its findings in a Latin American manner. As historian José Moya has stated, "A focused interpretation of scattered studies could demonstrate that, as broad categories go, this one has more historical significance and cultural meaning than other continental labels such as Europe, Asia, and Africa." Indeed so, for Latin America was a racial idea (like "Africa") that has undergone a moral upgrading (unlike "Africa"), as did that originally imperialist and racist idea, "Mitteleuropa" (Friedrich Neumann), which after 1914, through nostalgia, acquired the meaning of a mythical time of coexistence of nations and races, of tolerance and fruitful cultural promiscuity. And yet, whereas post-1919 "Mitteleuropa" implied the old "*saggezza asburgica*" (Habsburg wisdom), as Claudio Magris put it—the art of "postponing the end, of delaying dusk," finding an "ironic and painful arrangement"—the expression Latin America in the twentieth and twenty-first centuries has implied a presumably blissful ethnic exit from Western history through an un-ironic encroachment on a Western cliché.[60]

As a historian, in showing US Latin Americanism's limitations, I only highlight the enduring power of the term Latin America. "Area studies can very rapidly become parochialism," Sanjay Subrahmanyam has taught us, commenting on the category of South Asia. He goes on to say that "it is as if these conventional geographical units of analysis, fortuitously defined as givens for the intellectually slothful, and the result of complex (even murky) processes of academic and non-academic engagement, somehow become real and overwhelming. Having helped create these Frankenstein's monsters, we are obliged to praise them for their beauty, rather than grudgingly acknowledge their limited functional utility."[61] Indeed, I therefore conclude with a happy, if circumscribed and simple, historian's embrace of the concept. For the term is a malleable vessel ready to be filled with interesting, important, more-than-national histories, and not only Latin American ones. As I was writing this, I was, after all, the director of the University of Chicago's Center for Latin American Studies. I thus carefully embrace the term, like Father Guillermo Schulenburg, former abbot of the Basilica of Our Lady of Guadalupe, who neither believed in Juan Diego nor in the divine painting of the image, but who nevertheless had no doubt about the relevance of *mi santísima Virgen de Guadalupe*.

ONE

The Connotations of an Idea:
On the basic connotations of the term Latin America, though said connotations are further elucidated as the essay unfolds and are only stated baldly here

De vegades, cal ser pervers per misericòrdia.

—Joan Fuster, *"Aforismes i insolències"* (*Sagitari*, 1985), in Joan Fuster, *Indagacions i astúcies: Antología de textos assagístics* (Barcelona: El Garbell, 1995), 111

Latin America is a modern concept. This much we know. No one but the poets of the ancient lingua franca were considered Latins in seventeenth-century New Spain or in eighteenth-century France. Also, "Latin America" is a phrase that did not occur in spoken vernacular Spanish and Portuguese until recently. And there is that other certitude: "Latin America" alludes to history, language, and culture. In fact, it constitutes a lasting confirmation of racial beliefs. Thus, as a modern, highbrow conjecture about culture, but indeed about race, the term Latin America is unable to designate a rapidly changing reality. It is not surprising that the term has undergone two centuries of semantic reincarnations. But, so far, I believe, every rebirth has been a renewal of belief in the term's ability to designate the same region, people, and phenomena as it has from the outset—the Bilbao Law for Latin America.

In fact, "Latin America," more than as a name, has served as an ossified metaphor whose lasting linguistic presence bears witness to itself—a metaphor and an institution that have captured poetically, as it were, important beliefs and empirical data whose collective meaning no single concept seems capable of capturing in various European languages. As Giambattista Vico believed, to conceive metaphors is to grasp the intricate relations of phenomena that at first sight appear dissimilar. In poetry, as María Zambrano believed, "the metaphor has a deep, prior role in culture. . . . Its function is that of defining a reality unfathomable to reason, which can be captured in another way, . . . a form of continuity with long-distant times and mentalities." Hence the importance and indispensability of metaphors in historical knowledge. Thus also their danger: they tend to ossify, to serve as mental routines and not as attempts at knowing or at deciphering. Ossified historical expressions that, for those in the know, truly work as vital metaphors—such as "*las dos Españas,*" "*la España invertebrada,*" or "the frontier in American history," "melting pot," or "community"—become a way of avoiding something that is otherwise hard to understand.[1]

In brief, through its changing historical meanings, the metaphor of Latin America has conveyed the following meanings.

1. The encounters of modern empires. Thus it has meant imperial agendas or resistance to empire: the French Empire vs. the Anglo-Saxon; the Spanish Empire vs. the American (US); or the new race, the Cosmic one, Ariel, vs. the old races; or the notion of internal colonialism, say, in thinking of Latinos/as in the United States, or of the Guatemalan national economy, or of Nahuatl speakers within Mexico. Thus the term has incorporated the following.

   —Anti-Americanism: specifically, anti-US expansionism and Catholic anti-Protestantism. Over time anti-Americanism in "Latin" latitudes has sometimes become, as in France or Spain, a form of anti-Semitism (for "everybody knows," said certain forms of nineteenth-century European Latinism, that Slavs or Germans have Jewish blood; or, "everybody knows" that the Jewish lobby controls the United States). Anti-Americanism also has been expressed as protest against something huge called "the System" (for "everybody knows" that the United States controls world capitalism and globalization). José Enrique Rodó's *Ariel* (1900) was for long this anti-Americanism's overused metaphor—"No se puede exigir una ingenuidad más uruguaya" (A more Uruguayan naïveté cannot be demanded), said his contemporary Julio Herrera y Reissig of Rodó's book. As early as 1926, Mexican writer (then resident in the United States) Martín Luis Guzmán already considered the Ariel trope "a set of established ideas almost always a priori . . . which has been maintained over a century of practical nullity and with neither time nor calm to think."[2]

   —Violence. Latin America as a concept has not only included violence as part of its history (what history escapes this characterization?), but has incorporated a fascination with redemptive violence. That is, it is not that Latin America was or is violent, but that Latin America means love for some kind of violence—which is so visible in the acceptable Spanish loan-words in English that resonate with the Latin in "Latin America": pistola, cacique, caudillo, sombrero, cojones, guerrilla, junta, desperado, cañón, capo, narco, desaparecido, incommunicado. Violence was part and parcel of the Bolivarian dream as much as of the fascination with the Che Guevara–like Latin America or with the current praise for the "struggle" of anti-system protesters, whether indigenous people or new revolutionary hipsters.

—Latin America has meant support for the very large (i.e., Latin America itself, the empire of the Cosmic Race, a Latin or Iberian empire, *hispanidad,* or a federation of indigenous people) through the defense of the very small (i.e., local mores, "communities," languages, powers, privileges, traditions). This has implied belief in the unchanging nature of what is defined as local, authentic, and real, or at least belief in a very slow pace of change. This assumes a locality that nevertheless, through the very use of the term Latin America, does not need to be specifically demarcated historically, geographically, or politically.

2. From its old meaning as an alternative West, *latinidad* as applied to America (the continent) has come to mean non-Western. Thus Latin America has meant "imitation of the West" or a radical non-Western ontology; a different, non-Western, non-modern, anticapitalist notion of time and space, or an "alternative modernity"; or a postcolonial reality (not as in the United States or Canada, but as in India). Also, as "China" was often used in English or German, "Latin America" has meant a sort of "state of nature" used to illustrate fossilized (in time and space) forms of primitive communism, oriental despotism, or, also, ideal community.[3] Regardless of the morals drawn, the assumption remains the same: in the 1870s, amateur anthropologist Lewis H. Morgan (1818–1881), assisted by Adolph Bandelier (1840–1914), concluded that the Aztecs were a communitarian "gens," which had no notion of private property, forming a primitive democracy. Morgan inspired Marx's oriental communism and Engels's take on the origins of private property. This was an evolutionary view that, to be sure, does not resonate with any current view; but the same utopian equalitarianism and communitarianism is maintained nowadays, for instance, by "coloniality" studies of Latin America.

3. Latin America has meant the endemic collective failure of modernization; in other words, backwardness *als Beruf*—what Juan Villoro called "*la utopía del atraso*" (the utopia of backwardness).[4] Over the course of the twentieth century, Latin America became the other name for underdevelopment, the example of the world's experiments in modernization *par excellence*, and the enduring triumph of backwardness—either because of these countries'

failure to become new nations like the United States, or because of their endemic violence and inability to overcome "path-dependent" sins against modernization. "Latin" thus has come to mean crony capitalism or fake liberalism.

—Until recently, Latin America has often embodied either very old or very new forms of modern antidemocratic thought: a defense of one oligarchy or another—criollos against stupid *pardos* who fought for their masters, as in Simón Bolívar's case; or the rule of the enlightened philosophers of the Cosmic Race, as in José Vasconcelos's case; or the elitism of masters of Spanish eloquence, as in Rubén Darío or José Enrique Rodó; or the leadership of the Communist parties against petit-bourgeois, anti-revolutionary peasants and Indians. As a proxy of antiliberal democracy, the term has also meant US Latin Americanism and NGO idealization of indigenous *"usos y costumbres"* vis-à-vis dirty party politics in modern democracies. The founder of twentieth-century Latin American Studies in the United States, Frank Tannenbaum, for all his support of the Mexican Revolution, his love of the bucolic, authentic, Indian Mexico, thought that democracy was not for Mexicans or "Latin" people. He welcomed Lázaro Cardenas's corporatism as a Mexican solution for Mexican problems—nothing to do with alien models of democracy. Even in the 1970s, no form of liberation theology, Víctor Jara– or Che Guevara–style Latin Americanism considered liberal democracy to be worth a rat's tail. Thus the transformation of the term in the 1990s: from "Latin" cum oligarchy or relentless populism (rarely democratic) to *Latinoamérica* cum the failure of democracy or the return of the authentic (indigenous, antiliberal) democracies.

—Nonetheless, Latin America has gradually and recently implied a form of not necessarily liberal and not always republican democracy. For the term has carried over a strong sense of communitarianism derived from its history, which blended old notions of the Catholic community (pity, solidarity, and compassion), Masonic thought, nineteenth-century French Catholic redefinitions of revolutionary *fraternité*, Iberian federalism and municipalism, and domestic struggles for local autonomy. At times, in speaking of Latin America these fraternal trends have been developed as local anti-elitism, anti-imperialism, and solidarity beyond certain classes and certain races—as in Martí and Bilbao. Other times, the fraternity intrinsic to Latin America has been used—as fraternity was used in Pan-Germanism or Pan-Latinism *à la* Italian—for quasi-fascist notions of the continental working class–as in Peronismo and Vargismo. And always fraternity and Latin America, thus conjoined, have implied an anti–Anglo-Saxon brotherhood. In sum, that Latin America has not often meant liberal democracy does not imply that it has not connoted one or another democratic experiment—understood as a form of social inclusion, opportunities, redistribution, or fraternity. The problem has been that intellectuals and scholars have tried to frame every democratic experiment either as Latin American—and thus brought in all the rest of the term's connotations—or as fake democracy, not truly liberal. I suspect, thus, that any truly new democratic stand from the left in the region would have to be indifferent to the idea of Latin America. To de-Latin-Americanize democratic experiments would allow embracing the practical—often unpleasant—nuances of ruling that lie beyond overused ideas of ethnic or cultural utopias. It would also demystify the ideal of a spotless liberal democracy. Fully embracing the term Latin America—from the left or the right—by exaggerating the element of *fraternité* in its content would be like fully adopting Pan-Germanism, Pan-Anglo-Saxonism, or the Cuban Revolution only because of their undeniably popular aspects.

—As a paradise of tradition, Latin America has included strong doses of anti-individualism. That is, belonging to the real Latin America meant, and still means, showing not individual interests (Bilbao) but some form of corporate, collective passions or desires (preferably ethnic, but in other flavors as well). Thus we find the odd characters often invoked in US Latin Americanism: "Latin Americans want this and are that," or "Latin American subalterns do this and that." What made art and letters Latin American, said Jean Franco in the 1960s, is that they were not individualistic forms of art; rather, they were concerned with collectivity.[5] Thus Latin America has been the involuntary and unfair complement of the avant-gardes of the twentieth and twenty-first centuries: a mainstream artist can mock or destroy any sense of identity, tradition, or canon; but a "Latin American" artist who mocks or destroys everything, including the notion of Latin America, is a fake.

—Latin America seems to be synonymous with a proclivity for economic failure; thus the term came to mean the failure of nineteenth-century development, and it means the same today, in spite of the fact that the region includes two or three of the largest industrial economies in the world. Regardless of economic models—Keynesian welfare states or market-oriented policies—Latin means failure, and a collective failure.

4. In cultural terms, to use Eugeni d'Ors's description of himself, Latin America has come to mean a *"vocación de abismo"* (taste for the abyss). That is, the term has borne contradictory assumptions about identity, authenticity, and history. These have involved the following.

—A form of antimodernism, anticapitalism, or anti-mechanization, commonly expressed in some version of "spiritual superiority," either of the

Latin people or of the native people; either of the hybrid races or of "all the good guys together."

—A moral imperative: victimhood; that is, evil is somewhere else, not in what genuinely constitutes Latin America.

—A bizarre appropriation of promiscuity as the patrimony of Latin America, a timeless and spaceless identity; thus, mestizaje, hybridity, and mixture have generally been considered to be the meaning of Latin America. The tropics are lusty, and so . . . Over time, as did the concept of "America" (the United States), the term has sanctioned one mythical way of controlling the uncontrollable: the unstoppable mixture of people, of ideas, of everything together at once. Thus Latin America has at times meant anti-black mestizophilia, as expressed by early twentieth-century defenders of continental "Latin" thought. But Latin America has also meant a sort of lasting Las Casas–like defense of the purity and innocence of the natives and thus a strong anti-miscegenation trend (purity and authenticity ought not to be spoiled by "alien" mestizo and European ideas or people).

—An addiction to authenticity and thus to the endless "Tepoztlán-like" existence of a region immune to change, often expressed through the formula that Latin means resistance—to modernization, imitation, assimilation, and impersonation. Latin is being what we really are, responding to our real circumstances, being faithful to our origins. It is authenticity not understood as intellectual responsibility and accountability (Kierkegaard) but as the genuineness possible only for unsophisticated but real people whose only *Dasein* is being what they are, were, and always will be. The obsession with authenticity, wrote the Portuguese poet Jorge de Sena in 1961, was "the cautious and conventional survival of the romantic appeal of the exceptional and of the morbid as morbid." This is the enduring, and always laboriously renewed, belief in a profound uniqueness (ethnic, cultural, historical) and difference vis-à-vis United States, the West, all that is not Latin. "This desire for originality," said Witold Gombrowicz in Buenos Aires, "is also an imitation of Europe." More recently, Brazilian historian Evaldo Cabral de Mello has described all notions of authenticity and identity as fetishes: "The notion of identity is an anthropological fetish that polluted history and the humanities, but that is just a vestige of an eleatic revival in a globalized world that, realizing itself to be so, global, strenuously seeks differences that could save it." This is difficult to maintain because, as the region was radically transformed economically, politically, and socially during more than half a millennium, it became harder and harder to construct and reconstruct an ontology of radical—that is, authentic—difference for the Latin part of the Americas. Thus the other implication of the term Latin

America, namely, a sort of historical genetics—the assumption that Latin America implies that some historical layers are fake, some people are inauthentic, and this is so because the recessive genes of authenticity in the term Latin America are always there, ready to appear at any moment, regardless of history. Hence any social movement or demand in any present can potentially be traced back to some paradise of authenticity *in illo tempore*.[6]

—Since it has meant the fight against fakes and imitations—of liberalism, of democratic ideas, of "white" ideas, of neoliberal models—that do not match the region's "real" reality, Latin America has been the name for a never-ending attempt to describe that "real" reality. Thus Latin America has revealed a reality that is, so to speak, real enough to make us aware of the models that have been imposed on it, but elusive enough to make that reality constantly unintelligible. In a word, these realities cannot reveal themselves on their own. Hence something else ought to be used to make them intelligible—something like God, as in Darío's poem against T. D. Roosevelt; or something like Marx's *Das Kapital*, as in the first *dependentista* thought; or something like the work of Slavoj Žižek, Alain Badiou, or Giorgio Agamben, as in current US Latin American cultural studies. In sum, Latin America cries out against parroting alien voices and yet calls for a new parrot to voice something that seems to be a voiceless reality. The only way out of this cycle is to assume that Latin America is just a constitutive part of that reality to which God or Marx, Žižek, Badiou, or Agamben belongs. But then what would the point of the term Latin America be? As I said, Latin America has meant a *"vocación de abismo."*

5. "Latin America," for all the above, has worked as a hunter's call to attract utopias—from ideas of the existence and unity of a pristine race to the belief in spiritual superiority over materialism; from one or another ideal conception of the Catholic community to the revolutionary emergence of the communist society or the reign of the indigenous epistemology and communitarianism. At times, the term itself becomes the utopia, as in Leopoldo Zea's 1950s Latin Americanism or in current US Latin American cultural studies, whose call is for "the affirmation of the distinctiveness of Latin America as a 'civilization' in the face of North American and European domination."[7] And I do believe that the twenty-first century needs new utopias; but the history of the term Latin America and its uses advise to look elsewhere for them. New utopias are not to be found through the hunter's call of "Latin America."

6. Latin America, from its origins as a concept to this day, has fundamentally been a changing version of a single, enduring, old, and seemingly insurmountable concept: race.

TWO

Iberismo and *Latinité*: A bit more elaboration on the intellectual milieu to which the "Latin" in Latin America has belonged, or an explanation of the multiple lives of *iberismo* and *latinité*

Or they might have known . . . let's call it a genius
For turning what's disparate into an us

—Peter Cole, *"On Coupling,"* in *The Invention of Influence (New York: New Directions Books, 2014)*

It does not make much sense to discuss the authenticity of the term Latin America. It was articulated by characters who, in truth, had no factual or logical way of embodying such authenticity. To argue either that the term was French in origin or that it had "real" Latin American origins would not improve the idea. In a way, if it was not entirely a bad idea, it is an example of a historically circumscribed thought that originated, as it were, at a bad time, in which old imperial languages were used to name new realities marked by the collapse of old empires and the massive formation of nation-states. Intellectuals, whose only *patrias* were their respective languages, conceived it. And in the nineteenth century, to be a Portuguese- or Spanish-speaking intellectual was, in every conceivable way, to live in French—not as the alien language belonging to France, but as one's own lingua franca.

More interesting than authenticity is to examine the large and complicated European and American intellectual milieu in which this idea, Latin America, originally made sense. For the idea was but one thread of a denser political and cultural fabric that involved *las Españas*, Spanish America, Portugal, Brazil, and France, but also the United States and North Africa, as well as emerging Pan-Germanism and Pan-Slavism. Allow me to explain this succinctly and all too schematically: in Europe, the idea of Latin

America was a peculiar adaptation of two late eighteenth- and nineteenth-century trends: on one hand, *iberismo*; on the other, *latinité*, understood in different moments either as regionalism in France (the South versus the North) or as *méditerranéité*. Both trends were geopolitical commercial strategies seeking to respond to the challenges that resulted from the re-alignment of European empires in the nineteenth century and from the emergence of many modern nation-states, nationalisms, and the industrial world. Both *iberismo* and *latinité*, in their many variations, at times included North Africa, as in some forms of Iberian Africanism that saw the origins of Spain in Africa—and thus argued for the Spanish Empire's right to African possessions. Africanism was also part of some forms of *latinité*, as in the French civilizing role in Algeria or Morocco or as in Italian Enrico Corradini's pre-Libyan call for the reenactment of Roman imperialism—"syndicalism, nationalism, and imperialism" as the hallmarks of the new Italy.[1]

Both *iberismo* and *latinité* were also important cultural agendas that included romantic searches for *Volksgeist* through the revival of local languages and traditions from the 1840s to the 1870s, as well as all sorts of racial creeds from the 1880s to the 1920s. Although neither trend materialized in any meaningful military or political reality, both had lasting cultural effects. Frederick Jackson Turner framed the importance of the frontier in US history and character in terms of *méditerranéité* and the spirit of *latinité*—the Western frontier being the US version of *méditerranéité*. Modern Catalan nationalism was defined within this context as *latinité* and *iberismo*, at times as the unity of Occitania and Catalonia (often linked to France as nation and empire), and at times as an Iberian inevitability (linked to Spain as an empire and as a confederation of nationalities). Another one of these effects has been very durable: the idea of Latin America.

જી

Iberismo was a cultural and political movement centered on Portugal and *las Españas*—here the plural is vital—in the aftermath of the Napoleonic Wars in Europe and America. It was a way to face the challenges of empire—threats to Portugal's possessions in Africa and India, Spain's cata-strophic 1898, or the Italian defeat in Adwa, Ethiopia, in 1896. *Iberismo* was especially visible and influential from the 1840s to the 1920s, and it was invoked during the early stages of the António de Oliveira Salazar and Francisco Franco dictatorships in the 1930s. As historian José Álvarez Junco has shown, however, it was never a truly popular idea; it belonged to intellectuals and had echoes in various political agendas.[2] Its original and main enemy was France, but this was gradually adapted to treat the United States as the bête noir or even Castile itself, as in some form of Catalan *iberista* nationalism—meaning Old Castile vis-à-vis local Iberian identities. *Iberismo's* main original claim was the belief in a common history and destiny for Portugal and *las Españas* vis-à-vis growing French hegemony, although Portugal's odd but lasting alliance with Britain often obscured the cultural and ethnic claims of *iberismo*. In turn, US policies toward Central America, Cuba, Puerto Rico, and the Philippines in the 1890s and 1900s made *iberismo* more intellectually appealing, whether in Madrid or in San Juan, in Montevideo or in Barcelona. As such, *iberismo* was a sort of imperial defensive alliance and a struggle for local autonomy, for regional cultures and languages.

In the history of the Iberian Peninsula or its American domains, to simultaneously defend *Imperio*, on one hand, and local laws, local kingdoms, or specific cultural or administrative units, on the other, was not at all a contradiction. As António M. Hespanha has explained, within the Iberian legal tradition, the imperial or royal whole "did not jeopardize, but rather assumed the specificity and irreducibility of the goals of each of the orders of creation." The wise emperor would expand, maintain, and protect the empire and yet respect, obey, and sanction the laws, mores, privileges, and institutions of the empire's many constitutive units. Thus in the sixteenth and seventeenth centuries, local sovereignties such as Portugal and Catalonia could revolt, accusing the emperor of breaking their local *fueros* and laws, which were the *raison d'être* both of their link to the empire and of the empire itself. At times, Portugal assisted Castile with money and men in crushing Catalan revolts. The busier the empire was somewhere else, the less autonomy would be lost in Portugal. Modern *iberismo* in the nineteenth century was an adaptation of these lasting principles to the new circumstances of the modern world. By the beginning of the nineteenth century, less than a century of Bourbon modern absolutism had not eradicated the many local sovereignties. *Iberismo* became a way to recast the old empire of the "composite monarchy" and its local autonomies.[3] The rejection by New Spain's criollos of the Bourbon reforms, for instance, or even Agustín de Iturbide's Plan de Iguala (Mexico's actual independence declaration), appealed to the old pacts to which *iberismo* gave a mythical dimension.

Thus the founding father of modern Catalan nationalism, Enric Prat de la Riba, in 1906 advanced both an autonomist and an imperial (Iberian) agenda: "Then it will be the time to work toward the unification of all the Iberian peoples, from Lisbon to the Rhone, into a single State, and if the renascent Spanish nationalities can make such an ideal victorious, if they can impose it, as Bismarck's Prussia imposed the ideal of German imperialism, the new Iberia will rise to the highest degree of imperialism; . . . it will be able to expand into barbarian lands once more, and serve the highest interests of humanity." For Prat de la Riba, *iberia* meant both the Spanish Empire (regaining importance in the Americas) and the union of Occitan- and Provençal-speaking people, for they belonged to the real Neo-Latin language, Catalan. In the same way, *Morsamor* (1899), the last novel by Juan Valera—one of Spain's most prominent writers of the second half of the twentieth century—was a monument to the imperial adventures of Portugal and Spain in an *Os Lusíadas* fashion. Valera and Portuguese writer Oliveira Martins believed that Camões had granted Iberia its identity. Equally, the influential Portuguese nationalist and *iberista*, António Sardinha, in 1916 considered that the best protection against Castilian imperialism was *iberismo*, which was also, in turn, the best defense against the attacks of other empires. And in Montevideo, in 1913, José Enrique Rodó believed that "South Americans" did not need to call themselves Latin Americans: "We don't need to call ourselves Latin Americans in order to raise a general name that includes all of us, because we can call ourselves something that implies a much more intimate and particular unity: we can call ourselves 'Iberoamericans,' grandsons of the heroic and civilizing race that has only politically fragmented into two European nations." Rodó included Brazil in the term, drawing on Portuguese *iberistas*. Thus, he argued, Almeida Garrett, "the poet of Portuguese national sentiment *par excellence* maintained that without prejudice to their independence, it would be entirely correct to call the Portuguese Spaniards, as well." Bearing in mind the difficulties of early proponents of the idea of Latin America in including Brazil in the formula, this was not a small twist in old ideas: Brazil was Ibero-American.[4]

Iberismo never went very far militarily, unless we consider the long-lasting *iberista* alliance between Franco and Salazar. At times *iberismo* was based on little more than a commercial agenda and was often the result of local politics and regional nationalisms that, in view of the peninsula's linguistic diversity, found in *iberismo* a way to reinsert diversity within an Iberian nation that could still function as what historian Josep María Fradera has called an "imperial nation." Not surprisingly, *iberismo's* founding modern document, *La Iberia: Memoria sobre la conveniencia de la unión pacífica y legal de Portugal y España* (Lisbon: 1851), was contemporary with the early articulators of the idea of Latin America. It was written by Sinibaldo de

Mas, a character who in his person embodied the many contradictions that *iberismo* sought to resolve. He was a devoted Catholic; a diplomat with long stays in colonial posts in Macao, the Philippines, and India; a Catalan; and both a philologist and a commercial strategist. He called for the spiritual, historical, and military union of Portugal and Spain as a natural, divinely ordained strategy against the French Empire and as the way to protect the uniqueness of the empire's composite elements.

As the nineteenth-century idea of Latin America, *iberismo* had a conservative, commercial, and monarchical character—as in the case of de Mas. It also had, however, a republican, federalist, and free-trade-block version as well, whose main proponent in Spain was the important Catalan federalist Francesc Pi i Margall (1824–1901)—who late in his life even wrote a fictional, as it were *indigenista*, dialogue between Hernán Cortés and Cuauhtémoc, praising the existence of a monument to the latter, and not to Cortés, on Mexico City's main avenue. For him, the Cuauhtémoc monument was a sign of local autonomy over Castile's cultural centralism; that is what *iberismo* meant, local autonomy and unity of empire. *Iberismo* also had a late nineteenth-century republican and Catholic, but also anticlerical, proponent in the great Portuguese *iberista* poet, Antero de Quental, who called for the strengthening of republican municipalities against old, centralizing, and dogmatic monarchies. And *iberismo* in the twentieth century even won an anarchist exponent in the interesting Aragon anarchist Felipe Araiz, whose *Hacia una federación de autonomías libertarias* (1945) called for cultural and historical unity—the *federalismo ibérico* constituted by strong autonomous municipalities. Nevertheless, the lasting consequence of the movement, in its many versions, was the influential cultural *iberismo* that enchanted a significant part of the Spanish American, Spanish, Catalan, and Portuguese literary mainstream from the 1880s to the 1930s.[5]

As a late nineteenth-century cultural canon, *iberismo* was an odd form of philological and legal patriotism in favor of the survival, study, promotion, and coexistence of local languages and institutions in the peninsula—the legacy of Rome—within the common literary and *pactista* tradition created and advanced by important *iberista* intellectuals. Juan Valera and Miguel de Unamuno in Spain and Antero de Quental and Fernando Pessoa in Portugal were great exponents of this paramount group of *iberistas*. But perhaps the most important legacy of this *iberismo* was the literary canon created by three Portuguese intellectuals—Almeida Garrett, Oliveira Martins, and Teixeira de Pascoaes—and four important Spanish philologists—Manuel Milá i Fontanals, Marcelino Menéndez Pelayo, Ramón Menéndez Pidal, and even Joan Coromines (a Catalanist *iberista*). Together, though in remarkably different ways, they created a canon of literary traditions—including, very significantly, the recovery of popular poetry—in Catalan, Portuguese, Gallego, and Spanish, in Europe, Africa, and America. They built a true "archive" of Iberian languages and literatures, which remains the crucial point of reference when speaking about *lo hispánico, lo latino, lo español, lo catalán*. This explains why in 1910 Joan Maragall, the most important Catalan poet of the early twentieth century—and, according to Unamuno, one of the best poets of Spain as a whole—responded to José Ortega y Gasset's criticism of *catalanismo* in purely *iberista* terms: "The Catalan question is the Iberian question, and until the relationship between Castilian Spain and Catalonia is treated in parallel with the relationship between Castilian Spain and Portugal, I doubt that anything with any basis can be said [about it]." And in 1918, Fernando Pessoa, one of the most insightful poets in any language in the twentieth century, wrote of Iberia, "the imperialism of the future," as of a dream: Iberia as the spiritual master of Ibero-America (not Latin America).[6] In the same way, the early twentieth-century US Spanish-speaking philologists were citizens of the *iberista* world.

By the 1930s, *iberismo* had become the patrimony of quasi-fascist intellectuals who supported, or tolerated, the Salazar and Franco regimes. But *iberismo* had a larger impact, both before and after these dictatorships. Many Catalan, Spanish, and Portuguese intellectuals became disenchanted with their quasi-fascist regimes in the 1950s and yet still supported an *iberista* cultural agenda. In the 1950s, the most important Catalan historian, Jaume Vicens Vives—who had supported the Franco regime, if ambivalently—interpreted the history of both Castile and Catalonia in *iberista* terms as part of a conflictive but common and inseparable *pactista* cultural matrix. Indeed, *iberismo* as a cultural legacy was so influential that even in the late 1950s, various prominent, disenchanted Catalan, Portuguese, Spanish American, and Spanish writers maintained it: Josep Pla in Catalan, Álvaro Cunqueiro in Gallego, Eugeni d'Ors in Spanish, Miguel Torga in Portuguese, and José Vasconcelos in Mexican, as it were.[7]

☙

In its origins, cultural *iberismo* was both a reaction and a part of another trend, *latinité*—a Franco-Spanish or Italian commercial and military alignment. But it was also at the roots of post-1898 *hispanismo* in the Iberian Peninsula and America. In Spanish America—but neither in Portugal nor in Brazil—*iberismo* as a concept often became *hispanidad* and, as such, parasitized the term Latin America. From the 1840s to the 1860s, *latinité* was the intellectual trend that gave rise to the imperial plan of *l'Amérique latine* during the French Second Empire. But *latinité* was much more than that; it was an adventure story with multiple plots: as much hashish-infused Neo-Latin ecstasy as the idea of *l'Amérique latine*, the French-led empire in America; or as much the unification of the entire Latin race as the union of classic *latinité* on both sides of the Mediterranean in view of Europe's decadence. *Latinité* was indeed a loaded term. By the 1940s, Josep Pla made fun of it in his ironic chronicles: "When the warm weather comes, in this country we smell like lamb's wool; in the winter, we smell like smoke from green pine branches. These must be the odors of the Latin race."[8]

The story is colorful. One of the first general histories of the term *latinité* was conceived by the Catalan architect, intellectual, and amateur Africanist Nicolau María Rubió, who wrote *La patrie latine: De la Méditerranée à l'Amérique* in 1945, while in exile in Paris. It reviewed the many attempts at *latinité* led at times by Castile, at other times by France, Italy, Portugal, or by Catalonia. For him, Christopher Columbus was neither Genovese nor Castilian—nor, as some argued, a Catalan—but *"un enfant de la Patria Latina"* (a child of the Latin Fatherland), which was "a prototypical image, inscribed at the very beginnings of our collective memory." Thus Rubió hinted at the far-reaching nature of *latinité*, which included precisely the domains that Columbus had incorporated into *latinité*—namely, America. Rubió, as a proponent of a Latin union on both sides of the *mare nostrum*, mentioned one of the first appearances of *panlatinité* in *Le hachych* (1843), written by the flamboyant Claude-François Lallemand, who was a medical doctor in Montpellier (an important location for our story, as we will see). In it, the protagonist, on a drug-induced trip, discovers not "erotic ecstasies" but *"des extases politiques"* (political ecstasies). A doctor invites the protagonist to consume hashish to see the truth of things—"The most remarkable property of hashish is that it excites the prevailing ideas of the person who has taken it; . . . his most complicated plans are disentangled with ease, his dearest projects realized without obstacle. . . . What clarity of ideas!" Thus the protagonist sees the need for "Neolatins" who could unite and protect the old local traditions of Latin peoples, for "we have renounced Roman traditions, despite our origins, because European civilization is advanced enough to go on without the aid of conquest." In a way, hashish revealed the need for *latinité* as a form of cultural confederation, a solution to the problems of imperial conquest and homogenizing modernization, for *"la santé du corps social"* (the health of the social body) depended on local freedoms. In the unmasked reality of hashish, Marseille would be the natural capital of a *latinité* formed by Spain, France, and Italy, a federation of brothers, not conquerors.[9] Here we already see the confederate and utopian cultural aspect that would eventually belong to the concept of Latin America, either in José Vasconcelos's version of a Cosmic Race, with its capital in the midst of the Amazon (Brazil), or in the more recent Bolivarian revolution, with its capital in Caracas.

These bizarre ideas soon achieved less gaudy expression in France due to the growing Pan-German and Pan-Slavic movements, which flourished from the 1850s to the 1900s. As I have argued, during his 1830s US trip, Michel Chevalier spoke the language of a superior, French-led Latin world opposed to the Teutonic and Anglo-Saxon races. But one of the founding documents of full Pan-Latinism was Prosper Vallerange's (François-Lubin Passard) *Le panlatinisme* (1860), whose title said it all *". . . confédération Gallo-Latine et Celto-Gauloise contre-testament de Pierre le Grand et contre-Panslavisme ou . . ."* (*". . . Gallo-Latin confederation and Celto-Gallic counter-testament to Peter the Great and against Panslavism or . . ."*). He was adamant, in view of the growing Pan-Slavism, "against which . . . there is no other remedy than Pan-Latinism."[10] Thus, before *latinité* became the intellectual fuel for the idea of Latin America, it already included connotations of resistance—similar to the connotations of resistance in the term Latin America; that is, the endurance of the last front against what modern times meant: change, inauthenticity, mechanization, loss of innocence. The irony is that cultural Pan-Slavism sustained similar ideas of spiritual superiority over hyper-modernized Germany or France, as best expressed in the voice of that melancholic Pan-Slavist Fyodor Dostoevsky: "The Slavic idea, in its highest sense, has ceased to be only a matter of Slavophilism"; it has "entered the very heat of Russian society; . . . it is . . . the notion of sacrifice, the need to sacrifice even oneself for one's brethren, and a feeling of voluntary duty by the strongest of the Slavic tribes to intercede on behalf of a weaker one . . . and thereby to found the great Pan-Slavic unity in the name of Christ's truth, that is, for the benefit, love, and service of all humanity and defense of all the world's weak and oppressed."[11]

But *latinité* had another connotation, the racial and cultural artichoke effect, which became a conceptual routine for all sorts of *latinité*, as much in Catalan-Occitan notions of the real Neo-Latin civilization as in the very idea of Latin America. Starting in the 1840s, *latinité* meant the struggle of the modern French North—entrepreneurial, individualistic, and rational—against the rural French South, where odd Romance vernaculars were still spoken and backwardness prevailed. The South was full of the people of the *"langue d'Oc,"* who still practiced the savage tradition that was also at the core of European and US stereotyping of Latin America: bullfights. These are the origins of the Félibridge movement, the advocates of the Provençal and Occitan troubadour tradition. Originally, this was a cultural movement against the centralizing powers of Paris and northern France, against modernization, industry, and linguistic homogenization, but it soon called for getting rid of the many French or Castilian leaves of inauthenticity in order to reach the core of the racial and cultural artichoke. In Latin America this would eventually signify the spiritual superiority of Latinos or of some authentic entelechy that needed to be de-Americanized or de-Westernized.

The poets and intellectuals of the Félibridge regionalist movement (especially Frédéric Mistral and Théodore Aubanel) advocated the spiritual superiority of the Latin South vis-à-vis the non-Latin North in publications such as *La Revue du Monde Latin* (1854–1880s), *La Revue Félibréenne* (in the 1880s), *La Feu, organe du regionalisme méditerranéen* (1917–1928), or, in Spain, the *Revista Española de Ambos Mundos* (1853–1855), and then the reconstructed version of the same *latinité* in periodicals like the *Revue de l'Amérique latine* (1922–1933) in the midst of US-sponsored Pan-Americanism. In these publications, a sense of *latinité* was aired simultaneously with emerging modern nationalisms—Provençal, Catalan, Italian, and Latin American nationalisms. To be sure, the Franco-Prussian War further "Latinized" both the Félibridge movement and French nationalism as a whole. Catalan intellectuals were part of the Félibridge Latinization and, curiously, Brazilians were also, through the significant input of F. J. de Santa Anna Nery and Comte de Barral in the *Revue du Monde Latin*—who did not promote unity with either Argentina or Mexico, but with Brazil as part of the civilization headed by France.[12]

In Italy, too, the Mezzogiorno allowed Italian and European intellectuals to imagine a pristine, traditional place that either had to be saved as a reservoir of authenticity vis-à-vis modern times or had to be overcome to reach a fully modern nation-state. Thus, from Pasquale Villari to Cesare Lombroso in the 1860s and 1870s, *l'uomo delinquente* was imagined through the analysis of southern Italy. But also, in 1906, writer and criminologist Napoleone Colajanni opposed northern Italy's racism using the Mezzogiorno. In his *Latini e anglo-sassoni (Razze inferiori e razze superiori)*, he criticized the concepts of Latin and Anglo-Saxon: "Some *noble* Anglo-Saxons can be savage, barbarous, corrupt, lazy, and stupid, just as some *degenerate* Latins can be civilized, honest, hardworking, and intelligent." For, if from the self-constructed notion of "*nazioni latine*" the anthropological element were to be excluded, what would remain would be "*aggregati diversi*" (various elements). In Colajanni's view, what had occurred was "*Latinizzazione*," a national and imperial project that "because of its intensity and geographical extent can in a certain sense only be compared to Aryanism [i.e., the Aryan race]." As Justo Sierra did with the idea of mestizos in Mexico, Colajanni believed that the Latins, like any other people, had no fixed racial structure; thus, the problem was not a matter of race but of education.[13]

In sum, whereas in *iberismo* the center was empire plus local autonomy, in *latinité* the key was somehow defined in the more modern terms of race identity. *Latinité*, understood as the Félibridge movement in France or as the Italian love/hatred of the Mezzogiorno, implied the imagining of a (geographical and/or human) reservoir of authenticity, of tradition, of real identity—that is, of utopian realization of the human species. Here one can already hear echoes of the lasting meaning of Latin America as a basin of unaltered traditions and authenticity. Indeed, these various *latinités* were what Spanish American intellectuals absorbed in nineteenth-century Paris—the brothers García Calderón, Enrique Gómez Carrillo, Pedro Lamas, and Manuel Ugarte, for instance. One of the great founding fathers of Pan-Latinism in Spain, the Dominican Francisco Muñoz del Monte, advocated the reenactment of the Crimean War's Latin-Anglo-Saxon alliance against the Slavs of the Americas (i.e., the United States), just as Parisian *latinité* had prescribed. José María Torres Caicedo, Francisco Bilbao, and Justo Arosemena advanced several variations on these *latinités*.

Curiously, by the late nineteenth century Garibaldi's Italy was absent from the prominent kind of Latin Americanism proposed by Rodó or Darío. This is odd, for, after all, Italy shared the same hero (Garibaldi) with Rodó's Uruguay, and Italian migration to South America was vast.[14] Moreover, Mexico's Juárez, in a peculiar form of transcontinental *latinité*, had furnished a poor blacksmith in Romagna, Italy, with a name for his son: Benito (1883)—Alessandro Mussolini must have admired Juárez not for being Latino but for having ordered the execution of Maximilian, the younger brother of Austro-Hungarian emperor Franz Joseph. Italy itself, in its imperial attempts in Africa starting in the 1890s, developed a notion of civilizing Italian *latinité* that shared many features with Spain's or France's articulation of *latinité* or *hispanidad*. After all, the nineteenth-century Italian influence in the world was vast, even reaching the Hindu and Indian nationalist Lajpat Rai, who in the 1890s used the Italian Risorgimento as inspiration. And yet, for all the dreams of a unified Latin America, Garibaldi did not seem to have had a strong appeal; he disliked very much the France of the Second Empire—that of *l'Amérique latine*—and he handed over his military victories, achieved in part with French support, to a monarch, Victor Emmanuel. A new, unified, monarchical Italy and an old and still extremely anticlerical Garibaldi fighting for France in the Franco-Prussian

War seemed to lack appeal for Spanish American intellectuals, who, by the late nineteenth century, were consensually republican and had abandoned radical anticlericalism. Imagine a Latin America with a fervent attachment to Garibaldi's unified Italy. It would have been an interesting experiment. Giacomo Leopardi, nevertheless, was part of the Catalan, Spanish, and Portuguese sense of decadence, especially after the appearance of the influential *Le pessimisme au XIXe siècle, Leopardi, Schopenhauer, Hartmann* (1878), by Elme-M. Caro. And of course, a very positivist reading of C. Lombroso's science was mandatory for Spanish American and Portuguese American scientists.[15]

Rome, however, did appeal to the strong Catholic gist of *latinité* in the Americas. Three contexts marked the assumption of a Latin American name and agenda by the Catholic Church in the 1850s: mid-nineteenth-century liberal reforms in Spanish America (often seen as Masonic complots); the Catholic confrontation against the challenge of liberalism (whose main exponents in the Spanish-speaking world were Jaime Balmes and Juan Donoso Cortés); and the mid-nineteenth-century threats to the Jesuits and the Vatican state, first by France and later by the Garibaldi-like (anticlerical) unification of Italy. In such circumstances, the influential and wealthy Chilean priest and politician—a close relative of Diego Portales—José Ignacio Víctor Eyzaguirre (1817–1875) advanced the project of a Colegio Pío Latino Americano in Rome. It was funded in 1858—always directed by a Jesuit—in order to educate the elite priests of Spanish and Portuguese America. The goal was to keep a unified reactionary front against the secular and liberal temptations in the American republics. As did Balmes, Eyzaguirre believed that Catholicism was the only civilization available for both Europe and America. "Half a century of bloody revolutions," he argued in *Los intereses católicos en América* (1859),

> . . . is the terrible holy teaching for America, that America seeks to rumple the faith she received from her elders and pretends to emancipate from the Church that granted her all the goods of Civilization. . . . America owes everything to the Church, to religion, to her faith; America was happy when religion was the basis of the actions of her governments; to the contrary, every time that governments combated religion, . . . their power eclipsed, their injured peoples ignored their authority and each Republic and each State fell down into a storm of bloody discords."[16]

As was the case with that other Catholic and Chilean proponent of the idea of Latin America, Francisco Bilbao, French liberal Catholicism

(Lamennais) influenced Eyzaguirre. The latter, however, took the common post-1848 reactionary route (closer to Balmes and Donoso Cortés than to Lamennais). Though Eyzaguirre never used the term Latin America in his 1850s writings, he supported the idea of a Latin American seminary, making use of Rome and centralized religion as the spine of the real and only possible civilization for the Americas. The college trained 1,504 priests from 1858 to 1957, and sponsored the I Concilio Plenario Latinoamericano (1899), which seeded the mission of a Latin American Church, which became an important institutional reality in 1955 with the creation of the Consejo Episcopal Latinoamericano (CELAM). Of course, by the 1960s a branch of this Catholicism would radicalize in a very Latin America–oriented fashion: liberation theology. All in all, this 1850s Catholic Latin Americanism was more linked to the Pope and reactionary Catholicism than to any idea of Latin American unity other than God, as a 1940s Colegio Pío's hymn affirmed:

> Hijos todos de América ufanos
> de la Virgen vayamos en pos;
> Ella quiere que seamos hermanos
> Ella quiere llevarnos a Dios.

> (All claiming to be proud sons of America
> Let's follow the Virgin
> She wants us all to be brothers
> She wants to take us to God.)

And yet, by the 1920s this early Catholic *latinité* had to face that old *latinité's* conundrum: Brazil. In 1927, the Brazilian clergy requested—and was granted—permission from the Vatican to open its own seminary in Rome. Though an all–Latin American seminary had been active for more than half a century, the Brazilian Episcopate maintained that "for us it is more convenient to have a College or Seminary that would be truly ours, exclusively ours, where our language would rule, and our habits and customs would gain due importance, providing a more homey ambiance in which the activities of our priests would be better performed."[17]

℞

Latinité was also consumed in an odd kind of Latin America: French Canada. There it was part of French Canadians' sense of unique sovereignty,

Latin and Catholic, during the second part of the nineteenth century. Catholic nationalists in the 1860s were pro-Maximilian, hoping for a strong Catholic counterweight in North America—all the better if led by French institutions and language. The French Canadian press was mobilized in favor of the French invasion of Mexico, and Honoré Beaugrand (1848–1906) (later mayor of Montreal) fought for Maximilian in Mexico. By the end of both the US Civil War and the Maximilian Empire, Canada's 1867 Constitutional Act furnished Quebec with significant cultural, religious, and political autonomy. But nationalism boomed in French Canada in the last part of the nineteenth and early twentieth centuries, as it did in the rest of the world. As Michel Lacroix has shown, French Canada's "Latin network" expanded in 1920s Paris through the interactions of French, Canadian, Spanish, Mexican, Argentinean, and Chilean artists and intellectuals—around *La Revue de l'Amérique latine*. By the end of World War I, such nationalists as the influential Catholic historian and leader Lionel Groulx (1878–1967) considered that the realignment of empires in Europe, as well as the booming American and Canadian Anglo-Saxon capitalism, would destroy French Canada's uniqueness. The solution was independence.

By the 1920s, a strong trend of French Canadian nationalism had, as it were, fully Latinized; first, by following the strong French pseudo-fascist *latinité* à la Charles Maurras (1868–1952)—the originally *Félibréenne* (Maurras was from Provence) and strong pro-*latinité* version of anti-Protestantism, anti-Semitism, antiliberalism, and nationalism of *l'Action Française*. And then, after the collapse of France in World War II, this Latinization continued by making French Canada a part of the Latins of America, advancing a common *latinité* with Latin America. It was a timid political agenda, but it had strong cultural connotations that resonated with both the history of the term Latin America and the history of French Canadian nationalism.

In the 1940s, in Montreal, the Union des Latins d'Amérique and other Canadian initiatives supported this common *latinité*, built over old nineteenth-century ideas, over networks of Catholic solidarities created, especially with Mexico, during the Cristero War, and over Maurras's style of anti-Anglo-Saxonism. But in the French Canadian version, it was also a *latinité* against US-sponsored Pan-Americanism. Members of this trend defined their new nationalism in old *latinité* terms, as did Jean-Paul Trudel in the 1940s: "The Mediterranean people—France, Italy, Spain and Portugal—upheld this Greco-Latin civilization and brought it to the New World with the crucifix. Sadly, the war now threatens to annihilate that civilization. This war brought the Americas closer together, and favored connections between French Canadians and Ibero-Americans. Our task is to bring back the world to faith, to the Christian spirit of the Middle Ages, and the Humanism of Ancient Greece and Rome."[18]

After World War II, French Canadian Catholic nationalism tamed its own "Latinizing," but always kept an eye on Latin America. Oddly enough, by the 1990s the idea of Latin America would gain a Canadian imprint through the influence of 1970s Canadian multiculturalism—very much seen as both a solution and a way to weaken French Canadian separatist feelings. French Canadian and Catalan missionaries in Bolivia, Ecuador, and Peru were, before the full *"mondialisation"* of multiculturalism, the pioneers of this odd *multikulti* "Canadization" of the idea of Latin America. It was a nice moral twist for another morally dubious racial and cultural Latinizing.

ᏫᎡ

As was the case in the 1860s with Vallerange's anti-Slavic Pan-Latinism or Michel Chevalier's anti-Anglo-Saxon Pan-Latinism, *latinité* was fully racialized by the 1890s. The pro-*latinité* Provençal regionalists of the 1890s sought to "affirm," to "proclaim" "the proof of the existence of a Southern Race through the centuries."[19] For northern anti-regionalists, such as the reactionary French nationalist Gaston Méry, *"le Méridional voilà l'ennemi"* (The South, there is the enemy), for it represented *"la race la plus détestable"* (the most hateful race), a *"péril latin."* In the same sense, the old literary renaissance of the Catalan language eventually became, for some important authors, an issue of race, as in Pompeu Gener. Just as Vallerange believed in an Aryo-Gothic race, Gener believed in the Catalan race, thinking it superior to the Castilian race, which, for him, was full of Jewish influence. The same could be said about Valentí Almirall's quasi-racial distinction between the Catalan and Castilian characters. In Italy, before the defeat at the hands of the Austrians at Lissa (1866), historians like the influential Jean Charles Léonard de Sismondi maintained the idea of the degeneration of the Latin people of Italy, mostly coming from the South, but in cultural and historical terms—the influence in the Mezzogiorno of those other Latins, the Castilian monarchies. By the 1890s, world-renowned Italian intellectual Guglielmo Ferrero (1871–1942) also believed in the decadence of the Latins (Italians) but as a product of racial degeneration derived from the hypersexuality of southern Italians.

In the same way, as in the racial *latinité* of the notion of Latin America after 1898, late nineteenth-century Spanish and French regional nationalisms were but the expressions of race, of nature, as the Catalan periodical *Som, Serém! Cap al'Esser* said, echoing the ideas of the founding father of modern Catalan nationalism, Enric Prat de la Riba: "We believe in Nature, the creator of nationalities. She made us Catalan, and we cannot be anything but Catalan." And like the idea of Latin America, Catalanism meant the gradual removal of layers of imposed inauthenticity and belief in an indisputable racial essence. In 1904, Prat de la Riba, returning from Occitan lands, believed that the Catalan nation was there, in Occitan lands, if only the "layer of Frenchness" could be extirpated; if only *"aqueixa crosta nova forastera"* (that new and alien scab) could be withdrawn, the real nation would emerge. If, for the Venezuelan writer and politician Rufino Blanco-Fombona or for the Brazilian nationalist Eduardo Prado, the idea was to de-Americanize (de–United States) Latin America in racial and economic terms, for Catalan nationalist Joan Bardina, the idea was to de-Castilianize Catalonia, in racial and economic terms, of course. If there are defects in "our race," said Bardina, it was due to *"un xich de semitisme, una malura kabilista [sic], que ens han encomanat els castellans"* (a bit of Semitic [blood], a cabalistic illness, with which the Castilians infected us). In turn, Basque regionalism, after centuries of being a struggle for *fueros* and local autonomy within Iberian pacts, became a modern nationalism in fully and forthright racist terms in the writings of its founding father, Sabino Arana (1865–1903).[20]

Iberismo had imperial Spanish and Roman (religious) connotations, but it was also based on a strong and lasting, romantic, anticentralizing attempt to rescue, say, the Occitan or the Provençal languages as the true spirit of the *Volk*, as the essence of an identity linked to *urbanitas*, to civic virtue and notions of the authentic self. This was the modern version of romantic philology's assumption of language as the axis not only of a people's culture but of its political existence. For Johann G. Herder, for instance, Europe had no right to impose language and religion on other peoples. "Did the Americans need a European culture?" wondered Herder, "The Spanish brought them no such things."[21] Regionalist movements challenged the strong modernizing and centralizing trends of modern European states, but also at times supported the imperial role of European states in non-European scenarios, just as such liberal nationalists as Alexis de Tocqueville or Max Weber did.

Post-1898 Spanish American *latinité*, however, was defined in racial terms—not that, for US and European observers, Latin America ever meant anything other than race. But for writers in the Spanish of the Americas, their race was Latin not because it was not Castilian or not Slavic but fundamentally because it was not Anglo-Saxon. Here is the old lasting meaning: "Latin" meaning to be naturally and ontologically not the United States. In the early twentieth century, Blanco-Fombona and the popular Colombian novelist José María Vargas Vila put this in the same terms as the other *latinité* nationalists, only assuming a different enemy: "El yanqui, he ahí al enemigo" (The Yankee, there is the enemy). And the nemesis was defined in racial terms. As early as the 1860s, José María Torres Caicedo, residing in Paris, pioneered *latinité* for Spanish America in confident racial terms: "La raza de la América latina / Al frente tiene la sajona raza— / Enemiga mortal que ya amenaza / Su libertad destruir y su pendón" (The race of Latin America / Is facing off against the Saxon race— / Mortal enemy that is now threatening / To destroy her liberty and her flag).[22] To be sure, in some few advocators of its name, "Latin America" meant somehow the end of certain forms of racism—Francisco Bilbao in the 1850s, and most notably José Martí in the 1890s. But to even conceive the concept "Latin America," between the 1880s and the 1950s, un-racially or as pure anti-racism would be as taking as face value the irony of the vulgar Brazilian saying, "*freira no puteiro.*"

CR

The old *iberismo* was originally more historical and cultural than racial, but starting in the 1870s and until the 1930s, it was racialized in biological terms. By the 1920s, in its *falangista* version, *iberismo* had also acquired strong racial connotations in the derived notion of *hispanidad*. Either culturally or racially, however, *iberismo* was always a reaction to Mediterranean *latinité*, which advanced common commercial and cultural interests among France, Spain, Italy, and Mediterranean Africa. *Iberismo*, however, had no *avant-la-lettre* translation to Spanish America, other than as a form of *hispanidad* that rarely included the Portuguese-, Catalan- or Gallego-speaking world. Before 1898, Spanish American popular xenophobia (often directed at Spaniards), as well as writers and philologists, criticized *hispanismo*, especially given the total disdain with which local languages and literatures—Spanish *mexicanismos, chilenismos,* or *peruanismos*—were treated by great *iberistas* such as Menéndez Pelayo. His masterful history of Spanish (all Iberian) literature covered Portuguese, Gallego, and Catalan literatures in depth, but virtually ignored any Spanish American authors—with such notable exceptions as Juan Ruiz de Alarcón and Sor Juana Inés de la Cruz. But after 1898, *iberismo* was made American (as in the continent) via an odd hybrid: the well-established *latinité* consumed in Spanish America in tandem with *iberismo* understood as *hispanidad*.

Thus, unlike Bilbao or Sarmiento in the 1850s, the great masters of Latin America as a cultural, racial, and anti-US entity, from the 1900s to the 1930s, were all translators of *latinité* into *hispanidad*: José Enrique Rodó, Rubén Darío, José Ingenieros, Manuel Ugarte, and José Vasconcelos. And they often, as in Italy, Portugal, or Spain, supported an authoritarian "racial" state. "Algunos escritores solían ser mercadería alquilada o comprada por tiranuelos de América" (Certain writers used to be a commodity bought or rented by little American tyrants), wrote the great Guatemalan art critic Luis Cardoza y Aragón, in his memoir, recalling *hispanismo*'s gilded age. With elegance, he concluded: "Darío, Gómez Carillo, Tablada, Chocano, Díaz Mirón, Vasconcelos, Salomón de la Selva, Barba Jacob and a few more; it's a list of men of genius and talent and also of [men who] simply had no shame. Their laughter is not amusing. But I'm no policeman, and I remember their beautiful passages best of all."[23] I say the same.

Indeed, this transcontinental translation of *iberismo* into *hispanidad* included lots of friendly fire, making use of the same racial weapons with which the superiority of *hispanidad* was advanced against Spanish America. Ramiro de Maeztu hated Sarmiento and Bilbao for attempting to de-Hispanize Spanish America by getting closer to US republicanism (Sarmiento) or French radical Catholicism (Bilbao). The Spanish writer Julio Camba saw the great Darío as a black drunk: "El lenguaje es negro, el pensamiento también" (His language is black, as well as his thought), as did Valle Inclán and many other Spanish intellectuals vis-à-vis Darío, *el divino mulato americano*. But Darío, while in New York City, used *hispanidad* for more than rejecting Anglo-Saxon materialism:

> Casas de cincuenta pisos
> Millones de circuncisos
> Y dolor, dolor, dolor.

> (Fifty-story houses
> millions of circumcised men
> and pain, pain, pain.) [24]

CR

Most modern European and American nationalisms, from the 1880s to World War II, were simultaneously anti-imperial and imperial; such is the nature of the modern nation-state, as Josep María Fradera has shown with his "imperial nation." US nativism and imperialism coexisted as much as

Mexican nationalist anti-US imperialism coexisted with the strong belief in the right to complete the conquest of the *"indios salvajes"* of the northern frontiers—in alliance with the United States—as well as with the right to influence Central American affairs. Modern Catalan nationalism, as E. Ucelay-Da Cal has shown, was a neo-imperialist regional *regeneracionismo* influenced by the Cuban experience. And Napoleon III attempted to create not only a Latin empire, but also a Franco-Arab empire, as inspired, for instance, in Saint Simonian Ismaÿl Urbain's notion of a French-led Latin-Arab Mediterranean—an idea that had more appeal than the Latin empire in America for the Provençal nationalists, who had been part of Mediterranean commerce for a long time. Also, having lost Cuba, some Catalan nationalists found Mediterraneanness more useful than a mythical Latin or Iberian union with America. Other *catalanistas*, centered on the important political figure of Francesc Cambó, promoted a *hispanista* agenda in the Americas from Barcelona so as to renew the cultural hegemony of Spain in the Americas, with Catalonia at its head. Ironically, unlike Catalan or Provençal nationalisms, Vasconcelos, Rodó, and Darío did not oppose the Spanish language; on the contrary, they made it the core of Latin America, the imperial kingdom of the Spanish language vis-à-vis the English language. Their regionalism was also imperial and local.[25]

Latin America came to mean anti-US imperialism in the 1900s, and especially after the 1960s, but in the *hispanista* version of the 1900s, the idea of Latin America supported the guiding role and spirit of Spain, which included commerce, language, religion, and political culture. Vasconcelos's *Indología* utopia was, like the fantasies of Catalan nationalism about being the head of Iberia, a renewal of the guiding role of Castile, only this time with a new race, the Cosmic Race, at the head. The regional and imperial projects inspired by Latinity were behind the Saint Simonian Michel Chevalier's idea of *l'Amérique latine* and the Iberism of Miguel de Unamuno or Joan Maragall, which easily became José Vasconcelos's *La raza cósmica* (1925) or José Enrique Rodó's *Ariel* (1900). Small wonder that, in his Hispanic universalism, Unamuno wrote to Uruguayan writer Carlos Vaz Ferreira (1907) recommending the best Spanish poets (from Spain): Jacint Verdaguer for the entire nineteenth century, and Joan Maragall for the beginning of the twentieth century (both wrote only in Catalan and were the cultural pillars of modern Catalan nationalism). The nineteenth-century Provençal, Catalan, or Occitan sense of authenticity and uniqueness (a language as a unique worldview) emerged in the idea of Latin America as a unique *Weltanschauung*, which, though it was expressed in Spanish, proclaimed itself the alternative to the decadent West. That is, Latin America was to foster an alternative civilization for an era in which civilization itself seemed to be in decline. It was never such a civilizational option, but it is a lasting empire: the Spanish language.

ନ୍ଧ

Both *iberismo* and *latinité*, in various versions and with various connotations, meant an alternative (to the assumed decadence of the West) but also a synthesis, a mixture, an amalgamation—of cultures, races, and imperial interests. Various forms of Portuguese, French, Catalan, and Spanish nationalisms claimed some sort of racial or cultural purity; thus, the mestizos were the others. But in fact, when nationalisms were invoked either in terms of *iberismo* or *latinité*, purity was only a manner of speaking, for indeed the theme was the intellectual acceptance and articulation of mixture, of the right mix. Portuguese and Spanish *iberista* intellectuals did not claim *pureza de sangre*; among them there were influential *hebraistas* and *arabistas* who collected documents, scientific treaties, poems, and dictionaries of the peninsula's Muslim and Jewish past—Menéndez Pelayo, Pascual de Gayangos, José Antonio Conde. They constructed an orthodoxy by rescuing forgotten heterodoxies, as Menéndez Pelayo did in his magnum opus, *Historia de los heterodoxos españoles* (1880, 1882). In France, Pan-Latinists such as Vallerange or Chevalier affirmed the superiority of the hybrid: the Latin as the blend of Roman, Celtic, Gallic, and Greek traditions. So, for Spanish American intellectuals, in Paris or in Mexico City, the advantage of assuming a position in favor of either *iberismo* or *latinité* was that this represented an approved form of mestizaje. In fact, in an era in which nonracial thought was inconceivable, to be able to accept and defend mestizaje was vital for intellectuals in the Americas, who could hardly sustain national or continental notions of racial purity. Of course, some late nineteenth-century Argentinean and Brazilian intellectuals defended racial purity, but the moment they spoke of *latinidad* or *iberismo*, they had become pro-mestizaje.

The real intellectual, scientific, and political struggle was over what kind of mestizaje it would be. But that is why both *iberismo* and *latinité* claimed uniqueness vis-à-vis other common pan-isms of the nineteenth and early twentieth centuries, which supported absolute racial and cultural purity. Nicolau María Rubió put it in a nutshell: in the diaries he kept while exiled in German-occupied Paris, he wrote, "Latin is synthesis. Germanic means anti-synthesis; a cold and frightening racial purity."[26] The same essential meaning has percolated from Vasconcelos to Leopoldo Zea, from Rodó to Arturo Ardao, or from Richard M. Morse to Walter Mignolo.

The black, the Moor, the Indian, and the Jew were the controversial ingredients that the various *iberismos* and *latinités* worked out. Within the peninsula, the Jews and the Moorish factors were constantly mentioned as positive or negative contrasts in nineteenth-century regional nationalisms claiming a federation of either Pan-Latinism or pan-*iberismo*. Thus, for Catalan nationalists, the Castilians were too Moorish or too Jewish; for the Castilians, the Portuguese were too African or too Marrano. But when speaking in the broader terms of *iberismo* or *latinité*, the center was synthesis. *Iberismo* and *latinité* in Spain and Portugal at times included *africanismo*, at least in mere intellectual terms—from the archaeological Spanish debate about the African origins of Spain to Franco's *africanismo* and from the nineteenth-century Portuguese promotion of miscegenation in Portuguese Africa to Salazar's long defense of a multiracial empire. The legacy of African slavery was a difficult historical burden to bear, but intellectual *africanismo* and embracing the right small quota of Jewish and Moorish cultural influence were signs of *latinité* and *iberismo*.

Thus, in Spanish America before 1898, *latinité* meant accepting mestizaje (insofar as it was Indian and European) within the French/Roman-Catholic synthesis. After 1898, *latinité* meant the same, only within *hispanidad*. Thus, locally in Peru or Mexico there were long-lasting, radical defenses of the indigenous past, present, and future in the respective nations (vis-à-vis a European destiny). There were also long-lasting radical understandings of the nations as petit Europes (vis-à-vis any idea of mestizaje or *indigenismo*). But by and large, speaking in terms of Latin America meant taking a position in favor of synthesis and thus accepting mestizaje, either as the natural consequence of what *latinité* meant (mixture, synthesis) or as a temporary station on the road to a final white *latinité* via education and immigration. In 1890s Argentina, thus, Manuel Ugarte had no doubts: "No one can cast doubt on the fact that the border of Mexico is the boundary between two civilizations. . . . They are two antagonistic entities that taken together represent a contrast of interests and ancient habits and a historical and geographical dilemma that cannot be resolved." But the mestizo as actor was what characterized Latin America, "Condemned to live between two circumstances with the ancient laziness of his origins and much of the pride of the European, passed over in some republics by the white man as an inferior, considered in others as illegitimate by the Indian, the mestizo vegetates and multiplies in a no man's land that his own lack of enlightenment perhaps makes fatal. Because, unlike what occurs in some countries—Germany, for example, is divided like a piece of furniture into drawers and compartments corresponding to each group—in

Latin America all liquids, whatever their density, are mixed together in the same glass." Thus, for Ugarte, Thomas Dixon's *The Leopard's Spot* (1902) was unthinkable in Latin America, but, as he claimed, not because Latin Americans already had a drop of *"sangre exótica en las venas"* (exotic blood in their veins), but because Latin America meant the repudiation of *"los errores que hacen ley en los Estados Unidos"* (the errors that are made law in the United States). In pre-revolutionary Mexico, Justo Sierra was a convinced *mestizofílico*: Mexico was an extension of the great syntheses that the Iberian Peninsula and its spirit had produced through centuries in Europe and the Americas. In post-revolutionary Mexico, Vasconcelos was the master of Mexican mestizaje and *hispanidad*, of a great new synthesis intended to take the reins of the decadent Latin European world. Both Sierra and Vasconcelos were also opposed to any black ingredient in the new synthesis, as each clearly expressed in travel writings about the United States and Brazil, respectively.[27]

◌঵

The "Latin" in Latin America began its long life in this bizarre intellectual milieu. And there seems to be no stopping it—*latinité* has always been criticized and always manages to come back. In 1934, prominent French writer Francis de Miomandre considered *latinité* a very controversial question that some people would have liked to eliminate "with the stroke of a pen or a burst of laughter." But, "we must believe that they are mistaken, since it returns periodically as the question of the day," because, for him, *latinité* stood for nothing other than basic human values.[28] Yet, soon afterward, Portugal, France, Italy, and Spain would begin their bloody descent into the most inhuman values, making the worst ideological use of their respective *latinités*.

THREE

The Question of Brazil: An inevitable note on Brazil's historical "Yes, but no thanks" to the idea of being Latin American

Le Brésil est un présent du xvie siècle, offert par le hasard à l'avenir.

—F.-J. de Santa-Anna Nery, *Le pays des Amazones: l'El-Dorado, les terres à caoutchouc* . . . *(Paris, L. Frinzine et cie, 1885), xii*

Escute. Há ocasiões em que eu me sinto enquadrado no meio natal. Sou um com a minha gente. Nessas ocasiões sou brasileiro como os que mais o sejam . . . E como é bom ser brasileiro! Contudo, não é o único bem da vida. Daí amanhecer, outros dias, norueguês ou tchecoslovaco (mais freqüentemente, francês). Isto é o que eu chamo de *liberdade espiritual*. Este, sim, o maior bem da vida. Ser. Mas ser tudo. Não somente brasileiro.

—Letter, *Carlos Drummond de Andrade to Mário de Andrade, December 30, 1924, in Carlos e Mário, Correspondência de Carlos Drummond de Andrade e Mário de Andrade (Rio de Janeiro: Bem-Te-Vi, 2002), 79*

In Brazil, *iberismo* had a very different trajectory. To my knowledge, it was never appropriated in its Spanish American hybrid *iberismo-latinité* version. It became, first, an institutional historical mark that precisely explained Brazilian exceptionalism vis-à-vis the *latinité* of Spanish America. There was, to be sure, a Brazilian *americanismo*, at times derived from *iberista* exceptionalism (as in F. J. de Oliveira Vianna, Richard M. Morse, or José Guilherme Merquior), and at times appearing as a local form of pro- or anti-US ideology (as in Manoel Bomfim, Eduardo Prado, or Manuel de Oliveira Lima). But not until the emergence of dependency theory did Brazilian intellectuals fully embrace the expression "Latin America." Moreover, *iberismo* became a way to deal with something that *latinité*, in its European and American hybrid forms, did not confront: the stain of slavery. And finally, *iberismo* without *latinité* became an instrumental way for Brazil to deal with the US factor. That is, Brazil's *iberismo* served its imperial concerns, which could not afford the strong anti-Américanism (anti–United States) implied in pre- and post-1898 Spanish American *iberismo* and *latinité*.[1]

ᘒ

Since the mid-nineteenth century, Brazil's intellectuals and popular culture have often either ignored or rejected the categorization of their country as part of Latin America. In fact, Latin America and Brazil have maintained a mutual ignorance, which nevertheless did not prevent the great empire of Brazil from being generically included in the term, Latin America, starting in the twentieth century. For long, Brazil was often characterized as it was in the 1850s edition of an influential German dictionary of politics and jurisprudence (*Das Staats-Lexikon: Encyklopädie der sämmtlichen Staatswissenschaften für alle Stände*, originally produced by Karl von Rotteck and Carl Theodor Welcker), which described it as "more closely associated by its constitution with Europe than with the other countries of the New World; it is outside of the Americas' [*amerikanischen*] system, giving it a peculiar importance."[2] To be sure, nineteenth-century Brazil was not the fifth empire that Father António Vieira envisioned in the seventeenth century; but it was the most stable and largest empire of the Americas.

Brazil's history developed an *iberista* mark, the institution of monarchy, which made Brazil un–Latin American from the outset. As historian Ricardo Salles put it, commenting on the internal formation of a Brazilian identity, which included the monarchy and slavery: the emperor, the monarchy, and its representative institutions marked the "*respetabilidade*" (respectability) of Brazil vis-à-vis Europe "in comparison to the 'primitivism' and instability of the other Latin-American nations." Despite slavery, this mark was indeed respected in the world, for, as Salles pointed out, the other optimal American solution, the United States, also included slavery within republican institutions after experimenting, as did Brazil, with the possibilities of saving the institutional English legacy. Latin America, thus, was Brazil's symbolic and material enemy by embodying both republicanism and "*barbarie*." Giving up Brazil's unique Iberian mark, said Joaquim Nabuco in the 1890s, seemed "*um atentado contra a história*" (an assault against history).[3]

Before the 1860s, Brazil understood itself as the non–Latin America, and in fact, rather than assuming the burden of *latinité*, many of the new countries emerging out of the former Spanish Empire would have liked to follow Brazil's institutional solution to the world crisis started by the Napoleonic Wars. In 1807 Portugal became a piece of a larger whole overnight, the Lusitanian Empire: the regént king and the court moved to Rio de Janeiro. In Rio, the crown was the gravitational force that held together a vast empire. Unlike the old viceroyalties of New Spain or Peru, Brazil was almost half a continent, and remained unified and relatively stable in territory and structure throughout the nineteenth century. The monarchy was the state, and the state was the empire, a confederation that offered protection and stability vis-à-vis the many European and American challenges and against domestic revolts (especially worrisome because of the persistence of a vast slave economy). This institutional arrangement for long seemed a much better option than what Spanish America went through from 1810 to the 1860s. What explained the integrity of the empire also explained the survival of the political regime (the monarchy)—namely, the un–Spanish American mark: slavery and a politically enlightened elite devoted to civilizing an American scenario beyond regional differences.[4]

In September 1815, a new imperial order was declared in Rio—the United Kingdom of Portugal, Brazil, and the Algarves. Brazil became a kingdom among kingdoms. Soon after that, Dom João was crowned in Rio de Janeiro—like Charles V, he had been a regent king during the life of his insane mother. Never before, and never since, has a European king of a vast empire been crowned in America. When European concerns made the king's return to Portugal inevitable, his son, Dom Pedro, led the Brazilian independence movement (1822). Thus emerged the independent *empire* of Brazil, whose institutional arrangements and territorial integrity were maintained until 1889—not without serious difficulties and challenges, especially during the First Empire (1822–1832) and the Regency (1832–1840). This would leave a lasting institutional, legal, political, and military mark on Brazil that would have important consequences for the country's un–Latin American history.

This is the Iberian institutional history that Brazilian intellectuals and politicians constantly invoked throughout the nineteenth century. From the moment of independence on, they defended their exceptional path and the mark left by Iberian institutions: through the imperial monarchy, transformed in various ways, nineteenth-century Brazil fought hard to differentiate itself institutionally and culturally from Spanish America. In the late nineteenth-century, Brazilian intellectual and diplomat Oliveira Lima, comparing Latin with Anglo-Saxon America, still maintained that Brazil was un–Latin American: for him, Brazil had escaped Latin America's *"tentação liberticida"* (temptation to destroy liberty).[5] Indeed, regardless of cultural or ethnic affinities, rather than bringing it closer to the ethereal concept of Latin America, Brazil's imperial interests held it relatively aloof, except of course from the Río de la Plata, Bolivia, and Paraguay. But that was no Latin American love; it was the business of empire.

Brazil's interests vis-à-vis Bolivia, Paraguay, Uruguay, and Argentina should not be seen as an embrace of the idea of Latin America, but as the projection of Brazil's imperial profile in the Southern Cone. These interactions can be seen as the necessary complements of the growth of the regional importance of Brazil in the Southern Cone, not as Latin Americanism per se. In the late nineteenth century, Brazil and Argentina were, together with the United States, Australia, South Africa, and Canada, the world's most important examples of "new development," attracting immigration and investment, and becoming important regional powers. So both countries, Argentina and Brazil, engaged in mutual cultural, political, diplomatic, and even military (the result of a massive imperial war in which Argentina and Brazil fought together) recognizance. But this was not about Latin American "modernity" or integration. Was Australia about Anglo-Saxon modernity and integration? Were 1890s interactions between France and Russia about Slavic modernity or about mutual interests in the collapse of the Ottoman Empire and the balance of power in Europe?[6]

In 1825, for instance, the governor of the Bolivian province of Chiquitos requested and gained protection from the Brazilian province of Mato Grosso, thus nurturing Brazil's imperial goals and reputation in the region. Similarly, when Spanish troops threatened Chilean and Peruvian ports in 1864–65, Brazil lent its ports to the Spaniards, threatening its supposed neutrality—though Brazil had more to fear from its neighbors than from Spain. Indeed, Brazil conceived itself as a *"bastião da civilização cercado de repúblicas anárquicas"* (bastion of civilization surrounded by anarchic republics).[7] Thus, over the course of the nineteenth century, Brazil engaged in three wars with or against the Río de la Plata nations. In 1825 it battled the Provincias Unidas del Río de la Plata over the Provincia Cisplatina (Uruguay), which resulted, through the United Kingdom's mediation, in the independent nation of Uruguay. In 1851, Brazil allied itself with the provinces of Entre Ríos and Uruguay against the Argentinean dictator Juan Manuel de Rosas. Finally, in the 1860s Brazil joined forces with Uruguay and Argentina against Paraguay, resulting in the devastation of Paraguay and the annexation of part of Paraguay's territory. And Brazil's imperial nature was not lost on the rest of the world. In 1871 and 1872, Brazil became the internationally sanctioned legal intermediary during the Alabama claims—the US claims against the United Kingdom for its support of the former Confederate states. Brazil played this role not because it was the largest country in the mythical Latin America, but because it was the empire of the South, an internationally recognized power that could successfully serve as an intermediary between two powers—supporting US claims, of course.

Starting in the 1850s, in the various congresses and meetings attempting a Latin American Union, Brazilian diplomats played an ambivalent role, and at the end never actually supported the union, not even rhetorically. These congresses, which called for some kind of continental unity, were held in Panama (1826), Lima (1847–48), Santiago (1856), Lima (1864–65), and Washington (1889–90). Brazil participated only in the last of them, a fully US-sponsored Pan-American congress.[8]

By the end of the nineteenth century, the presence of the Brazilian emperor, Pedro II, at the 1876 World Centennial Exhibition in Philadelphia, openly displayed Brazil's radically different approach to the United States vis-à-vis Spanish America; an approach that made it by definition non–Latin American. And understandably so; US imperial gains in Mexico and the Caribbean not only were not of concern to the Brazilians, but also offered protection against Brazil's true enemies: Europe and its neighbors. Influential diplomats like the Baron of Rio Branco or Joaquim Nabuco brought Brazil and the United States closer through diplomacy and further enlarged the distance between the myth of Latin America and Brazil. During the interwar period and World War II, Brazil reinforced this "special" relationship with the United States, not as a "sellout" banana republic, but as a strategically allied empire that was aware of its own limitations and its real cultural, military, and commercial interests. This is the extent of Brazil's Latin American character.

CR

To be sure, there were some reciprocal *intellectual* attempts to Latin-Americanize Brazil, but not many. I believe, though it would be hard to test, that before the Cuban Revolution, it would have been inconceivable for the general public in Brazil to consider itself Latin American. The strong Brazilian sense of belonging to a region, its large population of African descent, and massive immigration from Southern and Eastern Europe and Japan make it hard to believe that the country could have had a widely dispersed popular sense of Latin Americanness. Being Latin American was, like *iberismo* in the peninsula, a matter for intellectuals and politicians. Starting in the 1970s, through the effects of the Cuban Revolution and the influence of various exiled intellectuals, and also thanks to post-1990s global ethnic agendas, Brazil's popular culture became somewhat more acquainted with the idea of Latin America.

Prominent Brazilian sociologist and former president Fernando Henrique Cardoso claimed that, during their time in exile in the mid-twentieth century, Brazilian intellectuals fully discovered the existence of Latin America. Before that, Spanish American intellectuals had no real place for Brazil. For a time they admired it, but after the 1860s they either ignored or feared it, depending on their location. One could produce an anthology of Peruvian, Brazilian, Mexican, and Argentinean writers and statesmen who cited Brazil as a model to be imitated in the 1830s and 1840s. For instance, the Mexican politician and historian Lucas Alamán described the trade-off that 1808 and 1814 had meant for Mexico and Spain in Brazilian terms: "This project [bringing the royal family to New Spain to escape Napoleon's invasion] would have had the greatest results. . . . Mexico could have won its independence without violence or turbulence, like what happened in Brazil."[9] Indeed, in the first half of the nineteenth century, thinking of Brazil was a way to jettison the burden of the concept of Latin America.

The early proponents of the term Latin America in the 1850s were republicans or liberals like Francisco Bilbao, who had no place in his idea of Latin America for a slave monarchy, though by the 1870s the crown was clearly in the abolitionist side. But others, such as Alamán, felt admiration for Brazil's unique history. Commenting on Brazil's peculiar institutional setting, Justo Arosemena—that great promoter of a South American union—explained Brazil's independence as a virtuous solution vis-à-vis the chaos in Spanish America: Brazil's independence "was rather a friendly goodbye, sanctioned by her parents, by the grown daughter. . . . The monarchy, liberalized as much as possible, was transplanted so smoothly in Brazil that there seems to be no resistance."[10]

One could also elaborate an anthology of Argentinean, Paraguayan, and Bolivian intellectuals who feared Brazilian imperialism. Prominent among them was the Argentinean Juan Bautista Alberdi, who wrote many critical articles about Brazilian imperialism during the Paraguayan War. But all these pro- and anti-Brazilian writers, by and large, had nothing to say about Brazil as part of Latin America.

Between the 1830s and the 1940s, very few books about Brazil or translations of Brazilian books were published in Spanish America. There were some Spanish and Argentinean translations (of Nabuco, Oliveira Lima, J. M. Machado de Assis, Eduardo Prado) and a few Argentinean books about Brazil, naturally. In Mexico, before the translations of Machado de

Assis's *Memórias póstumas de Brás Cubas* (1951), Sérgio Buarque de Holanda's *Raízes do Brasil* (1955), and before what was published as *Interpretación del Brasil* (1945), by Gilberto Freyre, there was nothing about Brazil other than diplomatic pamphlets published in Spanish during the 1910 Centennial celebration; a book about Brazil written by the former Mexican ambassador to Brazil, Alfonso Reyes; a history of Brazilian literature published by Alfonso Reyes's friend and protégé, Ronald de Carvalho; and, finally, another pamphlet by Stalinist intellectual Vicente Lombardo Toledano, which ambivalently condemned Getúlio Vargas's revolution in Brazil. There was, nonetheless, an important Brazilian book translated into Spanish in 1918, by a Mexican in exile, Carlos Pereyra: Eduardo Prado's *A ilusão americana* (1893)—published in Spain as *La ilusión yanqui*. Pereyra was a strong Mexican antiliberal, an enemy of everything American (United States), and a vociferous and prolific enemy of the Mexican Revolution. Catalan writer Josep María de Sagarra, who shared the same hostel in the Madrid of World War I, described him as a strong, pro-German writer who had "una mala llet del temps de Moctezuma molt ficada en la pell" (a bad temper from the times of Moctezuma really infused into his skin). Of course, as we will see, Prado's book was an ideal component for Pereyra's Mexican anti-Americanism, but not important evidence of his knowledge of Brazil.[11]

In Argentina, by 1911, there were such prominent intellectuals as Manuel Ugarte, who, from a pro–Latin American Union point of view, sought to include Brazil. But Ugarte's Latin Americanism was expressed within the booming and relatively stable Argentina of the 1890s; his claims were less a defense of racial or cultural union than an argument against the triumph of nationalism in the Southern Cone, both in view of the economic and political success of countries like Uruguay, Argentina, and Brazil, and of the fear of US imperialism after 1898. "For the majority, patriotism consists in closing one's eyes," he wrote, for "young nations, like conceited women, cannot live without flattery." For Ugarte, Argentina and Brazil were particularly nationalistic, unable to see their shared history and what they had in common with the rest of Latin America vis-à-vis, of course, the United States, the "lamp or [the] sun" before which all Latin American republics appear, "according to their distance and volume, either as butterflies or satellites." But Ugarte was indeed an advocate for the inclusion of Brazil in the entelechy Latin America, though he had few followers.[12]

In fact, Ugarte was following the lead of an Argentinean critic and diplomat, Martín García Mérou, who published *El Brasil intelectual* (1900), one of the very few books in Spanish published before the mid-twentieth century that dealt with Brazilian culture. It was a detailed review of the literary history of Brazil and showed that, although very little from Mexico or Peru reached Buenos Aires, at least something was available. Garcia Mérou's treatment of Nabuco, especially of Nabuco's book on José Manuel Balmaceda, is especially revealing—he called Nabuco "the Brazilian Macaulay." Even before the 1900s, romantic Argentinean poet José Mármol lived in Río, in exile during Juan Manuel de Rosas's regime in Argentina, and later missed Río, for, as he wrote from Montevideo to his protector José Tomás Guido, he was "tired" (*aburrido*) of democratic calls like those of Esteban Echeverría and the May Revolution (independence revolution) in Buenos Aires. In early twentieth-century Argentina, things were not very different. Borges—granted, not an ecumenical reader of the Latin dimension of the continent—unashamedly admitted his ignorance about "*la lírica del Brasil*." This, he said, was not the result of animosity, but of an "indolent belief, perhaps erroneous but not illogical": his and his friends' libraries had nothing astounding to show about Brazilian literature.[13]

In turn, Mexican José Vasconcelos published two books with strong Brazilian content: *La raza cósmica* (1925), a pro-mestizaje manifesto resulting from a trip to Brazil, Uruguay, and Argentina; and *Indología* (1927), an interpretation of Ibero-America, including Brazil, in which he used the term *Indología* "to designate this new vital historical current; . . . Indología in the sense of a science of the Indies, a science of the universe, not of the ancient or modern Indies, nor of the geographical Indies, but of the Indies in the sense of Columbus's fantasy that the earth was round, of the unity of the species and the harmony of cultures." He located the capital of his mythical Cosmic Race in the middle of the Amazon. By the late 1930s, however, he feared Brazil's diplomatic proximity to the United States and its lack of *hispanismo*, of real *iberismo*; for, more than of Latin America, Vasconcelos spoke of *iberismo*: "No one can deny Brazil's enormous progress; but they are trying to hide the fact that it is the Portuguese spirit that is flourishing there, [that spirit] which once dominated the seas and spanned the world." In addition, Alfonso Reyes, Mexican ambassador to Brazil (1930–1935), was indeed a great promoter of Brazilian literature in Spanish; the mainstream Brazilian literati truly considered him their interlocutor. His intellectual approach to Brazil, however, seems closer to *iberismo*—à la Menéndez Pelayo—than to Latin Americanism.[14]

In sum, throughout the nineteenth century and well into the 1920s, properly speaking, Latin Americans read the same authors—not because they read each other but because they read Walter Scott or Emilio Castelar; Victor Hugo or Lord Byron; Leopardi or Pérez Galdós; Queirós or Rabindranath Tagore. Of course, at times *costumbrista* authors from Peru and México did read each other—and even wrote to each other, as did Ricardo Palma and Ignacio M. Altamirano—but the borders among Latin American languages (Spanish vs. Portuguese, Spanish or Portuguese vs. Quechua or Nahuatl, or Quechua vs. Nahuatl) were a lot stronger than those between the American Spanish or Portuguese vis-à-vis French, English, Italian, and even German. Not only fancy intellectuals, but also other people who knew how to read and write in the Americas culturally inhabited not Latin America but a language with all its complex global connections.

With notable exceptions, the Portuguese and Spanish realms of things had ignored each other in the continent. For instance, perhaps the only fully extraordinary style in the late nineteenth-century Portuguese or Spanish of the Americas was that of Brazilian J. M. Machado de Assis (1839–1908). In a region whose intellectuals had considered ideas of either Latin or Iberian unity throughout the nineteenth century, one would imagine that Machado de Assis's remarkable Portuguese prose would have had wide diffusion in Spanish—as had, for instance, the novels by J. M. Eça de Queirós (1845–1900), a Portuguese master of his language, which were amply admired and translated in Spain (at times by such important writers as Ramón del Valle Inclán). But Portuguese and Spanish have been so aloof from each other in the Americas that Machado de Assis remained virtually unknown in Spanish until the 1950s. There seems to have been an early Uruguayan 1900s translation of a few of Machado de Assis's works—made by Julio Piquet, a friend of Rodó. I have found also a rare translation of *Esaú e Jacó*, made anonymously and published in Buenos Aires in 1905. Better known were the translations, published in Paris in the 1910s, by the prominent Spanish writer and polyglot Rafael Cansinos-Asséns and by the bohemian critic Rafael Mesa y López—Benito Pérez Galdós's last secretary and friend. But the fact is that such an important Brazilian writer as Machado de Assis was virtually unknown in Spanish until the mid-twentieth century, when the lucid Mexican philologist Antonio Alatorre translated *Las memorias póstumas de Blas Cubas*—thanks perhaps to the 1950s Latin Americanist moment of the influential Mexican state-owned publishing house El Fondo de Cultura Económica, which widely dispersed Machado de Assis's novels in the Spanish-speaking world.[15]

ন্ধ

Latin Americanism within Brazil has been both a marginal intellectual trend and, often, a way of defining Brazil itself—precisely as an image that produces no reflection in the Latin American mirror. By the 1890s, there were odd mirror effects at work: Spanish America hardly translated, studied, or knew anything about Brazil, while Brazilian intellectuals rarely cared about Latin America, other than as a negative contrast. But in the twentieth century, Brazilians used the Spanish language as the instrument of their domestic cosmopolitanism and non–Latin American existence. As A. Cândido explained it: "Higher education in Brasil from 1940 to 1960 would have been practically impossible" without the Spanish, Mexican, and Argentine translations of the classics of philosophy and social science.[16] Various generations of students in Brazil read Marx, Heidegger, or Weber in Spanish. Practically all Brazilian scholars and intellectuals have read Spanish; very few Mexican, Colombian, Argentinean, or Cuban scholars and intellectuals count Portuguese as part of their intellectual equipment. Curiously, regardless of the institutionalization of Latin Americanism in the United States, the general trend prevails: US Brazilianists often at least read Spanish, whereas a US Mexicanist or Peruvianist would rarely bother to read Portuguese.

The real Brazilian concern with Spanish American literary trends was originally of European inspiration, read in French or English. Voltaire's or Marmontel's eighteenth-century interest in Peru, said Cândido, inspired the Spanish American motifs of the prestigious eighteenth-century Brazilian poet Basílio da Gama, who wrote about Tupac Amaru after the manner of Voltaire:

> Ferindo a vista os trêmulos cocares,
> Animoso esquadrão de Chefe Augusto,
> Rompe as cadeiras do Espanhol injusto
> E torna a vindicar os pátrios lares.

> (With quivering crowns to dazzle the eye,
> Brave Squadron of Chief Augusto,
> Break the cruel Spaniard's rule
> And once more defend the native land.)

In the same way, the visibility of the writings of Darío, Rodó, or the brothers García Calderón in Paris made *latinité* accessible in Brazil. As late as 1931, Brazilian writer Prudente de Moraes Neto told Alfonso Reyes that it was through Valéry Larbaud—the prominent French writer who introduced Spanish, English, and German writers into the French literary canon—that he had learned of the existence of one of the masterpieces of

Argentinean literature, Ricardo Güiraldes's *Don Segundo Sombra* (1926). To be sure, Alfonso Reyes's friend Ronald de Carvalho and, later, Erico Veríssimo were somehow acquainted with Mexico in an uncommon way for 1920s and 1940s Brazilian intellectuals, thanks to Reyes and the world appeal of the Mexican Revolution. But before the effects of the Cuban Revolution and the influence of the intellectual exiles of the second half of the twentieth century, there were only a few important Brazilian writers who were concerned with the idea of Latin America: Joaquim Nabuco, Silvio Romero, Eduardo Prado, José Veríssimo, Oliveira Lima, Oliveira Vianna (from a fully *iberista* position), and Manoel Bomfim.

Joaquim Nabuco was known and admired in Argentina and Uruguay, but it would be fair to say that he was completely unknown in the rest of the continent—perhaps with the notable exceptions of Alfonso Reyes, Pedro Henríquez Ureña, and José Vasconcelos. But Nabuco's many writings were not suitable for any kind of *latinité*. He was critical of Spanish American political experiments. In 1890, he wrote to Rio Branco, celebrating the development of the new Anglo-Saxon nations and criticizing the new Latin nations, that "perhaps it could be worth while to show how Canada, Australia, and the English colonies have fared under the parliamentary system. These, like those rampant republics of Spanish America, are also young countries, yet their citizens are free men who do not, and will not, ever suffer the same humiliation inflicted on their subjects by the Santa Annas, Barrios, Rosas, Guzmán Blancos, and tutti quanti."[17]

In turn, Veríssimo, although he really did introduce Spanish American writers into Brazil, had no room in his thought for any Latin Americanism other than the ecumenical republic of letters formed by writers aware of literature in Portuguese, Spanish, French, and English. In turn, Oliveira Lima's *iberismo*, too sensitive and at times too favorable to the United States, went against what the very idea of Latin America stood for. As Arosemena and other South American liberals had done in the 1860s, Oliveira Lima reinterpreted the Monroe Doctrine, the bête noir of Latin Americanism, in a positive light. For his part, Eduardo Prado's strong anti-Americanism, in *A ilusão americana* (1893), was sustained in monarchical terms, in conservative *iberista* ideas of a lost paradise of order. This was at odds with 1900s Latin Americanism, which was certainly antimonarchical, if not liberal and democratic. Prado was thus very critical of Juárez's republican Mexico (allied with President Lincoln during the US Civil War) and of everything in Spanish America, for "the frenzy of imitating the United States has been the ruin of America." For his part, historian Oliveira Vianna was concerned with Brazil itself and its Iberian matrix, but as he defended

Brazil's *Sonderweg* here and there in his many books, he both rejected and criticized nineteenth-century Spanish American republicanism. He advocated a unique form of anti-Americanism, based on the idea of synthesis—the optimal individualist, republican, and industrial US model merged with improvements drawn from Brazil's Iberian, corporatist, and pluralistic tradition.[18]

But there were also Brazilian supporters of Mexico's struggle against a Latin empire in the Americas. As Paulo Moreira has shown, in the 1860s Machado de Assis wrote some poems and essays praising Mexico's struggle against the French Latin empire. It appears that Machado held Maximilian and Carlota in great esteem, but he revered Mexico's resistance against a foreign intervention. Machado de Assis, however, did not support Mexico in the name of a Latin American Union but of an America free of European interventions. This ambivalence echoed that of the Brazilian government in the 1860s, when both the emperor and representative chambers officially recognized the Mexican Empire—after all, Maximilian was Dom Pedro II's first cousin and had visited Brazil as a young Austrian navy officer. The emperor, however, never sent an ambassador to imperial Mexico or did anything to assist his cousin, for, as Maximilian's Mexican envoy in Brazil concluded, relations with the Lincoln administration were much more important for Brazil than relations with Maximilian's empire in Mexico. Some Brazilian intellectuals, however, like Fagundes Varela, as Moreira shows, were fully Juaristas, and being Juarista in 1860s America was being pro-Lincoln and anti–French imperialism, not an advocate of that very French idea, *l'Amérique latine*.[19]

Romero and Bomfim's debate over Bomfim's *A América latina: Males de origem* (1905) is a well-known chapter in the history of racial thought in Brazil. Romero was the most important historian and literary critic of the early twentieth century, while Bomfim was a medical doctor, sociologist, and psychiatrist whose reputation did not equal Romero's. Romero despised miscegenation and predicted the gradual whitening of Brazil, thus departing from typical Latin Americanist arguments in favor of mestizaje. In their *iberista* debates with the prominent Portuguese statesman and intellectual Teófilo Braga, both Romero and Braga used each other's mixed race as an insult: for Braga, Romero was mestizo; for Romero, Braga was *"um cigarro oriundo das Açores."* But Bomfim, a scientist, saw nothing wrong with mestizaje: "In the history of Latin America there is no factor that proves that the mestizos have degenerated in relation to the essential qualities of the races that begat them." Indeed, Bomfim's book at first sight seems to be a pro–Latin American manifesto, defending mestizaje and the civilization of indigenous peoples. He praised Paraguay's Guaraní ethnic profile; for him, the Guaranis would have reached great standards of civilization if not for the devastation caused by Brazilian imperialism. But in fact, neither Romero nor Bomfim was a friend of the idea of Latin America or of any inclusion of Brazil in such a semantic landscape. Romero sustained Brazil's uniqueness and rejected the racial chaos and promiscuity of Spanish America; Bomfim actually rejected race *tout court*, and thus inevitably had to reject the very idea of Latin America—wise man. For him, Latin America was already a racial category, and nothing good could come from it: "The most unfortunate part of all this is that we ourselves, the Chileans, Mexicans, or Brazilians, . . . because we encounter the concept so often, because of the clarity and simplicity of its terms, will end up admitting that such a thing as Latin America must exist, like those who damn us with that epithet; in other words, we will believe that we suffer from some essential inferiority, a sort of ethnic original sin that renders us all incurably degraded, sharing a single fate."[20] These un–Latin American positions have been typical of Brazil for a long time. In Brazil, wrote Brazilian writer Afrânio Coutinho in 1969, "Every day we feel less Latin."[21]

CR

Thanks to Brazil's *iberista* exceptionalism, unique views of Brazil as a mestizo nation rather than a racial democracy began to emerge in the twentieth century. Regardless of the validity of Gilberto Freyre's or Buarque de Holanda's interpretations of race in Brazil, the fact is that both had used the Iberian roots of racial and cultural synthesis to open the image of Brazil to plural legal codes and traditions—just as Brazilian anthropologist J. Baptista de Lacerda or diplomat and writer Oliveira Lima had done in more racist terms. Young Buarque de Holanda read the strong *hispanidad* of Latin America in such authors as Rodó and Francisco García Calderón, but used it to reject Brazil's un-American (i.e., US) destiny, not to affirm its Latin American nature: "Imagine the inferno that would emerge from the bonding of these completely different civilizations." The mature Buarque de Holanda used *iberismo* as a way to construct a racial profile of the nation; a profile that those who defined "Latin America" based on *latinité/iberismo* did not even conceive of until the second part of the twentieth century, when Fernando Ortiz in Cuba and Gonzalo Aguirre Beltrán in Mexico expanded the idea of Latin America to include some blackness and cultural pluralism. In the late twentieth century, the few great proponents of Brazil as Latin America, such as Darcy Ribeiro, combined this lasting Brazilian *iberismo* with the fully *indigenista* Latin Americanism of the 1970s. Thus Ribeiro's Latin America was a defense of indigenous people and blacks as a civilizational option. Also, since the 1980s, scholars such as Richard M. Morse—and to some extent José G. Merquior—had maintained the Latin Americanness of Brazil based on *iberista* arguments: Iberia as an alternative enlightened West, which translated Brazil into a Latin American *Sonderweg*. This was an Enlightenment based less on John Locke than on the sixteenth-century Spanish political philosopher Francisco Suárez, based on non-individualism, on mestizaje, and on what José Vasconcelos saw as the advantage of uncontrolled desire—which actually fascinated Freyre himself as well as Morse—as a path to a new civilizational option born from lust.[22]

Over the last few decades, Brazilian commercial and strategic interests in the Southern Cone have grown, as has a small school of Latin American studies, thanks to more and more translations and new Brazilian books about Latin America—although there are not many compared to the number of books translated from English, French, or German, or the production of histories of Brazil, Portuguese-speaking Africa, and the racial connection with the United States. In 2004, Brazil's most prominent, fully Latin Americanist scholar, Maria Ligia Prado, still believed that "it is undoubtedly very difficult to continue down the path of Latin American studies in a country that insists on looking to Europe and the United States as intellectual models. Latin America, in general, is seen as a minor or secondary area, in which political passions take precedence over serious and rigorous study. Thus, the historian who is committed to Latin American themes and fascinated by considering Brazil in this broader framework, must make a greater effort and be twice as disciplined in order to maintain his/her arguments. After all these years, I continue to think that it is much more stimulating to see Brazil alongside the countries colonized by Spain than to keep looking only at Europe."[23]

&

To be sure, speaking in English, Brazil is undeniably and characteristically "Latin American." Whatever "Latin America" may be, however, it is something that Brazilian history has rarely sought. This is not out of ingratitude; it is simply a fact. Brazilians, one might say, ought to learn to want to be what they are. Or maybe just to be what they want to be.

FOUR

Latino/a and Latin America: A succinct note on the reciprocal intellectual and political effects between the term Latino/a in the United States and the very idea of Latin America

Em lugar de ser culpado da nossa desnacionalização, eu fui uma das melancóli-
cas obras dela.

—J. M. Eça de Queirós, *"O Francesismo" in Obras de Eça de Queirós, vol. 2 (Porto: Lello
& Irmão, 1979), 1647*

Nowadays, whether one lives in Chicago or San Pedro de Macorís, the Dominican Republic, one has to be careful. The doorbell may ring at any moment, and one could carelessly open it to find a social scientist at the door
asking how one identifies—Black? White? Mestizo? Hispanic? Latina? The
pollster could be carrying a palette in her hand to contrast one's answer
with the actual color of one's face (an unfair thing to do: our buttocks,
not our faces, are the keepers of our true color). And even in San Pedro de
Macorís, the person at the door could be, say, a Harvard professor, ready
to determine, through DNA analysis, that one is 50 percent black and thus
an Afro-Latin American, unconscious of, or in denial about, one's own real
identity. A robust statistical finding, which surely makes one black . . . or
white, or Indian, or a Jew, or all of the above. But the lesson is this: the
twenty-first century began as the nineteenth century ended: obsessed with
race. US TV shows and Internet sites about DNA lineages, and one academic paper after another confirm the current dictum: racial being deter-
mines consciousness and not the other way around. Hence, through this
neolinajero fixation (fixation on searching for lineages), such a relatively
new term in US political, academic, and commercial parlance as "Latino/a"

and that old term, "Latin American," reinforced each other semantically, thus gaining political and philosophical power.

Neither the terms (Latino/a, Latin America) nor their recent US marriage of mutual convenience, I believe, reflects as neat a historical conclusion and as nice a political strategy as have been often advanced both by a trend in US Latin Americanism and by "Latino/a studies." Both names are charged with undesirable and uncontrollable racial and historical connotations. Although nearly 40 percent of the US population will soon be classified as Latino/a, it is not such a statistical fact that would maintain the semantic powers of the terms "Latino/a" and "Latin America"; it is the belief in race that makes impossible opting out of using those terms in current US identity politics. I know that. I merely want to submit a list of historical scenes as evidence of unwanted side effects that require a more cautious and less automatic and naïve use of both terms and their marriage.

Having passed the Mexican, Hispanic, greaser, Chicano, and Mexican-American stations, we have reached the Latino/a station. The last term has been canonized since the 1970s and is now widely used in consumer culture, in scholarship, and in politics. The story is well known in the histories of US civil rights, census data, and the emergence of ethnic identities in twentieth-century US politics.[1] Latino/a is assumed to be a cultural, panethnic, historical, political, and linguistic category all at once. And yet, it exists and survives because of its undeniable racial denotations within a particular racial order and a peculiar fear of disorder—that of the United States. Not that Mexico, Spain, or Peru is free of racism; they constitute their own racial orders and disorders. But it is only in the United States, or from United States, that the term Latino/a has any meaning. In all possible senses and with all possible connotations, there would be no Latin America and no Latinos/as without the United States.

Sociologists have studied US ethnic identity formation, showing that the African American experience and the peculiar racial order produced by the one-drop rule, together with the massive migration of Mexicans, Cubans, Salvadorians, Puerto Ricans, and Dominicans to the United States in the twentieth century, have determined specific ethnic positionings. Large-scale continuous assimilation, miscegenation, and English monolingualism, of course, have also been facts of life for "brown" people. The constant renewal of immigration, however, as well as the black-white polarized US racial order, have created the ethnic identity Latino/a within a market that demands either an assumed racial neutrality (white) or a clear degree of ethnicity. But it is not that Latinness–whatever it might be—can be found in US history as an essence, always there, waiting to be uncovered and cherished. As historian Andrés Reséndez showed, in the territories between old New Spain and the United States, in New Mexico and Texas, in the first half of the nineteenth century, "a person was not a mission Indian *or* a Mexican, a black slave in Mexico *or* an American, a foreign-born colonist or a Texan, but could be either depending on who was asking."[2] Two structural forces, not often in synchrony, Reséndez argued, swept the region over time and determined the limits of social and political identification: states and markets. Thus the trajectory of the mythical ethnic identity, Latino/a, is not a history of a genetic or cultural or empirical actor, but that of variegated and contested processes of becoming and unbecoming—consumers, citizens, taxpayers, voters, labor force, criminals, terrorists.

As was often the case in the frontier regions of emerging states, in the Manitoba region of North America the expansion of the beaver fur trade fostered alliances among Europeans, colonists, and different native groups; it also gave rise to new groups, such as the Métis, who later fought both for and against new nation-states. Catalan speakers in the Pyrenees region did the same during the sixteenth and seventeenth centuries, maintaining commercial and political alliances with different crowns and assuming either French or Spanish institutional disguises, until what were contingent identities became their only political existence in the era of strong nation-states. And in both Manitoba and Catalonia, the case could be made—as Métis or Catalan nationalists often have made it—that their ethnic or cultural uniqueness deserved either an independent nation-state or special cultural recognition within nation-states. In the case of the United States and Mexico, the Mexican-American War seems to have clearly demarcated the possibilities of political and cultural identification in New Mexico, Texas, Arizona, and California. But in fact the process was not very different from that of many frontier regions of "wannabe" nation-states. Native groups from all over New Spain, not only from the northern frontiers—Criollos, and all sorts of mestizos—were, for long, subjects of the Spanish Empire, fighting wars of conquest against local natives, allied with other locals, capturing and enslaving *"indios bárbaros"* in *"guerra justa,"* and being captured, assimilated, and enslaved by local natives or Christianizing *"indios mansos,"* expanding commercial routes and political alliances, often speaking French or Spanish as lingua franca. As Ramón Gutiérrez has argued, the parameters of political and cultural identity were, above all,

God and king and then many variegated local (peninsular and American) possibilities.[3]

After 1821, both Indians and non-Indians were made Mexicans by decree, reshaping the parameters of negotiation of their local political and cultural existence. The Treaty of Guadalupe Hidalgo, which completed the US conquests of the former Mexican territories, made of the former New Spaniards, or Mexicans, or *indios mansos amestizados*, or Californios, or Texans, all of them, white by treaty, and they would defend that status for nearly a century—by calling themselves Spaniards, Mexicanos, Californios, or Nuevo Mexicanos, meaning white by treaty. And they did so against a racial order that did not respect the citizenship (whiteness) that such an order had granted them. "*Mexicano* responses to such insults," says Ramón Gutiérrez, "came in two forms. First they crafted distinctions in Spanish that were understood only within their linguistic community, and secondly, they created larger panethnic identities that were hemispheric and global in reach, far beyond the boundaries of the national geography in which they found themselves."[4]

In such a way, then, the global language of *latinité* and *iberismo* became the patrimony of those who were "white by treaty." But this cannot be seen as the defense of good rights with bad racist and imperial weapons. Rather, it ought to be seen as the creation of political identities that, seeking to oppose land dispossession or racial discrimination, maintained nevertheless the racial order: old Mexicanos in the United States claimed their *hispanidad* or *latinidad* to defend their imperial and racial rights against local Indian groups, whom they fought and killed (often in alliance with the "Anglos" that discriminated against them), and fully participating in the anti-black social order. *hispano, mexicano*, or *latinoamericano* in the United States, from the 1850s to the 1940s, meant above all a way to say: "we are not blacks"—as was also the case in many forms of *hispanidad* in Mexico, Argentina, or Peru.

Starting in the 1970s, markets and the state—understood as a polity that granted services and protection through complicated mixtures of typologies of race, class, and citizenship—gave rise to the "Latino" cluster: somehow designating a homogenous ethnic group sharing a common authenticity that encompasses old ideas of *latinité*, contemporary US identity politics, and deep-rooted Washington Irving–like views of the Hispanic world. As Arlene Dávila demonstrated, the entelechy "Latino" has worked well for a nation believed to include people of various nationalities with unique cultures, ethoses, and languages. This belief, Dávila argued, was "fed and maintained by sources as varied as the precept of contemporary US multiculturalism, nineteenth-century ideas of Latinidad developed by Latin American nationalist ideologies, and Anglo-held beliefs about 'Hispanics' evidencing the varied sources that are strategically put into service in the commercial representation of Latinidad as forever needy of culturally specific marketing." Authenticity thus becomes a commercial and political necessity. Therefore, Latinos are structurally linked to an imaginary "Latin America"—somehow encompassing Spain—and hence allowing access to a political and commercial market at the cost of eternal exclusion, exoticism, and invisibility: "Latinos are continually recast as authentic and marketable, but ultimately as a foreign rather than intrinsic component of US society, culture, and history, suggesting that the growing visibility of Latino populations parallels an expansion of the technologies that render them exotic and invisible."[5]

Making people exotic and invisible involves fear of assimilation, of being actually the same as the "others": thus exclusion and self-exclusion arise because of racism or because of fear of becoming like them ("Anglos" or "Latinos"), or of being overwhelmed (by the browns, by the blacks). As late as the 1990s, Samuel Huntington once more reacted to this fact with fear of the Mexicanization of the United States—fear that the "genuine" cultural and racial order of the United States would be overcome by an unstoppable brown tide of un-American Spanish speakers. And as I write this, one more in the long list of US populist and nativist messiahs, Donald Trump, vows to clean the country of eleven million exotic rapists. This latest messiah wants to be president, and he might succeed, but not in making America white and great again by erecting—better said, making Mexicans construct and pay for—a nearly two-thousand-mile wall, the sanitary cordon for a mythical US identity. This is extreme, but it is not news. This is what the prominent Swiss American biologist Louis Agassiz feared during the US Civil War. He wrote to a friend, "Can you devise a scheme to rescue the Spaniards of Mexico from their degradation?," and upon learning of the Confederate bombing of Fort Sumter (1861), said, "They will Mexicanize the country." Mexicanizing meant not only political instability and violence—the Civil War made the United States one with the Americas' modern violent struggle to create unified nation-states—but it also meant racial chaos and promiscuity like that imagined to predominate in Mexico, which was supposed to emerge from the end of slavery.[6]

In a way, however, post-1990s Latino/a activists have also accepted this promise, reacting to the same basic fact (the two-hundred-year Mexican presence in the United States) by making assimilation—cultural, racial, and linguistic assimilation—the bête noir of a presumed Latino ethnic identity. Hence, in the 1990s, Chicano poet Nephtalí de León could ask in English: "Why should a pinche Gringo / tell our Raza / where to go?" And writer Richard Rodriguez becomes the Mephistopheles in the Latino/a creed for being a prominent assimilated writer in the English language— "I never had an adversarial relationship to American culture. I was never at war with the tongue." And yet his books are shelved according to racial categories: "In either case I must be shelved Brown. The most important theme of my writing now is impurity. My Mestizo boast: as a queer Catholic Indian Spaniard at home in a temperate Chinese city [San Francisco] in a fading blond state in a post-Protestant nation, I live up to my sixteenth-century birth." For, as he argues, "how a society orders its bookshelves is as telling as the books a society writes and reads." At the University of Texas, the Benson library, which is the largest Latin American collection in the United States, also houses the Latino/a collection, for, one must conclude, the many English-writers of "Latino" origin, the experiences of millions of Americans, belong there and not in the large and adjacent Center for American History at the University of Texas.[7]

Invisibility, however, is the most silent and uncanny result of US Latinidad: I myself, dressed as a janitor, would be materially invisible for my colleagues and administrators at the University of Chicago. And yet the mere possibilities of exoticism and invisibility intrinsic to the term "Latino/a" turn out to be an unrecognized privilege if compared to the inability of African Americans to be exotic and invisible.

∾

After the Holocaust, an ethnic marker should at least have the verisimilitude of cultural and historical validation. For the term "Latino/a," such validation, rather than from Mexico itself, has come from the idea of Latin America. But if the complicated histories of how we came to have and use both terms—Latino/a and Latin America—are considered, such a linkage can be supported only by a belief either in an ideal and mythical/cultural matrix or in a racial atavism. Presumably Latino/a has implied unity in history, unity in oppression (resistance), and unity in language/culture, more than it has implied race. And this sense of unity, it ought to be clearly stated, is an important post-1960s political strategy. But that does not mean that it stands up to the minimum of empirical and conceptual—and even ethical—rigor. In other words, these are important myths, but they remain myths, nonetheless.

Third- or fourth-generation Mexicans in the United States cannot be considered on a continuum with sixteenth-century Chiapas, or twentieth-century Merida, or twenty-first-century Buenos Aires. *Latinité* and *iberismo* do indeed have something to do with the history of how we have come to accept "Latino/a" as a respectable word. We have Latino days, the Latino community, Latino heritage, and Latino music, but are there Teutonic days? Is there a Teutonic community? Teutonic heritage? Teutonic music? To be sure, the history of Mexican Americans intersects with Mexico, but not with Mexican history per se—understood as a body of nationalist historiography. Mexican Americans and Mexicans share a history, indeed—the history that Mexico as a whole has shared with the United States during the last two hundred years, which to this day remains foreign to those other historiographies known as "American history" and "Mexican history." Both realms have been constructed under the presupposition that, regardless of a few obvious chronological or thematic intersections, they are mutually exclusive stories; one is precisely what the other is not. The broader shared history of North America is also made invisible by the very notion of a Latin American history. The category of Latin America inevitably implies the separation of the story into two ontologically different histories (American history cum European history, Mexican history cum Latin American history). It is the persistent belief in race, however, that keeps the idea of "unity in history" intact and makes such unity potentially expandable to any time or place where an *ad hoc* racial subject can be found.

Unity in oppression, of course, links the history of Mexicans, Salvadorians, and Guatemalans in the United States—and their histories in Mexico, in Guatemala, and in El Salvador. But, on one hand, this oppression cannot be reduced to what the idea of the Latino/a implies: that is, a history of Anglo/white/criollo oppressors vs. brown/Indian/black oppressed peoples. Every day, Salvadorian immigrants face the oppression of the local brown or indigenous coyote, the brown Mexican police and army, and the Latino border patrol. In turn, a simple ride on bus 55 in Chicago, from Hyde Park to Midway over East 55th Street and Garfield Boulevard, reveals the complicated and tragic map of oppression that cannot encompass all people of color together. Once the opulence of Hyde Park is left behind, there are blocks and blocks of total desolation and institutional abandonment—except for the presence of a police state. This is a huge African American ghetto abandoned by elite and working-class whites as much as by elite and working-class Mexicans. At some point, one reaches a huge, vivid, alive but poor Mexican neighborhood, which has distinguished itself, as much as Hyde Park has, from the African American ghetto; blacks in such a large Mexican barrio are as suspicious and as unwanted by police and residents—in the streets or as clerks in restaurants and stores—as they are unwanted in Hyde Park. Moreover, longtime Mexican American residents of Chicago are, for Mexican newcomers, as much part of the oppression as white bosses.

Indeed, in the name of good analysis and useful politics, we need to be more specific. What kind of oppression, when, and how? The fact that networks of solidarity emerged, as they did among Filipino and Mexican agricultural workers during César Chávez's struggle, is not decipherable through ethnic essences, but through the understanding of specific historical circumstances. Without specificity, the ethnic Latino's unity in oppression is better treated—morally speaking—in Marx's timeworn terms: that is, as a universal principle of class.

In turn, unity of culture, epitomized by the value of language—by and large the Spanish language—is a myth, perhaps a politically useful one, but a myth nonetheless—unless, of course, we reduce culture to a limited number of words and to some consumerist ethnic markers in cuisine, religious rituals, and family mores. Otherwise, commonality of culture through a mythical, deep-rooted "Latin" *Weltanschauung* is gone before one is even able to identify oneself as Latino/a. For calling oneself Latino has been the essential sign of Americanization.[8] When the term in use was "Hispanic," a 1930s *corrido* recorded in Texas among Mexican immigrants mentioned this process, which is the same one that time and time again Mexicans, or Argentine immigrants, have repeated ("I did not know I was Latino until I came to the States"):

> Hablar no quieren muchos paisanos
> lo que su mamá les enseñó
> y andan diciendo que son hispanos
> y renegando del pabellón.

> (Many of our countrymen don't want to speak
> the tongue their mothers taught them
> but they keep on saying they're Hispanic
> and yet they deny our flag.)[9]

Nowadays it is a *delito de lesa etnia* (crime against ethnicity) to highlight the importance of language in the Latino and Latin American senses of belonging. Yet it remains uncertain what Latin America might be beyond language. What is clear is that it must involve the Spanish-speaking world, as well as the many speakers of various incompatible indigenous languages. For all the talk of bilingual education, year after year US statistics show that the great majority of Latinos/as do not speak any Latino language. Their world is the United States, their language English. A great early twentieth-century *iberista* from New Mexico, Aurelio Macedonio Espinosa, in telling, in Spanish, the story of the eighteenth-century love of Doña Concepción Argüello for Count Rézanov in the San Francisco Presidio, idealized the time in which all the children of Spain in California spoke beautiful Spanish. But by the 1900s, Spanish newspapers in New Mexico were clear: "New Mexican Hispanics differ culturally from Mexicans or Latin Americans in general; they are de-Hispanicizing themselves, forgetting their language, their traditions, and the innate feeling of being Latin American." For the *hispano-nuevomexicano* was a US citizen, an American who *"piensa en inglés"* (thinks in English). Of course, these were merely the opinions of some Spanish newspapers in New Mexico. But from the 1840s to the 1930s, this press was the most important expression of the long Spanish-speaking presence in what is now the United States. A review of the Spanish newspapers in New Mexico, Texas, and California, from the 1900s to the 1930s, reveals not a Latino (*à l'américaine*) ethnic consciousness but a blend of concerns: local grievances and issues that often involved conflicts with state and federal governments, and both English- and Spanish-speaking "oppressors"; a deep concern with Mexico's politics, especially enhanced by Mexican literati exiled in the United States; and what can be called a serious *iberista/hispanidad* sense of belonging, reproducing not only the same sense of unity and superiority of the Iberian matrix of civilization but actually reproducing articles by Spanish and Mexican authors through syndicated op-pieces bought in Mexico, Spain, and Argentina. One can find in these US Spanish newspapers many essays by Ramiro de Maeztu, Miguel de Unamuno, José Pla, Miguel Bueno, José Vasconcelos, and Martín Luis Guzmán.[10]

Today, to be sure, it is scandalous to de-Latinize a self-identified Latina just because she does not speak Spanish fluently—or read and write it. Latino/a, it is argued, indicates an alternative epistemology, an ontological existence beyond language. But, on one hand, in the United States can we conceive of a unity in culture beyond language (command of Spanish) that yet excludes English (the actual linguistic existence of Latino/as)? On the other, the history of the Spanish language in the United States has a less ethnical and more complicated story. Beyond the myth of some kind of Latino proximity to the Spanish language—or of more proximity than those whose ancestors did not speak Spanish—as the materialization of a culture par excellence, language is a mere triviality. The vast literature on "Latino-ness," the many novels, poems, treaties, and monographs, are all not only written in English but also meant for a specific, English-speaking audience. The notion that George de Santayana and William Carlos Williams, as well as prominent current writer Junot Diaz, write in either Spanglish or another ontology in English highlights the importance of a vague, but loved, ethnic mark imposed over the complexities of language—a mark that is considered of course more important than both the overwhelming normative powers of English and Spanish and the actual way languages evolve. The truth is that race is more important than language as a source and habitat for US *latinidad*.

But if, just for a moment and all too experimentally, we leave the category of race aside, then the Latino/a can be said to be part of the English-speaking world. This is not an insult. It is a fact, and nothing can be done about it. Whatever complex cultural or political positionings the word Latino/a implies, they do not refer to the complexities and nuances of the Spanish-speaking world. I do not see a problem here. It is not that existing in Spanish is such a wonderful thing, or at least mainstream world scholarship's complete intellectual disdain for scholarship in Spanish would suggest as much. It is merely something Spanish speakers do; their children might not. The Spanish language is indeed an intricate cultural realm not shared, say, by a Latina scholar and a Bengali subalternist. But the latter two are part of the same academic mainstream; they participate in the same production of English words. Scholars writing in Spanish could say, "Tu subalterno es mi hegemónico." "Don't humiliate yourself and don't give up hope," wrote philosopher Carlos Pereda, advising young philosophers in Spanish. There is no way to join any famous Agora in Spanish, and thus the only decent thing to do in Spanish, said Pereda to the young, is to "try to get into one of the many places halfway between knowledge and ignorance, between power and impotence."[11]

The fact is that, without language, cultural sameness is hard to maintain in a massive consumerist society that is home to the world's lingua franca. A cultural unity beyond language is either a tempting call for institutions that would support legal and political coexistence in a multilingual milieu, as in the European experiment of the 1980s. or the old modern business of monolingual unity based on some kind of genetic trace—in other words, right back to race. Of course, there is the Jewish, more-than-linguistic sense of unity. But as shown by the pre-Holocaust antagonism between Sephardi and Ashkenazy Jews, or by the cultural differences between Yiddish- and German-speaking Jews, language was the center of different Jewish identifications. Languages are, in the modern world, not only a matter of Herder-like *Volkgeist* but also, very importantly, a matter of sociocultural status. It is a hierarchy, even in terms of accents (better a German than a Spanish one in US English)—to such an extent that, as some historians have argued, if not for the power of Islam (David Wasserstein) or of the Holocaust itself (Peter Novick), the Jewish sense of unified cultural identity would have fragmented in the midst of many linguistic, national, and class distinctions.[12]

The origins of the current US concept of Latino/a, therefore, have little to do historically with the linguistic preoccupations of *latinité* or *iberismo*, except in some old uses of the Spanish language in Texas and New Mexico and their links to the Spanish-speaking world as a whole. In fact, if history can teach us anything, it is that the trajectory of Mexican Americans, whether descended from immigrants or not, is by and large a history of struggle against the ethnic marker, defending either the "white by treaty" status or a sort of racial limbo that could allow Mexicans in the United States to negotiate their social status depending on the moment and circumstances, as they have done for centuries in New Spain or Mexico. The history of the proud embracing of the ethnic marker through various forms of ethnic politics, multiculturalism, anti-assimilationism, or nativism is a rather short and recent one. It is an important narrative, even vital; morally speaking, it is the right history. But it is a US-specific story for which the category of Latin America is merely a nonsensical and, unfortunately, inevitable addendum.

ʒ

Antimiscegenation laws offer a window through which to observe how Mexicans defended their racial limbo. In 1908, Dr. Raphaël Anatole Émile Blanchard, from the French Academy of Medicine, wrote about what he called the mestizo paintings: that is, the eighteenth-century *castas* paintings that are today invariably included in any US Latin American history textbook. Blanchard argued, wrongly I believe, that mestizos were left with no real social place within New Spain's social hierarchy. Thus, he maintained, Spanish authorities sought to measure the degree of *"mesticidad."* "Castilian pride," thought Blanchard, could not stand promiscuity. Before Blanchard, E. T. Hamy, one of the founders of nineteenth-century physical anthropology, had studied similar paintings, which were found in a Paris museum, and he interpreted them as degrees of degeneration. Nothing to do about that: no one in the United States, France, England, Germany, or

Spain, between, say, 1850 and 1920, could conceive that racial miscegenation was biologically, culturally, or morally commendable. Consider this: the last antimiscegenation law was repealed in the United States in 2000.[13]

Porfirian and early revolutionary Mexican *mestizofilia* was reinforced by its very proximity to the United States. It was appropriated in odd ways by the US racial legal system. The constant flow of Mexican and US citizens between the two territories reinforced the self-identification of Mexicans as something rare, mixed, and odd: not black, not Asian, not Spaniards, nor pure Indians. Simply Mexicans. In 1921, in Arizona, Joe Kirby nullified his marriage with Mayellen—a Mexican American—by proving that she was black. When interrogated, she said her mother and father were Mexicans, "What do you mean by Mexican . . . Indian, a native?" asked the judge. "I don't know what is meant by Mexican," she responded.[14] The limbo, mestizo existence of Mexicans made them in the United States what mestizos were in the hierarchical structure of colonial times—that is, a matter of daily and local negotiation.

From the 1830s to the present, not one of the many US antimiscegenation laws specifically included Mexicans. At times Mexicans could prove to be white; at times they were considered Orientals, or Mongolian, or blacks, but it all depended on specific circumstances—class, region, language, skin color, gender. The ambiguity of being "Mexican" was even sought by some African Americans, as economist Paul Taylor showed. He found many cases in 1930s Chicago in which foremen caught African Americans pretending to be Mexicans in order to be hired in the packing industry. The prominent 1941 antimiscegenation case (*Pérez v. Sharp*) was advanced in California not because Andrea Pérez was Mexican, but because she was considered white, and her husband was black. Andrea asserted her non-whiteness to avoid being subject to California's antimiscegenation law. But the interracial Catholic civil rights networks embodied in her lawyer, Daniel Marshall, constructed the case by appealing to constitutional freedom of religion and won the case on religious terms, for Mexicans could not be fully and always accepted as anything in the United States. Therefore, they often defended their limbo status, at times claiming Spanish descendants, at times, above all, denying any Asian or black traces in their *linaje*. By the late 1970s, the Chicano movement had transformed the antiblackness common in *latinidad:* Chicanos had shared with African Americans the same history of oppression. This was a political strategy, of course. Was it empirically and, above all, ethically a robust argument?[15]

Of course, lynching people of Mexican descent became the expression of what historian Richard Hofstadter (*The Age of Reform*, 1955) called ethnic nationalism, an expression of anguish about lost status and extinction. According to William D. Carrigan and Clive Webb, more than five hundred men of Mexican origin were lynched in the United States from the 1870s to the 1930s—a debatable high figure, I would argue. Except for some well-known cases, Mexico's history has no record of massive lynching or killing of US citizens, but it does offer ample evidence of the killing and harassment of Spaniards and Chinese. But it would be intellectually far-fetched and politically unjust to argue that the vast and growing Mexican population in the United States was caught in the not-negotiable cage of blackness. In turn, mestizaje in Mexico clearly functioned as an odd form of nationalism, ethnic indeed, but aiming, by its own praise of mixture, to overcome ethnicity with nationality. I do not call this paradise, but it represented a different racial order than that of the United States.[16]

⁊

The term Latino/a has had a very complicated history with the Spanish language in the United States. To be sure, Latino/a has prevailed over US Hispanism's aristocratic notions of culture. But Latinidad also has exposed the internal political and cultural contradictions of Spanish-speaking *letrados* in the United States.

Richard Kagan, a historian and a *hispanista*, coined the term "Prescott's paradigm," and US Hispanist James Fernández came up with "Longfellow's law."[17] On one hand, Prescott's paradigm involved the realization that US scholarly interest in the decadence of Spain coincided with the growth of US imperialist ambitions; on the other, Longfellow's law put forth the idea that such a peculiar preoccupation with the decadence of Spain was marked by US power over Latin America. But in reading such early US Hispanists as William H. Prescott, George Ticknor, Washington Irving, or H. W. Longfellow, I fail to determine which one is stronger: a US view of Spain biased by Latin Americanized US eyes or a US perspective on Latin America already "Spainized" by the persistent intellectual struggle for the name (Latin America? Hispanic America? Ibero-America?). The old *iberista* innuendos—racial, religious, cultural—percolated into US perspectives of, say, Mexico or Mexicans in the United States.

During the nineteenth and twentieth centuries, Spain and Mexico were ideal mirrors for reflecting whatever meaning America (the United States) was to have. But cultural crossings between Spain and the United States echoed romantic ecstasy, which, since the eighteenth century, had become a common trope in European languages. I mean not only the expansion of empires but the vice of getting out of place—in cultural, historical, and chronological terms. In the United States the ecstasy became the temptation of a long and ancient history—vis-à-vis the brief history of a nation believed to have started from zero—and the nostalgia of authenticity and tradition—vis-à-vis rapid industrial change and the destructions of "communities." Thus, starting in the late eighteenth century, nostalgic worship of tradition and self-assumed civilizational superiority were commonplace in European languages when dealing with encounters between Britain and Spain or between Germany or England, on one hand, and southern Italy, Portugal, Spain, or Greece, on the other. Following Kagan and Fernández, allow me to call this the *"barret mexicà* (Mexican sombrero) law in the Barcelona Ramblas." Simply stated: in the United States cultural things are demanded in Hispanic versions, just as Mexican sombreros are bought in the Barcelona Ramblas. The *barret mexicà* is the US stereotype of Mexicanness that passes as generic Hispanic, even as Catalan. The Pakistani retailer who sells the sombreros functions as a *hispanista*—he furnishes clients with what they demand. It makes no sense to ask the retailer not to sell as Spanish or as Catalan a Mexican sombrero, precisely because of that insurmountable law of the *"barret mexicà"*: namely, triggers change (it could be Andalusia or Oaxaca), but it is the same ecstasy. Thus triggers fuse and blend in the eyes of the searcher for ecstasy. The trigger could be handsome brown young bodies on the beaches of Sicily, or it could be La Alhambra, or Tepoztlán, or Taos; the effect is very similar, as expressed by the great US *hispanista* George Ticknor upon reaching Spain for the first time in 1813:

> There is more national character here, more originality and poetry in the popular manners and feelings . . . than I have found anywhere else. . . . I speak not at all of the highest class—what seems mere fiction and romance in other countries is matter of observation here, and in all that relates to manners, Cervantes and Le Sage are historians. For, when you have crossed the Pyrenees, you have not only passed from one country and climate to another, but you have gone back a couple of centuries in your chronology.[18]

Portuguese and Spanish *iberistas* of course opposed, as it were, the *barret mexicà* law, for it embodied either exotic views of La Alhambra or the Black Legend of Spain; either German and English fascination with Lope de Vega and Cervantes or the US gusto for Mexican burros, toros, fiestas, and sombreros. But neither US *hispanistas* nor peninsular *iberistas* ever foresaw the emergence of a native *iberismo* that was produced by US Spanish speakers: the "brown stain" in a lasting US Hispanism that imagined itself to be like

German *Romanistik*— that is, a highbrow treatment of the Golden Age literature of Spain.

Between 1890 and 1913, in addition to engaging in the Spanish-American War, the United States added Arizona and New Mexico as states of the Union—that is, the Hispanic challenge became apparent for US institutions and culture. At the same time that the "honorable freeing" of Cuba became an open and dishonorable imperialistic war in the Philippines, the Mexican population of Texas, Arizona, California, and Nuevo Mexico grew as a result, first, of the Gold Rush, then of the completion of railroad networks, and, finally, of the violence of the Mexican Revolution. By 1920, not only Texas and New Mexico were full of Spanish-speaking people; Chicago had thirty thousand Mexicans. In 1912, the constitution of the newly admitted state of New Mexico had no option but to sanction the inevitable: the Spanish language became one of the official languages of New Mexico. Vast Spanish-speaking populations, of either Mexican or New Spanish origins, characterized many parts of the United States. Moreover, large and important exile communities—from Mexico, Cuba, Spain, the Dominican Republic, and Nicaragua—contributed to a US Spanish-speaking cultural life.

US *hispanismo* became professionalized with very little concern for the history and culture of Spanish speakers in the United States. But there was a Hispanism produced by US Hispanics. US Hispanism could not remain for long immune to the input of the local Spanish speakers, who gradually introduced into the US academic treatment of Spanish Golden Age literature something that was always there from the outset: Mexico and the American Spanish. This led to the eventual prominence in academic *hispanismo* of people like the early twentieth-century New Mexican Aurelio Macedonio Espinosa, or the transformation, in Columbia, of a Spanish philologist, Federico de Onís, from an *iberista à la* Menéndez Pidal to an American pan-*hispanista*—a trend that would have been unthinkable either in Madrid or in Mexico City.[19]

The Mexican and Portuguese Revolutions in the 1910s, and Portugal's changing imperial role in Africa after World War I, impacted considerations of the Iberian world in the United States. Old Ticknor and Prescott Hispanism became *iberista* in its professionalization, still with a strong German philological mark, as was mandatory (Germany was the indisputable center of late nineteenth-century world philology). But the newly *iberista* US professional Hispanism included Portugal and Mexico in a way that would have been unthinkable in the *iberismo* of the peninsula. At Yale and other universities, Henry Roseman Lang institutionalized the study of Portuguese medieval and early modern literature. By 1920, the novels of the Mexican Revolution and the Mexican *corrido* had become subjects of US *hispanismo*. The *iberista* Federico de Onís wrote a piece considering the lyrics of a *corrido*, "*lo mero principal*" (The notion of the most important thing), translating it as "*lo espiritual hispánico.*" Mariano Azuela's *Los de abajo* (1915)—written in San Antonio, Texas—was translated as *The Underdogs*. Soon, through Federico de Onís, Carlos Castillo, Luis Leal, and later Renato Rosaldo and Américo Paredes, out of US university Hispanism emerged an "alien": the "brown stain" in US Hispanism, the study of the language and literature of Hispanos in the United States.

World War I divided the US political and cultural elites, and their debates occurred in tandem with the professionalization of the humanities in US universities. These debates, together with the lasting brown stain in US Hispanism, weakened the inevitable Germanic core of US philology. World Wars I and II devaluated the importance of the German language as second language in universities. US Hispanists with gusto took advantage, and launched Spanish, their own product, as the new fashion. During World War I, US Spanish teachers, in their journal *Hispania*, were clear: German *tot war*, what was mandatory now was to learn Spanish, which was the language of the United States anyway, the language of the then important Pan-Americanism; it was useful, and it was a return to Thomas Jefferson's love for the Spanish language and the millenarian culture of Spain. One of the founders of the Spanish Teachers Association, Lawrence Wilkins, said it clearly, "We in this country spell culture with a *c*. We have rejected unmistakably the *k* . . . . So I say, it is of culture spelled with a *c*, in the United States, in France, in England and in South and Central America, that I would speak today. And in the development of that culture, the study of Spanish is to play an increasingly large part."[20] The exchange, *Kultur* for *culture*, however, was for US Hispanists a poisoned kiss: Spanish indeed became the foreign language most studied on university campuses and in high schools, but at the cost of making plebeian what had always conceived of itself as the highbrow study of Spain.

The change of the *k* for the *c* was part of a larger transformation in US university culture. It was part of the logophilia of the last part of the nineteenth century, which, though heavily influenced by German philology, led to the study of many Native American languages and Spanish in the United States. That is, there emerged a new philology less attached to race and to a hierarchy of civilizations—thus the import of Franz Boas at Columbia, and above all Edward Sapir at Chicago and at Yale. These anthropologists were part of a cultural revolution based on the study of language; they examined native languages of the Americas and advanced the idea that each language revealed the mental structure of a distinct world, rather than being one of many different ways to represent one single world. Hence, notions of linguistic incommensurability and cultural relativism emerged. There were no better languages, or languages more advanced than others, but simply different *Weltanschauungen*.

Therefore, for instance, between 1900 and 1925, the University of Chicago had two philologists, very German in their training, George Tyler Northup and the German philologist Karl Pietsch, founder of the Romance Languages Department at Chicago. Both, together with Sapir, made of Chicago a center of Romanistic philology, and soon Mexico became a topic, first with the amateur anthropologist F. Starr and later with Carlos Castillo and Luis Leal, the editors of the first anthology of Mexican literature published in the United States (1944), and Robert Redfield, the most prominent Mexicanist in the first half of the twentieth century. Karl Pietsch trained Aurelio M. Espinosa at Chicago, who eventually became *the* expert in the Spanish of the United States between 1910 and 1950. Espinosa was one with his interlocutors and friends Menéndez Pidal, Franz Boas, and Pedro Henríquez Ureña. Like all of them, Espinosa was an *iberista*, a devoted philo-*hispanista*, who became a follower of the 1920s and 1930s expression of *hispanismo*: *la Falange*, along with many others in the US Spanish press between 1915 and 1940. As did many US Spanish-speaking intellectuals, Espinosa rejected any identification of U.S. *hispanidad* with Latin America or with any ethnic mark (they were Spaniards from North America).

Interestingly, the Spanish Civil War divided the pioneer US Hispanic *hispanistas*. Soon they saw two of their interlocutors—frequent contributors to Spanish newspapers in the United States—the *falangistas* Manuel Bueno and R. de Maeztu, both assassinated in Spain by one or another faction of the Republican coalition. Moreover, for *hispanistas* like Espinosa, an old Mexican and old Spaniard, as for many *hispanófilos* of Mexican or Spanish origins in the United States, the Spanish Civil War became a taunting political dilemma, not because of what happened in Spain but because of what happened with the Civil War in the United States. For people like Espinosa, the US support for the Spanish Republic was a matter of communists and of US Hispanists and scholars, often Jewish. On top of that, in Republican Spain, priests were killed. There were US brigades named after Lincoln and Washington in the Spanish Civil War, formed by communists and idealists, often Jewish, and even an important African American presence of labor leaders who had opposed Italian imperialism in Africa and found in Spain an anticolonialist crusade. There was no equivalent idealism among US

Hispanics or Hispanic *hispanistas*, but other Hispanists in the United States, like Leo Spitzer and Federico de Onís, became great supporters of the Republic in US universities. I cannot prove it, but I have the impression that divisions among *hispanistas* in the United States resulting from the Spanish Civil War led such scholars as Espinosa—who otherwise would never have supported the folkloric and strongly ethnic approaches of later scholars like Texan Américo Paredes in the 1940s—to participate in the Mexicanization of US *hispanismo* as a way to balance the insults received in the profession of *hispanista* during the 1930s and 1940s. All in all, in terms of their language, US Spanish-speaking *letrados* were deeply divided, more often than not uncomfortable both with the focus on the Golden Age of old US Hispanism and with the later efforts to ethnicize their language in the United States.

CR

In the first half of the twentieth century, to become Hispanic or Latino/a was to assume a degree of ethnicity that apparently made Mexicans or Puerto Ricans more than Mexican or Puerto Rican; it made them part of world *iberismo* or *latinité*. To be sure, among some New Mexican and Texan Spanish-speaking literati, there were some militant *iberistas*. Espinosa is emblematic in this regard. He was the most prominent, late nineteenth-century New Mexican philologist who collaborated with Franz Boas in understanding the popular ballads and stories collected in Mora, New Mexico; San Antonio, Texas; or in Milpa Alta, Mexico City. He also collaborated with the world logophilic movement, collecting Spanish *Romances*—thus he worked in tandem with Menéndez Pidal and Pedro Henríquez Ureña. He actually collected the *Romancero* of New Mexico's oral traditions. Espinosa, of course, disapproved of the idea of Latin America, as he explicitly stated in 1918 in an article that was soon reprinted by the Spanish government with a title that sounded like a decree: *América española o hispano América: El término América latina es erróneo* (1919). He believed that Spanish New Mexicans were part of an Iberian tradition, so for him the New Mexicans' oral tradition was "not a vulgar dialect, as many misinformed persons believe, but a rich archaic Spanish dialect, largely Castilian in source. . . . The indigenous Indian elements are unimportant, and only the Nahuatl of Mexico has exercised an important influence, being the language of a semi-civilized nation." His transcriptions of New Mexican Spanish can be seen as part of a continuum that includes those done in Galicia, Catalonia, Portugal, Mexico, or Castile, and they are truly part of an Iberian tradition expressed locally. In the 1900s, for Marcelino Menéndez Pelayo, Pedro Henríquez Ureña, or Aurelio M. Espinosa, language was not a homogenizing factor, but the source of real diversity. Just to hear it, here is an example of the living and diverse New Mexican language Espinosa collected (no need of translation; the point is in the flavor of the language): "Un cura le dijo a su sacristán que le cosiera uns güevos blanditos. El sacristán los echú a coser y los'irvió por un'hora. El cura ya cansau de esperar jue adonde 'staba 'lsacristán y le dijo:—¿quése los güevos? ¿qué todavá no 'tan? Y el sacristán le respondió–ya hasí un'hora que 'stan cosiendose pero tuavía no 'stàn blanditos."[21]

New Mexican Sabine R. Ulibarri was another *iberista*, a scholar of Iberian literatures and a writer of stories (in Spanish) about his "Tierra Amarilla," New Mexico. In addition, newspapers, popular romances, and *corridos* were, in their very use and transformation of the Spanish language, part of *iberismo*. Ideologically, however, they were linked to the history of Mexico and to the struggle for inclusion in their nation, the United States. Thus, one of these songs talked about World War II as follows:

> Año de nuevecientos
> cuarenta y uno al acabar,
> una nación amarilla
> nos vino a bombardear.
>
> Esta nación amarilla
> se llaman japoneses
> nos bombardearon las islas
> estos tristes feligreses.
>
> (At the end of nineteen hundred
> and forty one, a yellow nation
> came to drop bombs on us.
>
> The yellow nation
> is called the Japanese
> they bombed our islands
> those poor souls.)[22]

These local voices spoke of world and local events; their politics and morality were not those implied by the current term "Latino." The global connection to *iberismo*, however, was not, as recent scholars have implied, a sign of profound antiracism and democratization but a positioning within a cultural/racial hierarchy that could locate them in what they believed to be their rightful place: white by treaty or racially neutral, with "conquest rights" (no other name) over native Americans and, of course, higher than blacks. One song collected by A. M. Espinosa narrated the alliances among immigrants from Oklahoma and Illinois and local Indian groups (non-ethnic solidarities):

> Juriry, jari, camón
> dis'e vulgu americano
> comprende pero no quiere
> al imperio Mexicano
>
> todos los indios de pueblo
> se han hechu a la banda d'eos'
> disen qu'es nueva conquista
> la ley d'estos fariseos
>
> (How d'you do, howdy, come on
> say the American folks.
> They understand but don't care
> for the great Mexican Empire.
>
> All the Indian villages
> have already joined their ranks.
> "It's a new conquest," they say
> this is the law of these Pharisees.)[23]

Neil Foley has shown that many Spanish-speaking landowners in New Mexico and Texas used *hispanidad* to fight their segregation, but *hispanidad* involved racism against AfricanAmericans. New Mexican philologists like Espinosa made the same use of *hispanidad*. Such claims, however, had little to do with the idea of Latin America. In the 1930s, the most important Mexican American association, the League of United Latin American Citizens (LULAC), opted for this mix of terms: Latin, American, and Citizens instead of Mexicans or Hispanic. LULAC chose precisely that mix to diminish the importance of *ethnia* and race in their struggle. For three decades, LULAC fought against the segregation of Mexican Americans in Texas schools; they fought not for their traditions, their language, and their racial consciousness, nor even for their religion or against racism directed at African Americans. They fought for the right to be as racially neutral as whites and thus for full citizenship. LULAC also fought against further Mexican immigration, which would perpetuate the ethnic marker. New Mexican educator, scholar, and president of LULAC, George I. Sánchez, in the 1930s sought the educational inclusion of Spanish-speaking New Mexicans, not in order to maintain their ethnic purity but to reach full Americanism: their inferior "status," he argued, was "a result of the failure of the United States to recognize the special character of the social responsibility it assumed when it brought these people forcefully into the American society. . . . The legal right to 'life, liberty, and the pursuit of happiness' is an empty privilege when the bare essentials of Americanism and of social welfare are wanting."[24]

In sum, this was the struggle of "browns" everywhere in the United States until the 1960s. They were racialized, but their response was not full ethnic self-racialization. By the 1990s, however, this complex cultural and linguistic panorama became fully racialized on all fronts. Hispanic, first, and then Latino/a, Afro-Latino, and Queer Latino, were terms that advanced conjectures, in English, about an assumed common past, traditions, culture, and language, not only for Mexicans in the United States but for Cubans and Salvadorians, all of them one with the rest of the continent to the south. Race is indeed a powerful device.

⌘

At the end of the nineteenth century, Cinco de Mayo was the private celebration of Mexican towns in Texas, New Mexico, and California. These were indeed echoes of a very Mexican story, that of the civic canonizing of such heroes as Benito Juárez and Ignacio Zaragoza, and of the 1860s moment in Puebla when Mexico made a bid to win the world's respect. Thus on the fifth of May, Mexicans in the United States used to honor their Mexico, that of Juárez, but more importantly, their United States, that of Republican President Abraham Lincoln, Juarez's only ally in the world in the struggle against Maximilian and Napoleon III's *l'Amérique latine*. New Mexicans fought for the Union, and their Cinco de Mayo honored its Mexicanness as much as their Americanness. Truth be told, slavery was not their primary concern in joining the Union; they sought Union support against the attacks and the presence of various Native American groups. At least on that point, the Union fulfilled its promise; it contained or killed the Native Americans (not in order to satisfy its Mexicans but to make New Mexico suitable for railroads and massive immigration from the East Coast and Midwest).

With this vast new population in New Mexico, the old New Mexicans— "white by treaty"—were indeed dispossessed of their lands, and as former soldiers and loyal Americans, had to struggle for full citizenship. By the late nineteenth century, their Cinco de Mayo had become a way of claiming their right to belong to a nation that had made them second-class citizens. In the US Spanish media of the early twentieth century, Cinco de Mayo had clear local political meanings: it meant the liberal Mexican past, which was also American, and it meant critiques of some policies of the United States or the Mexican government and various other political and historio-graphical positionings. Often, however, the issue at stake was not ethnicity or race but the defense of their legal "racial neutrality," because that was the way to negotiate rights in the United States. Juárez was a hero for them because he had been a liberal, a patriot—almost never because he had been a Zapotec Indian. In 1892, a New Mexican newspaper, *El Mosquito* (Mora, New Mexico, May 5, 1892), recalled Juárez's liberalism and his re-publican honor, and asked Mexico to make peace with the new France, that of Adolphe Thiers and Sadi Carnot, which was closer to Juárez. The key questions for these early twentieth-century US Spanish speakers were local, national, and international—freedom and equity as represented by Juárez and Lincoln vs. reactionary forces, monarchy, imperial France, the Confederates, and the exclusion of Mexicans from the nations for which they had fought.[25]

Starting in the 1990s, "Cincou de Maio" became an "American" fiesta, in the same category as Saint Patrick's Day, but not as important as Thanks-giving or the Fourth of July. The celebration now has very little to do with Juárez, Zaragoza, Lincoln, and Puebla; it is not exclusively Mexican or Mex-ican American. It is the day on which celebrating is what is celebrated—diversity, Latino heritage. Latinos, by celebrating, become that which is celebrated: "Latinos" acting out their duty, the ethnic role that has been assigned to them by the ethnically marked, political, and consumerist cul-ture of the United States. Cinco de Mayo is therefore the day of tamales, piñatas, the "Cincou de Maio Sale," Dos XX, Budweiser, tequila, mariachis, and US diversity. George W. Bush used to hire mariachis, and in an un-conscious act of *iberismo*, enjoyed listening to *rancheras* sung in Andalusian singer Shaila Dúrcal's flamenco falsetto. Barack Obama, not a Texan after all, dined with Eva Longoria. It is a party for diversity, a sort of narcissism of an assumed diversity facing the mythical mirror of "racial identities," no matter that diversity pales before the homogenous inequality and consumerism that demands such markers (identities and ethnic ones) from those who would enter the political and economic markets.

To be sure, Cinco de Mayo is now criticized by advocates of Latino/a identity as that party of tamales, Guadalupes, Ricky Martins, toreros, and mariachis. Latino/a activism seeks to return Cinco de Mayo to what it believes Cinco de Mayo's historical origins were—its ethnic origins. Robert Con Davis-Undiano thus recalled that Zaragoza might have triumphed in Puebla, but "Mestizo and Zapotec Indians defeated the French." Now Cinco de Mayo celebrates ethnic people, Indians, mestizos, who give the celebration its original significance. In Davis-Undiano's words, "It says resistance. I'm standing. Don't count me out"; that is, cultural resistance, ethnic survival, not assimilation. Old New Mexicans, however—many of them veterans of the Civil War and of wars against Native Americans—had no place for the mestizo, Zapotec, or Nahuatl origins of Juárez and his troops.[26] The celebration has never been about the past, but about the present, the present in the United States—and rightly so.

In sum, there are and were many US Cinco de Mayos. New Mexicans celebrated their alliance with the Union for decades—and complained about the betrayal during Reconstruction, when the Union mistreated the nearly four thousand New Mexicans who had fought for the Union against Texas. They were, after all, the enemies of the idea of l'Amérique latine. They fought neither for an ethnic marker nor against slavery, but for full recognition within the Union. Today, for some Mexican Americans, Cinco de Mayo is a day on which gringos get money from Mexicans. For others, it is the Mexican "community's" sign of resistance. In the 1970s, for the Chicano movement, Cinco de Mayo celebrated the day on which Mexicans overcame fake empires and returned to authenticity; thus Zaragoza was seen as one with Che Guevara or Emiliano Zapata. But it is fair to say that, until the late 1960s, in the longue durée it was the ethnic marker implied by "Latino/a" or "Latin American" that Mexicans in the United States had fought against.

☙

The first Chicano scholarship had no use for the idea of Latin America, except for icons like Che Guevara, the Cuban Revolution, and the notion of internal colonialism. For its part, US dependentista Latin Americanism in the 1970s had very little to say about the struggle for civil rights by blacks and browns in the United States. However, most of the scholars active during the 1970s boom in US Latin American Studies were actually products of the struggle of the 1960s, and thus, in a way, their Latin Americanism was an illustrious part of the struggle. By the 1990s, with the crisis of Marxism and Latin Americanism as a whole, US Latin Americanism started to talk simultaneously of Latino/a and Latin America as one and the same thing. Sonia Álvarez, Arturo Arias, and Charles R. Hale explained how in the 1990s a task force within LASA made it a goal to overcome the wide intellectual and institutional gap between Latino/a and Latin American Studies; thus "the first queer studies panel took place at the XVIII Congress in 1994 in Atlanta; the first plenary session on US Latino studies was held in 2001 at the XXIII Congress in Washington, D.C."[27] At last, *latinité* was *toujours la même chose.*

Along similar lines, the 2010 edition of *The Norton Anthology of Latino Literature*, edited by Ilan Stavans, assumed a strange, more than four-hundred-year chronology and a flexible geography that included the United States, Mexico, the Caribbean, and, for that matter, Spain and all of South America. Latino/a literature turns out to be some kind of genetic message that includes both the fifteenth-century Dominican Spanish Marrano Friar Bartolomé de las Casas and the canonized US English-language modernist poet William Carlos Williams. (Indeed, some Puerto Rican blood did run in the poet-doctor's veins, but as modernist poets go Wallace Stevens was more Latino, if that means some poetic interaction with the Spanish-speaking world, thanks to his interactions with Cuban writer José Rodríguez Feo.) The Norton anthology states that the sixteenth-century Spanish traveler Álvar Núñez Cabeza de Vaca, the seventeenth-century nobleman Inca Garcilaso de la Vega (who wrote in Spain and in the kingdom of Peru), and the twentieth-century Catalan Felipe Alfau, who wrote in English, all belonged to Latino literature. Why not Fernando Pessoa or Jorge Luis Borges, who also wrote in English? Mexican performer and writer Guillermo Gómez Peña and the prominent English-language writer Junot Diaz are writers of "Latinidad," the anthology states. So is Chilean writer—in Spanish—Isabel Allende, but not Richard Rodriguez, who has never sought to be considered Latino. At the level of popular literature, the Norton anthology assumes an unquestionable continuum between 1900s border *corridos* and Ricky Martin's English rendition of "Livin' la Vida Loca." This is certainly an interesting remapping of academic canons, but it is possible only through some kind of essence that is difficult to accept unless one believes in a strong ethnic recessive gene.[28]

As Raúl Coronado has recently explained, the category of Latino could be useful for overcoming strong nationalistic storytellings, as the concept does not derive from or refer to any nation in particular. And yet to "Lat-

inize" eighteenth- , nineteenth- , or early twentieth-century historical subjects—whether they inhabited the former provinces of New Viscaya or Alta
California (or left any trace of their existence in Spanish)—is nevertheless
very much an act of nationalist history: that of the United States. One cannot presume that there are such things as "sediments" of *latinidad* (Coronado) or assume the Norton anthology's criteria on the basis of history,
language, or culture. This can be done only on the basis of some kind of
belief in an ethnic genetic message. Nevertheless, at last all of *latinité* has
been brought together. But in English.[29]

Discussions of race, at times, recruit their speakers according to class,
color, and ideology. That is, in academic parlance, to say "Latino" or "Latin
American" is to speak of race, but from a peculiar political position. It is
not that class and ideology grant access to the clairvoyance of ethnicity; it
is that those who do not accept such clairvoyance are from the wrong class
and ideology (or sexuality). As the prominent Latina artist and critic Coco
Fusco put it:

> With the exception of those who associate themselves with the leftist politics
> of the 1960s and 1970s, many of the middle- and upper-class Latin Ameri-
> can artists and intellectuals in the United States reject the notion of a unified
> Latin identity. Some of them don't even like to refer to themselves as Latinos.
> They don't like to use cultural identity as a term or even as a semiotic system
> with which to analyze their work . . . and do not support efforts made on
> behalf of the Chicano or Puerto Rican community. Many upper-class Latinos
> in the United States see making connections between politics and culture as
> regressive, and prefer to identify themselves as generic postmodernists. I live
> this every day with Latino gallery owners, artists, and intellectuals, who are
> for the most part criollos, who detest identifying themselves as minorities,
> and who see work produced by American artists of color as inferior, or of
> bad taste."[30]

Thus a Mexican American, or a Mexican, or a Guatemalan either em-
braces Latina as her own or is destined to live in an eternal false consciousness, because the United States constitutes the epochal cultural and economic center of gravity—as empire, as pole of attraction of workers and
scholars, as the assumed scenario of global media. Hence now, more than
yesterday but less than tomorrow, through this inevitable cultural and economic intermediation, both terms, Latino/a and Latin America, are mutually constituted: being a US "Latino/a is being Latin American as a de-
fault, if mythical, *in potentia*; and being Latin American is being Latino/a

in potentia—a matter of time: that is, of relocating oneself in cultural or geographical spaces in which a Brazilian or a Mexican or a Dominican becomes a Latino. But now this last possibility is not only a matter of a Mexican living in Los Angeles; it could also be a Latin Kings gang member in San Salvador or Barcelona. The power of the United States, and the increasing cultural weight of Latinos as in US culture, makes it possible, more than ever, for a racial category belonging to the specific US conditions to be assumed and consumed as a universal ontology.

Latino/a is the term in vogue on official documents, in consumer culture, and in academic settings, and is at times believed to be a word with a better pedigree than Hispanic, which clearly honors the Spanish imperial legacy. In turn, the field of Latin American Studies, in English and in its US setting, has for the last half century been the natural habitat of the term Latin America. Finally, in the twenty-first century the two fields are being linked institutionally. Like exotic orchids, however, out of their greenhouse habitat and detached from their peculiar attachment to race and ethnicity, these concepts would die out, both as related terms and as isolated concepts. And yet, in their own ecosystem, they have recently become indispensable to each other, regardless of their different and, at times, antagonistic trajectories as concepts and political agendas. This equilibrium, I believe, is intellectually far-fetched; its political utility, for better or worse, is confined to a US experience. It leads to an endless reduction to ontological mysteries and to an ethnic, if loving, barbarization. Thus Latino/a and Latin America can survive, coexist, and nurture one another. And yet, I do understand the political importance of the struggle embedded in the term Latino. I, however, am not sure that the ethnic obsession implied in the word Latino and its marriage with the term Latin America would result in justice and better social scenarios in the United States. But then again, what I have to offer as an alternative are these notes of caution. Whatever else I have to say—and I do have more—is as yet hard to sell intellectually and politically risky in the unsettling current US/Mexican scenarios.

FIVE

Singing *Latinoamérica*: A brief but obligatory detour into the question of the relatively recent, initially tentative, yet ultimately widespread embrace of the term Latin America, being an excursion into dustier corners of the author's memory in search of a vernacular singing of said tune: "Latinoamérica"

No la chiflen que es cantada.

—Mexican Proverb

In modernization theory models, the terms Latin America and "the masses" meant more or less the same thing: "backwardness." If we follow the logic, "the masses" in either Mexico or Peru, at all times, had been intrinsically Latin American. In turn, elites represented "modernity" when they were Westernized; otherwise they were simply as Latin American as the masses beneath them. Regardless of its unpleasant philological history, however, once in a while, the term Latin America has obtained a different moral charge. In these cases, the concept Latin America is recalibrated to connote nobility. Things, phenomena, ideas, have to be Latin American; that is, they ought to belong to the "masses" (by definition Latin American), not to the Westernized (un–Latin American) elite. The "modernity" of the elites becomes a morally dubious "fakeness," while the "backwardness" of the masses is redefined as the moral virtue of tradition and authenticity. Therefore if Mexico, Cuba, and Brazil are to enjoy such moral elevation, they must be the *real* "Mexico," the *real* "Cuba," the *real* "Brazil" by standing in for the larger universe of the palpably authentic continent-concept

Latin America. Otherwise they would not serve the purpose of standing for the masses; they would not sustain the appeal of the "non-Western." What I want to highlight is that in both versions of Latin America, a simple logic of the elite vs. the masses rules.

All this is a familiar story, but it conceals a lasting conundrum that goes way back: since the term's earliest articulation in the mid-1850s, "Latin America" has not been what one might call the commoners' widespread way of thinking or speaking. Nevertheless, the elite vs. the masses is, in history, an unstable and mischievous dichotomy. The global reach of the English language and US mass culture has made "Latin America," "Latino," and "Latina" commonplace terms in contemporary languages. Thus, from the standpoint of the present, it would seem natural that such labels and their connotations have always existed in popular vernaculars. And so the concept freely flows, for instance, in the song "Latinoamérica" by the Puerto Rican band Calle 13: "Soy América Latina, / un pueblo sin piernas pero que camina" (I am Latin America / a people without legs who nevertheless walks). In spite of these noble sentiments, the historical fact is that until the recent US-centered Latinization of everything tropical, Spanish, Portuguese, indigenous, brown, and exotic, the idea of Latin America was never fully embraced by the masses, commoners, or plebs of Mexico City, Cochabamba, or São Luís do Maranhão. Not in 1900. Not even in 1970.

There may not be a viable and rigorously empirical method to measure the popular diffusion of the idea from its mid-nineteenth-century origins to the present. There is, however, a domain where we may examine the concept Latin America "*de andar por casa,*" that is, in the realm of the quotidian, unrefined, and domestic—namely, popular music and poetry. That, and memory—my memory—because, due to a wicked and relentless *Musikbildung*, I command this realm almost by heart. Thus, rather than write a treatise to prove that the "subaltern does sing" and to the tune of Latin America, I am asking for a vote of confidence. I solicit the reader to trust my memory as a lens to observe the extension and embeddedness of a term in popular vernaculars.[1] Through this lens, I modestly but conclusively submit that the long trajectory of popular music and poetry shows, first, that Latin America has never really been a part of popular parlance; and, second, that in order to maintain its ontological purity, the term has mandated a quasi-religious faith in the hard and fast distinction between the real (popular and somehow non-Western), and the fake (elite, inauthentic, imitatively Western).

Please forgive me twofold: for trusting my own memory and for not offering complete translations of all this. To translate all would be betraying popular eloquence.

⌘

To live through "the popular" means to experience the continuous and promiscuous infringement of the line that separates the elite and the masses. Perhaps this is why Alejo Carpentier, unmatched connoisseur of popular music, once wrote, "I find learned the Latin American who, noting that all of our *campesinos* say 'Es malo atizar el fuego con un cuchillo' (It is bad to stoke the fire with a knife), is able to remember, there and then, that this sanction belongs to Pythagoras's precepts." More to the point: if one were to truly dissect, say, the origins of Afro-Cuban *lamentos* or those of the popular *habaneras*, one would have to rely on Natalio Galán's erudition. One would have to trace, along with Galán, the many varied interactions between highbrow and lowbrow that took place long before the emergence of the radio. These interactions involved Spain, France, Cuba, Mexico, Congo, Portugal, and the United States—the works of Frédéric Chopin, Camillo Sivori, Alejo Carpentier, Amadeo Roldán, Julián Fontana, and many other popular and elite musicians whose names have been lost to time. Regarding the origins of the very popular and traditional *habanera*, Galán explains, "The melody's intervals drifted about the Antilles (blending Portuguese and Spanish influences?), since who knows when. The music picked up its lyrics at sometime in the nineteenth century as it passed through France and Spain. Today it has emerged as an example of *afro-americano* folklore." Small wonder, then, that one runs into this music in the most unexpected places: characters in Alexander Lernet-Holenia's novel *Die Standarte* (1934), set in post–World War I Vienna, run into a street violinist playing the very popular Mexican *habanera*, "La paloma." The omniscient narrator informs the reader that this was the last song that the Austrian emperor of Mexico, Maximilian of Habsburg, heard before his execution, sung to him by a servant whose grief eventually led her to suicide.[2]

The term Latin America, along with its connotations, has remained largely absent in popular music and poetry. That is why popular music tends to undermine the category of Latin America. When a piece of popular music or poetry has been presented as emphatically Latin American, its potential mass consumption ends up contradicting its autochthonous Latin Americanness. To be sure, beginning in the late nineteenth century, continent-wide networks of musicologists and folklorists, along with local musicians and performers, began to look at popular music through the dichotomy of authenticity vs. fake commercialism—the latter often linked with imperialism. Yet authenticity and its opposite came in a variety of flavors: authenticity could be found, for instance, in Andean indigenous tunes, such as "El cóndor pasa," collected by folklorists as well as urban folk performers. Commercial fakeness was represented by proletarian "valses" in Lima, such as "Olga," "Cariño bueno," or even by Chabuca Granda's fabulous "Fina estampa" and "Flor de la Canela"—all known as "*música criolla*," meaning too vulgar, too urban, too Lima, not the indigenous highlands. Or not; for some, it was the Lima "*criollismo*" that was authentic, while jazz and rock and roll represented fake imperial commercialism. Authenticity could be found in Mexico's old *corridos* of the Revolution, while jazz and big band music were bogus cultural forms. Or not; for some, authentic Mexico meant countercultural rock bands, such as El Tri, who performed—in Spanish—in the proletarian quarters of Mexico City, while fake commercialism manifested itself in the extremely popular ballads broadcast by the great Mexican media conglomerate (XEW Radio and Televisa).

Regardless of the parameters of the dichotomy, the fact was that authenticity had very little to do with the actual popularity of the music. And Latin America, as a par excellence version of authenticity, has suffered the same destiny: authentic, perhaps, but never truly popular. A recent attempt to Latin-Americanize popular music and poetry had to admit that "according to reasonable estimates, nearly 90% of the music heard by the Latin American (*el latinoamericano*) is a commercialized, massive, and modernizing kind of music (*mediatizada, masiva y modernizante*)."[3] Could we not come up with similar "reasonable estimates" for "the American," "the European," or "the human"? Is this mass commercialism not the very nature of popular music? Is popular music too geographically uninhibited, too culturally promiscuous, and thus unfit for the conceptual purity that is Latin America?

CR

Two technological advances mark "before" and "after" in popular music and poetry: the introduction of audio recording and broadcasting—the phonograph and the radio. Before this momentous leap, we may find another, perhaps less spectacular, historical breakthrough in Europe and the Americas: the nineteenth century and its logophilia, a time when an army of philologists and folklorists dug deep into the local roots of European and American languages, amassing a great archive of words, ballads, and myths: Cherokee, Catalan, Yiddish, Quechua . . . Certainly, this linguistic treasure was not found in a pure state of *illo tempore;* it was found as it has always been: in a constant state of change. The nineteenth-century philological fever, however, collected its prize just before this state of cultural and linguistic change accelerated irrevocably, thanks to the industrial transformation of Europe and the Americas. The crusade included the nineteenth-century elaboration of dictionaries of localisms (*mexicanismos, chilenismos, peruanismos*) in local versions of the Spanish and Portuguese languages. Spanning the Atlantic, the philological crusade searched for Portuguese and Spanish *Romanceros* and *cancioneros* in oral traditions and old songbooks. They also documented and codified numerous indigenous languages. By the early twentieth century, all of this crystallized into an idea of a global *iberismo* or *hispanidad,* consumed at the time as "*el garbo hispánico*" (hispanic elegance), "*saudade lusitana*" (Lusitanian yearning), or "*el sabor caribeño.*"

All in all, not once have I spotted the term Latin America in my own obsessive reading of the findings made by these philologists and folklorists before the arrival of audio recording and broadcasting. Granted, this might be the result of not being obsessed enough. The term may indeed be waiting to be found somewhere in some obscure local *cancionero.* I doubt it. Popular songs, stories, and proverbs always change their meanings over time. They may become remote, even unintelligible—but rarely do they hide.

Popular songs and ballads are "archives" documenting centuries of promiscuous borrowing and stealing across regions, classes, and languages. In the early twentieth century, the Brazilian folklorist João Ribeiro traced the origins of many traditional animal fables from Bahía and São Paulo back to India (what he called the Pantschatantra) and Greece through Spain and the Muslims.[4] By the early twentieth century, many folklorists had of course found that all popular songs and ballads of the "Latin races" had something in common. But the discovery was indeed a tautology: "Latin races" appeared to share musical commonalities precisely because they had already been conceived as Latin races.[5] Still, at times, folklorists pointed out the interesting variations of shared tropes in, for instance, the consideration of the brown color in Andalusia and America. In 1917, the Andalusian folklorist Antonio Machado Álvarez (Demófilo) found that his homeland's folklore praised brownness, while in America brownness was disliked: "The steadfast determination with which the Andalusian praise brownness of skin is worthy of note; . . . their disinclination toward whiteness brings to mind the contempt with which white men in America view men of color." Then the folklorist included a telling example:

> Moreno pintan a Cristo,
> morena á la Magdalena,
> moreno es el bien que adoro,
> viva la gente morena.
> Lo moreno lo hizo Dios,
> lo blanco lo hizo un platero:
> vaya lo blanco con Dios,
> que yo lo moreno quiero.[6]

There is no better illustration of this widespread borrowing embedded in popular songs than the *romance* of *La Delgadina*. It is in essence the story of attempted incest. In its oldest versions, a king—or in some versions, a wealthy and important man—asks his daughter to be his mistress. After she refuses in the name of God and the honor of her mother, the father imprisons her, and she dies. A simple tragic tale, the beauty of which is in the untranslatable many renderings of the story. Consider, for instance, the version found in the early twentieth century, sung by Marta Rosaria Fernández, from Luarca, Asturias:

> Tres fijas tenía el rey,
> todas tres como una grana,
> y la más chiquita dellas
> Delgadina se llamaba.
> Estando un día á la mesa,
> estando un día á la tabla,
> la reparaba su padre,
> su padre la reparaba.
> —¿Qué me mira, padre mío,
> qué me mira pa la cara? . . .
> —¿Qué tengo de mirar, fija? . . .
> que has de ser mi namorada.
> —Non lo quiera Dios del cielo,
> nin la Virgen soberana;
> non lo quiera Dios del cielo
> que yo sea su namorada.[7]

Another rendering of the same story, sung by Próspero Baca of New Mexico, was found in the early 1940s:

> Delgadina se paseaba en una sala cuadrada
> con una manzana de oro que la sala relumbraba.
> Quedín, quedón, quedón, don don.
> Y le dice el rey su padre:—¡Ah qué linda Delgadina!
> ¡Ah qué linda Delgadina¡ Puede ser mi hermosa dama.
> —No lo permita mi Dios ni la reina soberana.
> —Apróntense aquí mis criados; encierren a Delgadina.
> Si le dieren de comer, la comida muy salada;
> si le dieren de beber, la espuma de la retama.[8]

And in Mexico City, if memory serves me right, it went something like this:

> Cuando salieron de misa
> su papá le platicaba,
> Delgadina, hija mía,
> tú serás mi prenda amada.
>
> Ni lo quiera Dios del cielo
> ni la virgen soberana,
> es un insulto para mi madre
> y perdición de mi alma.

I recall these lyrics, of course, largely for the simple pleasure of remembering, but the endurance of the words and the story serves to explain that if speaking "Latin America" had been widely common, the term would have percolated—as least as much as La Delgadina—in popular parlance. And somehow it would have reached my memory. The lack of circulation of the term, however, cannot be simply attributed to its conspicuously elitist origins. Nothing more elitist than late nineteenth-century modernist poetry: Amado Nervo, Juan de Dios Peza, Rubén Darío, Manuel Gutiérrez Nájera, Julio Herrera y Reissig, Leopoldo Lugones, or even José Martí. Some of these poets, as Carlos Monsiváis argued, were to a certain extent "popular" in their own time, thanks to urbanization and public education. Amado Nervo, Gustavo Adolfo Bécquer, and Manuel Gutiérrez Nájera were for long part of the collective memory of Mexico's urban working class. But these poets were not truly popular until their words were set to music

performed by Cubans, Puerto Ricans, and Mexicans, shellacked into phonograph records, broadcast over the radio, and sung by the earliest stars of
the Mexican silver screen. In this sense, modernist poetry gave shape to a
widespread brand of continent-spanning mass sentimentality. I recall one
poem by Gutiérrez Nájera as a bolero recorded in the 1930s: "Las novias
pasadas son copas vacías; / en ellas pusimos un poco de amor; / el néctar
tomamos . . . huyeron los días . . . / Traed otras copas con nuevo licor."
(Past lovers are empty glasses / where we once poured a little love / we
drank down the nectar . . . as the days fled . . . / New glasses, new spirits,
another round.) The connotations of the idea of Latin America, however,
never experienced this transformation into music.[9]

The concept did not gain popularity until the massive migration and the
resulting cultural and political influence of "Latinos" in the United States.
For long, the term had little tangible local use in Mexico, Brazil, or Peru.
This poses the question, first, of "the local" in popular music and how it
was affected by the introduction of the radio and the phonograph; and
second, it brings up the unavoidable matter of the massive migration of
people and ideas during the twentieth century. Always, but especially after
the 1930s, "the local" in Spanish and Portuguese popular music was given
shape by the simultaneous attraction and mixing of the domestic and the
cosmopolitan, the lowbrow and the highbrow. Tangos, boleros, *sones*, and
danzones were heard and sung everywhere, as they were adapted to local
rhythms and traditions. For instance, an old Spanish *copla* could be sung
and consumed as a Mexican bolero—for example, "Corazón loco" was
originally popularized in Spain by a Cuban singer, Antonio Machín, and
then made popular elsewhere by many performers. Sometimes, a Peruvian
vals could become a Mexican ranchera—like the beautiful "El Plebeyo,"
composed in the 1920s by the great Peruvian songwriter Felipe Pinglio, "*el
bardo inmortal*," a song that was, by and large, consumed around the world
as a Mexican *ranchera* sung by Pedro Infante: "Después de laborar, / vuelve
a su humilde hogar, / Luis Enrique, el plebeyo, / el hijo del pueblo, / el
hombre que supo amar" (The workday done, / he returns to his humble
abode / Luis Enrique, the Plebe / true son of the people / true lover of
love).

Still more important than the lowbrow/highbrow polarity were the
geographic/cultural coordinates of popular music production. These con-
sisted of three main axes: the Puerto Rico/Cuba/Mexico/US axis, the Río de
la Plata axis, and the Bahía/Rio/Minas/São Paulo axis. Each axis brought
together numerous local and international trends, blending rhythms and
melodies together, along with their respective human and cultural idiosyn-

crasies. Waves of migration fused the old and new, the high and low—musical voices emanating from Africa, Europe, indigenous America, and the United States. Beats blended and clashed. By the 1930s and 1940s, this frenzied musical promiscuity had reached new heights. Especially in the first axis, as the same musicians hopped across borders, splitting their time among orchestras in Mexico, Cuba, and the United States, switching from one day to the next: from swing to cha-cha, from big band jazz to mambo.

Between the 1930s and the 1970s, these axes of musical production and distribution gained further dominance due to the cultural isolation imposed upon Lisbon and Madrid by the regimes of António de Oliveira Salazar and Francisco Franco. La Habana, Buenos Aires, and Mexico City were true cultural Meccas for popular music. Meanwhile, Barcelona, Lisbon, and Madrid became consumers of the booming production of popular culture in the Americas. Hollywood and the US music industry captured these sounds and amplified them.

As with so much having to do with the adjoining yet aloof Spanish- and Portuguese-speaking worlds, the relationship between the Bahía/Rio/Minas/São Paulo axis and the other two axes was rather one-directional. That is, popular Brazilian music was influenced by the Spanish-speaking world, but not much the other way around. There were indeed Brazilian "folk" divas such as Carmen Miranda, *boleristas* such as Altemar Dutra, and popular avant-pop singers such as Chico Buarque and Caetano Veloso who could occasionally be heard in Mexico and Argentina. Yet none of these were as popular as Roberto Carlos, the first true Brazilian pop star in the Spanish-speaking world, something perhaps achieved because he sang, in both Spanish and Portuguese, the *"cursilería"* that both languages share. By the late 1970s, Roberto Carlos's "Amada Amante" could be heard on the radio in public buses in Morelia, Rosario, Oporto, Valencia, or Belo Horizonte, in both Portuguese and Spanish, "Es que tú, Amada Amante, das la vida en un instante" (Because you, Loved Lover, give your life away in an instant). But that was not singing Latin America; the interaction of all these axes had no place for that idea and its connotations.

Since the 1930s, however, during the strong Pan-American movement commanded by the United States around World War II, efforts were made to Latin-Americanize the music of "the other America." As Pablo Palomino has shown, US cultural diplomats fostered the creation of "Latin American music" as part of the Inter-American Alliance. The key figure in this endeavor was no less than the father of Pete Seeger, Charles Seeger, a musical New Dealer who directed the Musical Division of the Pan-American Union. These efforts did not result in the widespread popularity of Latin

America in music, but they set the stage for networks of musicologists in the continent to expand their horizons beyond the limits of national traditions. This effort joined the musical exchanges that took place in the Southern Cone, organized by the prominent German-Uruguayan musicologist and composer Curt Lange and then joined by the UNESCO-led projects in the 1950s of cultural world union. Besides, Weimar and Nazi Germany, it seems, loved Carlos Gardel, so captured Sérgio Buarque de Holanda in Berlin (1929), amazed at the, as it were, *iberista* German translation of the famous tango "*Adiós muchachos*") ("Adiós muchachos, compañeros de mi vida, farras querida de aquellos tiempos . . ."): "Zwei rote Lippen und ein flässchen Tarragona,/ Das ist das beste aus Barzelona." And Steven Spielberg's *Schindler's List* plays the music that retrieves in my mind the unforgettable *tango* lyrics: "Por una cabeza / todas las locuras, / su boca que besa / borra la tristeza / calma la amargura."[10]

Needless to say, the popular radio hits were not about "subaltern Latin American agency," but about mundane love—"Amor es el pan de la vida" (Love is our life's bread)—; about sex—"Vende caro tu amor, aventurera" (Set a high price for your love, adventuress). Many were about betrayal—"Tu mala canallada como tú, igual a ti, la tendrás que pagar" (Your foul treachery just like you, it's so like you, and you will pay)—and the resulting macho rage: "La encontró en el bullín y en otros brazos . . . le encajó 34 puñaladas, amablemente" (He found her in the cantina, in the arms of another . . . and, all politeness, he stabbed her thirty-four times). They were also about accompanying drunkenness—". . . que me sirvan de una vez pa' todo el año, que me pienso seriamente emborrachar" (Pour me enough to last me the year, I am seriously planning to get trashed).

To be sure, there were other lyrical subjects beyond the stereotypical "she done me wrong." There were local nostalgic landscapes: "allá al pie de la montaña, donde temprano se oculta el sol" (there by the mountainside, where the sun sets early), as well as songs about migration: "Aquí [New York] hace falta un tango . . . hacéme la gauchada, mandáme Mano a Mano grabado por Gardel" (This place [NYC] is lacking some tango . . . do me a *gauchada* [a favor] send me "Mano a mano" [a famous tango] recorded by Gardel"). The way that Latin America made itself felt among Spanish- and Portuguese-speaking poets and thinkers around, say, 1900—as a sense of spiritual collectivity as well as cultural and racial rejection of the "Anglo-Saxon"—manifested itself in boleros, rancheras, and *sones* and their lyrical content as an odd "we" of *machismo, saudade, nostalgia, sabor, arte, hermandad, tropicalidad,* or simply as "*la raza*" (as in Mexican norteño lyrics' use of "*mi raza,*" "*la raza,*" meaning both gang and ordinary people). There was, indeed, an unspecified "we," which could mean "Mexicans," "Argen-tineans," or some other collectivity brought together in its "*hispanidad.*" Sometimes this "we" represented little more than anti-US sentiment: "Pa' hacer pesos de montones,/ no hay como el americano. / Pa' conquistar corazones, / no hay mejor que un mexicano" (When it comes to stacking up the pesos, / there's none like an American. / When it comes to conquer-ing hearts, / there's none like a Mexican). But still, the term Latin America did not play a popular role—at least not until the 1960s, when the cultural impact of the Cuban Revolution brought local old folklore traditions into fashion in places like Argentina, Brazil, and Mexico. This turn was, by the way, very much influenced by the renaissance of folk music in the United States and Europe during the same decade.

For the late nineteenth-century Iberization of the term Latin America, one cannot overstate the importance of Spanish-speaking intellectuals in exile in Paris, New York, Santiago, or La Havana. There was another such migration. Following the Cuban Revolution and dictatorships in Uruguay, Argentina, Brazil, and Chile, all sorts of Spanish- and Portuguese-speaking people went into exile in the United States, London, Mexico City, and Paris. Beginning in the 1970s, these migrants changed the meaning of the term Latin America in popular music and poetry in Spanish and Portu-guese. And thus Latin America came into use—perhaps not yet in popular parlance—but certainly in the way a certain kind of "popular" music pre-sented itself to its middle-class consumers: university professors and their students, professionals, union members, and an increasingly widespread "progressive" urban bohemia. Folklorist revivals brought a certain mea-sure of fame to such Argentinean folksingers as Atahualpa Yupanqui and Eduardo Falú. They were popular in Buenos Aires, but also reached "pro-gressive" circles in Paris. They reached Mexico City's *peñas*—venues where this particular musical blend of folk and counterculture, the "*canción de pro-testa,*" was performed. The important Mexican band Los Folkloristas trav-eled the country up and down in search of old tunes, while such singers as Amparo Ochoa and Óscar Chávez began to sing even older songs in *peñas* and university halls. In London, Mexico City, New York, and Paris, exiles fleeing Brazilian, Argentinean, Chilean, and other dictatorships succeeded in concocting a powerful and hitherto unknown blend of local folk tradi-tions. These exiles produced, perhaps for the first time, a sound of truly continental dimensions. Mexican singers and songwriters performed and composed Argentinean and Uruguayan *sambas* and *milongas*, as well as Pe-ruvian *valses.* Argentinean "*cantantes de protesta*" composed Mexican *corridos* as well as militant ballads. Thus Uruguayan singer and songwriter Alfredo

Zitarrosa joined the Mexico City band Sanampay and sang about love and revolution. For Mexicans, this was the very definition of Latin American music and indeed it was—like never before. The concept was not in the songs themselves, as much as in the way they were consumed. *"Música latinoamericana"* became thus a scene, a genre, and a business.

At times, the Latin Americanness of the music was very specific, as in the tune by another Uruguayan exile in Mexico, Roberto Darvin, a true Latin American hymn: "Soy latinoamericano, soy latino . . . / traigo nueva la canción y alegre el vino / sé a dónde quiero llegar y sé el camino . . ." (I am Latin American, I am Latino . . . / bring a new song and cheerful wine / I know where I'm going and I know the way). Mercedes Sosa, Facundo Cabral, Alberto Cortés, and bands like Inti-Illimani, Quilapayún, and Los Calchaquis sang these kinds of songs for a decade or so. In those years, other prominent songwriters, such as the Chileans Víctor Jara and Violeta Parra, fell victims to fascist dictatorships, becoming the movement's martyred heroes. In time, this "progressive" trend reached the mainstream, gaining exposure in mass outlets such as Mexico's media conglomerate Televisa, and, starting in 1972, the Iberoamerican Television Organization (OTI) festivals: a kind of Pan-Hispanic version of today's Eurovision Song Contest. It got to the point when, in 1986, one Palito Ortega, a very popular Argentinean singer—more Barry Manilow than Pete Seeger—sang, "Yo señores, soy latinoamericano," "Donde nunca se marchita la esperanza," "Gente buena de corazón," (Dear sirs, I am Latin American, A land where hope never withers, A land of good-hearted people) . . . or something like that.

To be sure, the *canción de protesta* was nothing new. All sorts of popular ballads had long expressed social grievances and contestation, from Andalusian *coplas* to Mexican *corridos* and powerful old Cuban *lamentos*: "Pobe negrito que triste está, / trabaja mucho y no gana ná, / pobre negrito que triste está, / su mismo amo le está robá" (Po' little negro he feelin' so sad / workin' all day but ain't makin' a dime, / po' little negro he feelin' so sad / even the master be robbin' him blind). The new *canción de protesta*, however, was more ideological and militantly Latin American. That the new *canción de protesta* was formatted as Latin American was, somehow, evidence of the power of the term as second nature (it could have been phrased in the language of the Third World, decolonization, or world human rights). But this is not a proof of the common people's belief in such an idea.[11]

The actual meaning of Latin America in this new protest music was somewhat related to the meaning it had among turn-of-the-century Hispanophile intellectual elites who claimed "spiritual" superiority over Anglo-

American "machine culture." But the revival was imbued with a strong sense of support for the Cuban Revolution, a deeply felt anti-imperialism, and a kind of militant solidarity with different sorts of revolutionary guerrilla movements across the continent—much like the atmosphere in the United States during this time. What started as folk revivalism became politically *engagé* music, from Violeta Parra and Víctor Jara to the *Nueva Trova Cubana*. This *trova* was *nueva* in the sense that it was not the old romantic "*sonero*" Cuban *trova* of the 1930s, 1940s, and 1950s. It was new: consciously revolutionary, musically innovative, and authentically Latin American. Thus they sang of the coming continental revolution, a future viewed—it must be said—through a rather nationalistic lens: "*Madre patria y madre revolución*" (Mother *patria* and mother *revolución*); imagined in terms of redemptive violence: "*Y descubrió que la Guerra, era la paz del futuro*" (He discovered that war is the peace of tomorrow). The heroism of Fidel and Che was always emphasized: "*Aquí se queda la clara, / la entrañable transparencia de tu querida presencia, Comandante Che Guevara*" (Here remains the clarity, / the loving transparency of your presence, Comandante Che Guevara). To sing these songs was to sing Latin America.

Silvio Rodríguez and Pablo Milanés, leaders of the *Nueva Trova*, sang of Cuba and the Revolution, but they also wrote many extraordinary love songs, all which were consumed as authentically Latin American. Milanés also set to music many of the poems and part of the prose of José Martí. And so, young Argentineans and Mexicans growing up in the 1970s and 1980s—such as myself—retained Martí's prose, his old "Nuestra America," by heart, as a personal memory: "*Éramos una máscara, con los calzones de Inglaterra, el chaleco parisién, el chaquetón de Norteamérica y la montera de España.*" (We used to be a mask, with our English breeches, our vest *a la parisién*, our North American frock coat, and our Spanish *montera*.) But the collective memory of this progressive youth could not miss that Martí's own true love was more than "Nuestra América." It was war and poetry, it was his "*Versos sencillos*," and, thanks to Milanés, I still take pleasure in recalling these stanzas, which I dare not translate:

> Yo te quiero, verso amigo,
> Porque cuando siento el pecho
> Ya muy cargado y deshecho,
> Parto la carga contigo.
>
> . . .
>
> ¡Verso, nos hablan de un Dios
> Adonde van los difuntos:

Verso, o nos condenan juntos,
O nos salvamos los dos!

This widespread distribution of the poetry of José Marti—or Nicolás Guillén—represented a poetic education that came to be assumed, in the 1970s and 1980s, as a kind of Latin American *sociabilité*. At times these musical trends even restored their Catholic religious prehistory, such as when they adapted themselves to the Sandinista Revolution. Religious connotations insinuated themselves back into the idea of Latin America via liberation theology, as in Carlos Mejía Godoy: "Cristo ya nació en Palacagüina . . . María sueña que el hijo / igual que el tata sea carpintero, / pero el chavalillo piensa / mañana quiero ser guerrillero" (Christ is now born in Palacagüina . . . Such are María's dreams: / that like the father, the son will become a carpenter / but the kid's got ideas / "tomorrow I will be a guerrilla fighter") . . . something of the sort.

This kind of popular use of the term Latin America lasted until the late 1980s. It has now become part of baby-boomer nostalgia, my nostalgia. Last time I heard Pablo Milanés, he was singing old and gaudy boleros—not so badly I might add. My last recollection of Silvio Rodríguez is that he was dealing with a rapper son who went and escaped the island (". . . pero el chavalillo piensa mañana quiero ser rapero"). Meanwhile, the status of the *Nueva Trova Cubana* declined as the old *Trova* regained popularity, rediscovered by Ry Cooder and filmed by Wim Wenders for the documentary *The Buena Vista Social Club* (1999). Cooder found the old "*soneros,*" relics in the bars and streets of La Havana, eclipsed by the aging *Nueva Trova* and the old Revolution. Their wonderful rendition of old *sones* has gone beyond Latin America and become a music for the whole world. "World Music" perhaps to a fault, as the film's soundtrack became an inescapable background staple at bars, cafés, and restaurants all over Europe and the United States for more than ten years. Likewise, in her latest albums, Mercedes Sosa sang old tangos like the best of them, as well as rock duets with Argentinean avant-pop eccentric Charlie García.

Certainly, one could blame globalization, neoliberalism, or the Washington consensus for this demise. But the fact is that the Latin Americanist musical movement was itself a form of globalization, and it was about more than Latin America all along. It was, of course, marked by the appeal of the Cuban Revolution—while it lasted—but it would have been unthinkable without the counterculture that flourished in the United States and Europe in the same years. Its demise had more to do with the perishable fashions of popular music. Latin Americanism in music was, after all, a trend, and not fully popular. Within the continent and among its masses, this popularity was never comparable to that of Juan Gabriel (Mexico), Arturo "Zambo" Cavero and Óscar Aviles (Peru), Roberto Carlos (Brazil), Roberto Goyeneche (Argentina), Rocío Dúrcal (Spain), Los Ángeles Negros (Chile), Marco Antonio Muñiz (Mexico), Lucho Gatica (Chile), or José José (Mexico). These performers were true popular idols in the Spanish Americas throughout the 1970s and 1980s. By the 1990s, Spain had regained its cultural caché, and much of the Spanish-language rock that reached the Americas came from Spain. Independently, Argentinean rock had made it into countercultural circles in Chile and Mexico. Rock in Spanish had become not only acceptable, but popular and "progressive" as well. Latin American as a musical genre paled before the vibrancy of rock, salsa, rap, reggaeton, merengue, and so on.

Here, once again, Brazil deserves special treatment, for Brazil remained marginal to the Latin American music phenomenon, with the exception, perhaps, of Milton Nascimento. Of course Brazil also experienced a folk revival in the 1960s, and some of its "protest singers," such as Chico Buarque, Maria Bethânia, and Caetano Veloso, were idols of the "progressives" across the continent. However, by the 1950s, Brazilian popular music had moved in the very direction that Brazilian culture as a whole always seems to pursue—namely, de–Latin Americanization, beyond *charros* and Carmen Miranda. The so-called Bossa Nova and Tropicalia movements made Brazilian music a subgenre of international jazz—worldly music without the exotic intermediary of the Latin American concept. Antônio Carlos Jobim became one with Stan Getz and Frank Sinatra. International stars like Elis Regina, or Ella Fitzgerald, or even Amy Winehouse performed "Garota de Ipanema." However, the original beauty of the lyrics was lost in translation: Tom Jobim sang of a young woman whose walk on the beach of Ipanema filled the world with grace: "O mundo inteirinho se enche de graça" (The entire world was filled with grace). Thus the world "E fica mais lindo / Por causa do amor / Por causa do amor" (It gets more beautiful / because of love / because of love). In English the song's narrator is too self-absorbed to get the point: "The girl from Ipanema goes walking / and when she passes, I smile, / but she doesn't see. She just doesn't see." In any case, Bossa Nova and its worldwide popularity, had no place for Latin America, nor should it have. Later, David Byrne of the Talking Heads made popular Tropicalia and Brazilian pop among hipsters in the United States without intermediation of Latin America.[12]

Throughout the 1960s and most of the 1970s, Spain was kept at a distance from these trends. The country remained, by and large, a musical consumer, not a producer. While it imported Mexican and Cuban material, its own exports were for long little more than a kind of overcooked and Franco-flavored sub-flamenco *à la* Lola Flores: "¡Ay pena, penita, pena!."— something like: ""Oh grief, griefy, griefy grief!." And yet, despite the limitations imposed by political conditions, a protest-song movement indeed developed within Spain, in both Spanish and Catalan. There were important singers, songwriters, and bands like Jarcha: "Dicen los viejos que este país necesita / palo largo y mano dura / para evitar lo peor . . . Libertad, libertad, sin ira libertad . . ." (This country's old men say that what's needed / is a long stick and an iron fist / to keep the worst away, . . . but Freedom I say, Freedom without wrath, Freedom . . .). There were Joan Manuel Serrat: "y es que yo, nací en el Mediterráneo" (For it was in the Mediterranean that I was born) and Paco Ibáñez: "andaluces de Jaén, aceituneros altivos . . . decidme en el alma ¿quién? / ¿quién levantó los olivos?" (García Lorca's poem: Andalusians of Jaén, you haughty olive farmers . . . speak from your souls. Who? / Who uprooted your orchards?). In Catalan, there were Lluís Llach "Si tu l'estires fort per aquí, / i jo l'estiro fort per allà / segur que tomba, / tomba, tomba, i ens podrem alliberar" (If you pull hard over here / and I pull hard over there / It will surely fall / fall and fall, and then we'll break free) and Raimon: "Al vent, / la cara al vent, / el cor al vent" (To the wind / face to the wind / heart to the wind). The most elite of "progressive" circles—those who could purchase rare European records—consumed the latter two in Mexico and Buenos Aires. But the first two, especially Serrat, became important "poetic" references not only for their contemporary listeners of the 1960s and 1970s, but for four generations.

Ibañez and Serrat made their names by setting canonical Spanish poetry to music: Antonio Machado, Miguel Hernández, Francisco de Quevedo, José Agustín Goytisolo, or Federico García Lorca. Here lies the irony of what I call the "Machado Effect" in the popular "poetic instinct," an effect that goes beyond Latin America and the vogue of the *"canción de protesta."* To elaborate, poet Antonio Machado Núñez's father, Antonio Machado Álvarez, "Demófilo" (1846–1893), was a folklorist, a prominent collector of Andalusian *coplas* and popular songs. His son, Antonio Machado Núñez (1875–1939)—one of the greatest Spanish-language poets of the twentieth century—filled his poems with words and images from his youth in Andalusia and his family's intimate relationship with local traditions: "Mi infancia son recuerdos / de un patio de Sevilla, / de un huerto claro, / donde madura el limonero"; or "¡Oh!, la saeta, el cantar / al Cristo de los gitanos, / siempre con sangre en las manos, / siempre por desenclavar . . . Cantar del pueblo andaluz / que todas las primaveras / anda pidiendo escaleras / para subir a la cruz . . ." These lyrics were both set to music by Serrat and have become part of the memory of three generations of Mexicans, Argentineans, and Uruguayans. Music carried Machado through the decades. Today, it would be difficult to find a Mexican, an Argentinean, or a Peruvian older than thirty who does not know by heart "Cantares," a poem (1912) written by the son of a nineteenth-century folklorist and set to music by a native Catalan speaker: "Todo pasa y todo queda, / pero lo nuestro es pasar, / pasar haciendo caminos, / caminos sobre la mar." Today this song has enjoyed a lasting popularity far beyond anything that came out of the *canción latinoamericana* movement of the 1970s and 1980s. And thus, an old "elite" poem, more than one hundred years old, has had a more lasting impact than the folkish vogue of the self-consciously Latin American. Worse things have happened.

℘

Once more, in the twenty-first century, Latin America as a musical impulse lives on—and it spends most of its time in the United States, growing in popularity. There is Calle 13, and there is Marc Anthony, both from Puerto Rico. The latter named, by the way, not after the Roman general, but after the popular singer of Mexican boleros Marco Antonio Muñiz. And then there is reggaeton, the bit below by the Cuban group Gente de Zona: "Y se formó la gozadera / Miami me lo confirmó / Y el arroz con habichuela / Puerto Rico me lo regaló / Y la tambora merenguera, Dominicana ya repicó / Con México, Colombia, y Venezuela y del Caribe somos tú y yo / ¡Repicando!" Spreading from Puerto Rico and Panama to Miami and from there to Lima, Madrid, New York, and Mexico City, reggaeton has become unstoppable. Mexican popular music, in turn, has become the interminable tuba noise with lyrics that naturally express the US/Mexico popular world of love, money, violence, and social and geographical mobility ("Yo les puedo dar un TIP/ con dinero y troca nueva / caen morritas VIP"). I do not claim to know this music by heart, but it certainly is Latin America *comme il faut*, that is, made in the USA. Nothing wrong with that. It is just that I have run out of memory.

SIX

US-Centered Latin America—Part 1: On current US Latin Americanism and its challenges, or an explanation of the recent forms of survival of the term

He himself [Golovan] is almost a myth, and his story a legend. To tell about him, one should be French, because only the people of that nation manage to explain to others what they don't understand themselves.

—Nikolai Leskov, *"Deathless Golovan," in The Enchanted Wanderer and Other Stories, trans. Richard Pevear and Larissa Volokhonsky (New York, Alfred A. Knopf, 2013), 276*

Nowadays there is a lot more Latin America than *Latinoamérica*. The term feels much more at home in English. Without Latin America, I believe, *América Latina* or *Latinoamérica* would either be gone or would be a very marginal idea. Before fleshing out the limitations of the connotations of Latin America in current US-centered Latin Americanism, allow me to list some relatively recent challenges that have somehow affected the uses of the term Latin America.

☙

First, there is the end of the Cold War and the dismantling of welfare states throughout the world, but especially in the United States and various countries of the Americas. As Daniel Rodgers has shown, this came not only as a result of an evil force called neoliberalism, but also because of the exhaustion of old, state-centered welfare models of development. Throughout the immediate post–World War II period the models seemed to succeed in producing economic growth, some redistribution, and protection against the fear of revolution and war.[1] But by the late 1970s, these policies no longer worked. The welfare state, the social and industrializing role of the state, was put into question, both theoretically and practically, while the old fear of war remained contained in the all too real Cold War possibility of nuclear extinction. By the beginning of the twenty-first century, it was still unclear how Latin America would look beyond the inertia of the Cold War. In turn, the exhaustion of the old models and the success or failure of newer ones have come with an increase in inequality in countries like Mexico and the United States, and with a modest improvement in places with massive inequality like Brazil. All this has represented a serious challenge to the very idea of Latin America.

The term had for so long been theoretically and practically attached to the idea of state-oriented development (Keynesian, Marxist, or otherwise), that the end of welfare states brought obsolescence to old forms of Latin Americanism, both in English and in other languages. Recall what the early ECLA (Economic Commission for Latin America, UN) theories or the *teoría de la dependencia* were: calls for strong, state-sponsored modernization, for one or another form of a welfare state. Even for old-fashioned modernization theory, Latin American modernization meant nothing but the emergence of welfare states, both as engines of modernization and as guarantors of anticommunist stability. The intellectual founding father of modernization theory, Edward Shils, put it clearly in the 1940s: "modern" states were "welfare states" "proclaiming the welfare of all the people and especially the lower classes as their primary concern. . . . Modernity therefore entails the dethronement of the rich and the traditionally privileged from their positions of pre-eminent influence."[2] The US government at some point disliked Juan Domingo Perón's regime—more for its ambivalence toward the Allied cause in World War II than for its corporatist welfare state. But by the mid twentieth-century Mexico's and Brazil's hugely corrupt corporatist welfare states became the "miracle" models to pursue in US Latin American and world policies. Latin America became another name for a model of modernization, and that model was the welfare state—which was not necessarily democratic.

Starting in the 1970s, massive inflation, authoritarianism, and the growth of inequality and instability made it hard, by the 1990s, for the very corpus of development economics to recognize the category Latin America in the fashion of old dependency or modernization theory. As Debraj Ray has explained, the 1990s style of development economics did not reject as a whole the old, state-oriented development—à la Albert O. Hirschman—but advanced a view less attached to notions of absolute origins, of historical, cultural, and ethnic preconditions (i.e., Latin America); less about identities or ethoses and more about pragmatic, contingent macroeconomic policies.[3] The category of Latin America, thus, lost explanatory powers.

Now it is hard to speak of Latin American development, or even of imperialism, in terms of the good old *dependentista*, or modernization theory, or in Keynesian terms. What, then, is Latin American development? Cuba's revolutionary state-run utopia? Or Chile's stable but unequal market economy? Is it the economic model implemented by US-trained economists, as is the case in Mexico or Brazil (the same model, but clearly not the same results)? Or is it Venezuela's populist, oil-dependent, corrupt, and authoritarian welfare state? How can conventional Latin American anti-imperialism be reiterated when Brazil's and Chile's main commercial partner is not the United States but China? How to appeal to old forms of anti-imperialism, when for millions of Mexicans or Guatemalans the United States is either home or a desired destination; either the basis of local economies (remittances) or the axis of drug-related violence in South Chicago or Tepito, Mexico City?

It is indeed hard to articulate old forms of Latin Americanism in a post–Cold War, post-welfare-state era. Thus, over the last decades, adding, in a broad and vague fashion, the word *neoliberal* or *neoliberalism* to "Latin America" has often achieved the survival of the term ("Latin America"). Neoliberalism encompasses everything and nothing: the dismantling of the welfare state or the incorporation of constitutional multiculturalism and indigenous people into national systems of education; Chicago-style economics or the success of Mexican film directors in Hollywood; drug wars or obesity epidemics in Mexico or Guatemala—that is, neoliberalism as an almighty explanatory concept, loaded with a strong, negative ethical charge through a bombastic lack of specificity.[4] Hence, whereas the idea of Latin America in the post-welfare-state and post–Cold War era pales in meaning and importance, adding *neoliberalism* to it works as a lifesaver for the deep-rooted meanings of Latin America. Then, once more, things seem Latin American.

At times, current US Latin Americanism sees the region's states either as failed states or with the same abhorrence with which the US Tea Party sees its own. And through the overuse of the term *neoliberalism* in US Latin Americanism, the welfare-state agenda for the entire region has been replaced with a multitude of presumable engines of change: social movements, indigenous movements, NGOs, strong populist states (Ecuador, Bolivia, or Venezuela in the 2000s), but only if these are conceived as authentic. This is not only the result of the decline of the welfare state everywhere, but also of the long period of low economic growth and inflation in the 1980s, and of the loss of appeal of the Cuban and Nicaraguan Revolutions.

Thus the allure of, say, neo-Zapatismo or Chavismo (or whatever similar phenomenon comes next) in radical US Latin Americanism, as a sort of compensation for lost hopes. The lyrics have changed somewhat, but the music remains the same: collectivity, authenticity, utopia, messianic anti-imperialism, and an odd antimodernism. In the 1990s, US Latin Americanism left behind its support for strong welfare states and Marxist-Leninist revolutions; it became infatuated with indigenous movements, not because Indians were not mobilized before, but because now indigenous people seemed to be the engine of history, of Latin American history. If it was authentic and racially defined, then it was the right Latin America and the right sort of movement, whether it was Sendero Luminoso, neo-Zapatismo, or Evo Morales's regime . . . all new lyrics to be sung to the same old tune.

But how can Latin America still be a unit of historical, political, and moral analysis for social realities as varied as that of twenty-first-century Sandinista Nicaragua, of post-neo-Peronist Argentina, and above all those of Brazil, Mexico, and Chile? These three countries are very different expressions of the same experiments with ugly democratic procedures and unjust development strategies. To call them and see them as Latin American neoliberalism, as Latin American postcapitalism, as a Latin American neo-epistemology of power would be fine academically, but useless in any practical or seriously intellectual sense. Carefully considered, these countries critically challenge both the roots of the idea of Latin America and the hard myths of an ideal liberal democracy. They also challenge US stability. The extraordinary twentieth-century transformation of countries like Brazil or Mexico has quietly made anachronistic the category of Latin America in US political and economic circles: the very size and import of those economies make them untreatable as mere exotic, Latin American deviant cases. If their financial systems or their economies were to collapse, the US economy would be at serious risk—as happened with Mexico in 1994.

Or another example: isn't it clear enough by this second decade of the twenty-first century what has been true for more than a century? That is, that—leaving Latin America aside—Mexico has no past, present, or future to speak of outside of its real historical, human, geographical situation: the United States, the North American region, parts of the Caribbean, Cuba, and parts of Central America. And the same is true for the United States: what is the United States today, or what will it be tomorrow, without its complement, Mexico? Latin America, the name, and Latino/a, the term, are desperate attempts to reconnect with a (cultural, racial, and political) comfort zone where the world maintains the order that we assume it ought to have. As Thomas Holt has argued, "Race made sense of worlds that, in the midst of anxious change, were otherwise opaque, unpredictable, and inchoate."[5] Indeed, race is the epochal truth that we share with the nineteenth century. But that order does not exist. And I think it is actually dangerous to keep thinking in this way when discussing drugs, borders, and citizenship. This region, Mexico, the United States, and these people, Mexicans, Americans, who have no name or historiography in common, although they clearly do have a shared past, present, and future, urgently need a common understanding. They ought to be thought together, more than they need that other commonality implied by the idea of Latin America, which only obliterates the undeniable fact of the Mexico/US coexistence. So much for the Bolivarian dream of Brazil and Mexico joining forces. The assumed common history, Latin America, is indeed tautological but in fact useless for the understanding of the past and present of the United States and Mexico. There is much more, and more important, shared history between Mexico, Canada, the United States, and the Caribbean than the history shared between Mexico, Brazil, and Argentina. I am not speaking of love; I mean precisely the opposite: hate, war, human integration and contradictions; that is, a truly shared common past, present, and future.

In the same way, the growing world importance of Brazil has made Latin America, as an analytical category and a belief, a way of misunderstanding the past, present, and future of the giant Brazil, an old empire that has never stopped being one. Its large area of influence now includes many parts of the Southern Cone, Africa, and Portugal. Brazil is not only producing innovations in the form of the welfare state and the market economy, but consciously aiming to look un–Latin American. And Chile has become a stable democracy that, like Brazil, does not want to be identified as Latin American. It could be argued that this is just the legacy of Pinochet in some elite (as it were, Europeanized, mestizo, criollo) Chileans. It might be so; but I do not think that Chile's stable democracy would want to solve its many social problems through Latin Americanism, dreaming of a shared history with Paraguay, El Salvador, or Haiti, or joining the forces of postcolonial utopianism.

␞

The other great challenge for the US-centered notion of Latin America is democracy itself. I mean democracy not in its common metaphysical sense:

political modernity involves modern democratic representation, which implies institutions, which exist if and only if there are civic-minded citizens, whose existence also implies a democratic tradition. Without virtuous citizens, there are no institutions, thus no democracy, no representation, and hence no modernity. In Mexico and Brazil, and in US Latin Americanism, this pure metaphysics has produced a wave of disenchantment: arguments about democracy betrayed, stagnant democracy, incomplete democracy . . . because of the lack of a democratic tradition, of virtuous citizens, because of corrupt politicians, or because of neoliberalism. All this metaphysics is based on the idea that somewhere, sometime, democracy has been what democracy ought to be and has not produced disappointment. "The disenchantment," Adam Przeworski has said of democracy everywhere, "is as naïve as was the hope." "He who says participation," said Wanderley Guilherme dos Santos,

> says democracy (Rousseau); he who says democracy, says organization (Robert Dahl); he who says organization, says oligarchy (Robert Michels) or authoritarianism (as the facts tell). This is an example of a perverse series of transitive properties, paradoxes, and vicious circles which make the survival of fragile democratic regimes subject to random cycles, discontinuities and sudden surprises. It is possible to identify the attributes that are typical of a stable democracy, and the history of the emergence or evolution of the majority of these attributes can also be established. But, as far as I know, the S factor (stability) remains a mystery; I mean, the ingredient that makes it possible for these attributes to remain undisturbed for long periods of time in some cases but not in others, and whose absence can lead to the collapse of a democracy.[6]

Democracy and stability, thus, challenge the very idea of Latin America, because it ain't so, and because it is so. While democracy is seen as Latin American, it seems not to partake of our epochal crisis: that of democracy itself.

When I say *democracy*, what I mean is that ugly historical outcome, which is achieved with or against tradition (Uruguay and Chile, on the one hand, or Spain, Brazil, and Portugal, on the other); I mean electoral rules, a balance of power, and a political system that emerges from the masses or from the state, not to satisfy metaphysical principles, but to avoid tyranny and despotism. It emerges as a check on the power of tyrants and of majorities. I mean democracy as a balance of power precisely to ensure that rulers do not do much that is grandiose or maleficent (Edmund S. Morgan). Democracy, thus, is an ugly and imperfect, and yet less evil form of accountability, checks and balances, and distribution of resources. An ugly thing, but the human species has yet to come up with a better option.[7]

When Latin America meant anti-imperialism, wars of liberation, or the party's vanguard, the love of democracy—despite what many progressive movements claim today—was nowhere to be found. Until the late 1970s, very few communist or socialist parties or movements (Chile's Socialist Party being a great exception and a great tragedy) considered democracy anything but a structure of bourgeois domination. But starting in Argentina in the late 1970s, the entire region began to assume democratic features of government. Of course, all the region's democracies soon disappointed great expectations. There is now (2016) a generalized disenchantment with democracy in the United States, Spain, and Italy, but most especially in the countries of the Americas that put so much hope in the coming of democracy. Democratic procedures, democratic politics, have revealed themselves to be a nasty business. Curiously, in the midst of this current crisis of the "make-believe" of democracy, some progressive movements in Spain explicitly call for the Latin Americanization of southern Europe, as if Latin-Americanizing were the indispensable tilling of the soil in order to grow utopias of post-liberal democratic scenarios. Pablo Iglesias, the leader of Spain's Podemos Party, explained it to the *New Left Review*: "From 2011, we began to talk about the 'latinamericanization' of Southern Europe as opening a new structure of political opportunity. This populist possibility was theorized most specifically by Íñigo Errejón, drawing on the work of Ernesto Laclau."[8] Would this be the optimal creation of a new, hegemonic, populist option for twenty-first-century Portugal and Spain? And all because democracy, in Spain or Mexico, has proved to be a spiteful business. But where in the world is democracy not such a thing?

Some countries, like Chile, Uruguay, and Brazil, have consolidated functioning democratic regimes, and yet they too face many problems, and inequality remains—though inequality, for instance, in Uruguay is very different from that in Brazil or in Mexico. But are the majorities in Chile, Uruguay, and Brazil willing to give up this revolting business of democracy in the name of another oligarchic or populist utopia? They certainly would not want to see their democracies Latin-Americanized, if that means Venezuela's, Nicaragua's, or Ecuador's dubiously democratic Bolivarian revolution. Mexico, for its part, is a democratic regime despite the disenchantment of current progressive and conservative intellectuals who found the game too dirty for their hygienic ideas of democracy. I myself feel that the 2012 return of the PRI did mean the reoccurrence of old forms of unaccountability that we thought had been surpassed. But I am not willing to give up the dirty democratic game in the name of either a nationalist plebiscitary democracy or a hard-hand authoritarian regime. The myth of the strong state (authoritarian or otherwise) is long gone. But the odd surprise of the weakness of the state did not bring good news to any country. All this is a real challenge for the category Latin America, which has often implied ethnic or cultural collectivism, social engineering of the strong state—a strength that could hardly be achieved by democratic means—and utopian anti-individualism and antiliberalism.

In the 1980s, US-style comparative politics developed an entire school of thought about Latin American models of transition to democracy.[9] In a sense, the models were the result of the lasting assumptions of US Latin Americanism. After all, they were models derived—apples with apples—from the Portuguese Carnation Revolution and Spain's *transición*. These were "suitable" cultural models for Latin America. But once democracies flourished everywhere in the continent, the models were no longer in fashion, as happens with all theories in US academe. The problem was that democratic regimes (as disgusting as they seemed) made it harder to conjugate the lasting meanings of Latin America. Thus it had to be that if they were democracies, they were above all Latin American; that is, they were fake, somehow unfaithful to ideal types, matching neither great principles nor idealized local circumstances. No one doubts that messy Italy and corrupt Chicago were and are democratic, but Brazil and Mexico could not fit the model; they had a "path-dependent" problem, endemically Latin American.

US Latin Americanism has faced this problem by relying on the textbook existence of the region in order to argue, in brief, for two kinds of solutions to the challenge of democracy (no doubt an obnoxious pill to swallow); both are a response to the atavisms that the textbook existence of Latin America implies in English: on the one hand, what I call the "South of Nogales, Arizona, everything is Nogales, Sonora" argument; and on the other, the idea that real democracy can only be that maintained by culturally and racially authentic subjects. That is, first, and as I will elaborate below, the old argument about endemic, atavistic backwardness—the legacy of Spain, the lack of Protestant ethics, patrimonialist trends, corrupt states—explains the fakeness of democracy, of progress, of development, which is a comment on Nogales or Buenos Aires, Mexico City or São Paulo. Second, the argument that real, noncorrupt democracy, or true civic virtue, comes from the masses, an argument that is antistatist—that is, anti–Latin American liberal state—and culturally deterministic in equal parts, and is delivered with a twist: not just any kind of masses (not *mestizos*, not the urban poor who play the democratic game in huge national parties or unions), but those formed by authentically defined subjects according to a deep-rooted understanding of what it is authentic in Latin America.

 C&

Another challenge for US Latin Americanism has been violence. To be sure, violence has been historically endemic, for example, both to the United States and to Brazil. Moreover, as a whole, Latin America's violence rates are the highest in the world, but that obscures, for instance, that Chile's violence rate equals that of the United States, Bolivia's equals that of France, and then there are the extraordinarily high violence rates of Venezuela, Guatemala, Mexico, Honduras, and Brazil that support the high ranking of the region in terms of violence. The challenge I refer to is the changing nature of this violence. "Latin America," the term, has implied a fascination with redemptive violence, at times understood as ritual violence, liberating, and at other times as revolutionary. And the region has been violent, very violent. But some violence at certain times has been more important in defining the meaning of Latin America than other violence at different times. Latin America as a narrative testimony—from the English and French success of *Me llamo Rigoberta Menchú* (1982), to the memory literature on Chile and Argentina—was an important element in producing the world's awareness and agenda of human rights.[10] After all, such narratives prospered in the tragic soil of post-Holocaust accounts of genocide. But the recent uncontrolled violence—which we call, for lack of a better understanding, drug-related violence—that Mexico, Guatemala, Brazil, Colombia, and other countries are experiencing is challenging the old fascination with violence so dear to the idea of Latin America.

How are we to make sense of such violence? It is not revolutionary, it is not liberating, it is not redemptive. But it is popular, from the grassroots. So far US Latin Americanism has blamed neoliberalism and US drug policies—which are undoubtedly an essential explanatory factor for this violence. But US Latin Americanism has also fallen into the temptation of translating this violence into its intrinsic fascination with redemptive violence. Thus the popular culture around narcos and drugs is receiving Frida Kahlo–like treatment; it is being aestheticized, digested, as a very Latin American phenomenon, as a popular expression of resistance and solidarity. To display real walls full of the blood of the victims of recent violence in Mexico in a New York gallery could be an interesting exercise in disruptive art, but it is precisely what a circus of naked Brazilian or Mexican

Indians carrying their weapons did in many US and European world's fairs during the nineteenth century. What to do with El Chapo Guzmán? A neo–Subcomandante Marcos? A tropical version of George Soros? A new Pancho Villa? An excuse to force Mexicans in the United States to build a wall along the southern border? The problem is too tragic and too complex, and yet it remains to be seen what sort of idea of Latin America could result from this. But so far the idea looks like an old monkey playing old tricks.

Massive new violence might be better seen not through Latin Americanist lenses, but through the specific agendas of each country, which—despite US Latin Americanists' views of the state—will necessarily attempt to strengthen the state (legitimate monopoly of violence). It will also require the transformation of some US Latin Americanists into full Americanists, able to knowledgably and effectively critique and influence US policies. Conservative US scholars and politicians are further along in their crusade: linking terrorists with Mexicans, Guatemalans, Colombians. . . . If they succeed, the idea of Latin America may be lost or not, but certainly all of us, Mexicans and Americans, would be lost.[11]

Moreover, now violence in Latin America has a peculiar, un–Latin American component: the United States, not only as a champion of "the war on drugs," not only as the consumer of world illegal drugs and supplier of weapons, but also as the unprecedented world example of incarceration. The United States incarcerates an impressive percentage of its population (from 1 to 1.5%), and its jails are above all full of Latino/as, Latin Americans, and African Americans. So much for the exoticism, the utopia, the cultural aloofness of the idea of Latin America; it is at home, in jail. Furthermore, recent massive US repatriations have resulted in violent gangs going back and forth from Los Angeles and Chicago to Guatemala and El Salvador. To speak of "Latin American violence" in this context is to miss the point. The current violence is a problem addressable only by going beyond the category of Latin America. In the attempt to truly face the problem of the neo-prohibition era, of the world's new great migration, the category of Latin America *estorba*.[12]

℃℟

There is also the more domestic challenge that affects US Latin Americanist scholars: that is, the post-1989, post-1960s, and postmodern transformations of US academic life. Nowadays Latin America is a well-established academic stock, but not a very desirable one in the stock market of the social sciences and humanities in US universities. It is not what it used to be in the 1960s and 1970s. Moreover, the old Cold War funding of area studies has declined almost to the point of extinction, and there are doubts in many disciplines about the intellectual and administrative advantages of area studies, or of Latin American–centered subfields.

To be sure, among the social sciences, economics in the twentieth century was the most successful in achieving a "real" scientific and objective look—though, ironically, departing from a subjective principle: humans' maximization of desires. During the long reign of Keynesian economics, Latin America was an important unit of analysis, an academic industry that, as Arturo Escobar and Gilbert Rist showed, substantiated the world's belief in development as a scientific transformation based on reformatting cultural values and thus institutions.[13] But, as a result of the 1970s economic crisis, in which various developmental miracles started to show stagnation, inflation, and large-scale unemployment, the discipline underwent a radical transformation. Thus, what had been a marginal approach since the 1940s, the strong, neoclassical market-faith of the Chicago school, among other institutions, became mainstream, strongly sponsored by private interests and lobbying in the post-Carter realignment of parties' clienteles.

This brought about an odd result for the idea of Latin America: on the one hand, the concept became obsolete in the face of sophisticated, microeconomic mathematical models. Hence to have experts on Latin America in economics departments became less important than having experts in the discipline's new technical trends—who might or might not use Latin American data. On the other hand, the discipline has never been more Latin American, if by that we mean practiced by people coming from the Spanish- and Portuguese-speaking worlds. Not only have technocrats from all over the continent been trained in major US economics departments, but US-style economics is produced and maintained by the constant brain drain from the south. A lingua franca was developed, and now even in Brazil or Mexico, economics journals are often published in English. In a way, this is good news: the old ethnic and cultural atavism is no longer important to the discipline. Ideas are discussed beyond the hierarchical moral graduation so common in the humanities (which are as English-centric as economics, but in which ideas from Spanish and Portuguese are ignored as second rate, or idealized, included by quota, or as a proof of diversity or multiculturalism). But the fact is that economics needs the idea of Latin America less and less, except as an unchallenged, textbook-like category that is taken for granted, there to be used and abused according to models.

An influential book, *Why Nations Fall: Origins of Power, Poverty, and Prosperity* (2011), by MIT and Chicago economists Daron Acemoglu and

James A. Robinson, is a good example. The study departs from, and often returns to, the border between Nogales, Arizona, and Nogales, Sonora. It deals extensively with the Latin American past and present, meaning the textbook version, *comme il faut*, actually mostly based on English-language textbooks on Latin American history. The apparent simplicity and importance of the book's main argument is, nevertheless, radical for economists; that is, these are economists who accept the prevalence of politics over market theories: Great Britain and the United States "became rich because their citizens overthrew the elites who controlled power and created a society where political rights were much more broadly distributed." But the point is that in such an argument Latin America becomes an all-encompassing Nogales, whose atavistic, "path-dependent" Latin nature neatly proves the assumptions inherent in the model: "Why are the institutions of the U.S. so much more conducive to economic success than those of Mexico, or, for that matter, the rest of Latin America? The answer to the question lies in the very different societies formed during the early colonial period."[14] This is not, to be sure, a new argument for US Latin Americanism—it is a rephrasing of the colonial heritage dictum.

The book is emblematic of a currently influential style of social science based on one or two deceptively simple ideas. These ideas are, however, powerful when located within economistic reasoning. They offer two advantages: they allow the argument to escape the rigor of economic modeling through what is presumed to be historical analysis, and they furnish the argument with the conceptual beauty of "discovery"—simple but powerful ideas. Nowadays, many successful, US-style social scientists follow this formula. Every year a new book, by an archaeologist, an economist, a psychologist, or even a historian, gets published for "the general public" with a new neat idea: war was wonderful for the development of the species, violence is not growing but diminishing in the long run, or these are the x historical "apps" needed to achieve modernity. I myself am fond of this provocative conceptual logic. It inspires thinking, and above all rethinking. The problem is not that these approaches use the wrong history. It is that they are immune to historical specificity. No historiographical example could disprove their logic, for in their eyes, all specific histories are anecdotes, details that have no bearing in the larger models. In the same way that finding a successful reactionary Catholic *empresario* in nineteenth-century Brazil would be no threat to the power of the "Protestant ethic and the spirit of capitalism," dismembering the idea of Latin America into various complex histories would be no challenge to the social science bestsellers that have put forward a list of greatest hits, including "the colonial heritage," "the Protestant ethic," patent rights, patrimonialist values, war, or the effects of tropical heat.

Now, in order for the model to work, for simplicity to prevail, one has to grant physical and historical existence to the US textbook version of Latin America. The moment one zooms in a little bit on any location, then Latin America as a homogenous colonial or cultural legacy disappears, and the model becomes an overgeneralization requiring constant clarification; requiring, as it were, de–Latin Americanization.

Through un–Latin American specificity, it could be shown, for instance, as John Coatsworth has shown, that per capita GDP and economic growth in New Spain were higher than those of British America, and that the gap developed in the second half of the nineteenth century and, above all, in the twentieth century. Another zoom in would show that political rights were and were not instrumental to economic growth.[15] It all depends, as Adam Przeworski has shown, on conflict resolution, sometimes achieved peacefully with inefficient legal and often illegal institutions. Thus Brazil, regardless of its weak political rights, was successful in terms of economic growth. To treat Nogales as a metonym for Mexico, and thus for all of Latin America, is far-fetched as an explanation of what failure means and why nations failed: differences in institutional arrangements and legal histories were very significant. And if these differences are not considered to be important, then why have Mexico and Brazil been so different from the United States? By the 1800s, and all the way to 1861, political rights and the possibility of peaceful conflict resolution in the United States were not very different than in Brazil or Chile—if measured in the number of dead bodies, bloody violence seemed to be more a US institution than anything else. As Przeworski has shown, the United States had reached the equivalent of Chile's per capita income in the year 2000 by about 1950, Colombia's by about 1900, and Paraguay's by about 1800. These represent significantly different histories. And in 2000 Chilean per capita income was six times that of Nicaragua. So much for the explanatory powers of the US textbook version of Latin America. In turn, a zoom in on Brazil, in the heterodox way that Wanderley Guilherme dos Santos has done, would not only evaporate Latin America but also challenge US history's liberal democratic assumptions.[16]

◌⃝

The idea of Latin America has, to some degree, moved in a similar direction, though not as radically dependent on a mere textbook version, in two other disciplines: political science and anthropology. The days of Barrington Moore, of dense, historically informed arguments, are gone. What prevails are either formal, middle-range, ideal-type models or best sellers that develop a single idea or two—derived from rational choice theory, game theory, "big data," or law and economic models. These models, like some cultural-studies approaches, require *prêt-à-porter* history. They do what Marx, Weber, Moore, Albert O. Hirschman, or Alexander Gerschenkron used to do with a great deal of history and imagination, simply by reframing the US Latin American history textbook in different scientific languages. The subfield of comparative politics—once led by Latin America experts (Juan Linz, Philippe Schmitter, Guillermo O'Donnell, Adam Przeworski)—has been superseded by ahistorical quantitative models used as software to run data produced by an unquestioned hardware: the textbook version of Latin America, a mixture of long-standing prejudices about what Latin means and decades of Latin American history textbooks à l'américaine.[17]

US-style comparative politics, ahistorical as it is, has been producing important and revealing discussions of democracy, electoral politics, violence, collective action, and the politics of financial sectors in many Latin American countries. More and more, these tend to blend ethnographic work—in situ interviews with decision makers, common people, and popular leaders—with massive data collection, from the types and frequency of social protests to public opinion surveys at the national and very local levels. The best monographs published every year mostly deal with one or two countries, and it is becoming acceptable to compare apples and oranges—Argentina vs. Australia, Mexico vs. India. In the long run, this may lead to the extinction of the category of Latin America—not a great loss—and the emergence of different cultural and geographical units of analysis to deal with the problems of electoral politics, financial bailouts, and political violence. The problem remains that, as Adam Przeworski argued decades ago, the dummy Latin America still has appeal as an inevitable, if not desirable, unit for comparison. No new model, as yet, seems to be more logically, empirically, and morally seductive than that of the idea of Latin America. And the larger the comparison, the more general the model, the more appealing the category becomes as an available synthetic axiom of "things are like this"—a collection of long-standing prejudices and established knowledge.[18]

The concept of Latin America in anthropology, with its insuperable link to exoticism and its seemingly unstoppable proclivity for grand theory, would seem to have followed a very different path than it has in economics or political science. After all, anthropology has been guided, as Brazilian anthropologist Eduardo Viveiros de Castro put it to Great Britain's association of social anthropologists, "by this one cardinal value: working to create the conditions for the conceptual, I mean ontological, self-determination of people. Or peoples to be more exact."[19] Whereas, in US economics and political science, Latin America works as an unchallenged cultural assumption—which occupies one hour of the eternity represented by formal models—in anthropology, Latin America has often worked as a better Blake-like promise: eternity (i.e., an entire grand theory) in no more than an hour (a little town, a dozen informants). A narrow case study in Chiapas or São Luís do Maranhão, blended with lots of grand theories—that casts doubt on any epistemological, political, or moral assumption—becomes an entire *Weltanschauung*, an alternative approach to life, language, politics, sex . . . Often a racial or ethnic axiom is indispensable in order to achieve this knowledge, making the knowledge produced all the more Latin American, all the more non-Western, all the more unlike us. Important US Latin American anthropologists in the 1930s (e.g., Robert Redfield) idealized the peace and solidarity of "indigenous" towns, which were baptized as "communities"—the word for *Gemeinschaft*. These "community studies" became Latin America *tout court* in the 1940s and 1950s. Then, by the 1990s, what was idealized was violence—as has been done in the last two decades by the most influential US Latin Americanist anthropologist, Michael Taussig. Both idealizations belong to the very name Latin America.

Nevertheless, in US anthropology departments, grand theories seem to prevail more and more often, and mainstream institutions want to hire approaches, not regions or countries. But the discipline itself commands in situ participant observation; that is, a year or more of experiencing a town, a city, in Brazil, in Colombia, or in Mexico. The conventional connotations of Latin America are being challenged by the grand theories and by the growth of ethnologies not of "communities" but of monstrous *Gesellschaften* (Rio, São Paulo, Mexico City, Bogota). More and more revealing ethnologies of shantytowns all over the world are made beyond the conceptual constraints of the term Latin America. But this new work has to overcome three temptations: first, that of the grand theory that makes people in a Rio favela sound like fancy English-speaking Bengali intellectuals of the 1990s. Second, the temptation of the Latin American textbook, which often bewitches the best studies in their mandatory "historical context" chapters. Thus interesting ethnology often appears sandwiched between a historical-context chapter (summary of textbooks and commonplaces about the site in question as a Latin American country, done through US Latin America textbooks) and a bombastic "grand theory" conclusion that, curiously, invokes star thinkers from all over the world (though always in English translation), but very rarely a single thinker in the language, or of the place, that is being studied. Of course, to *document* an ethnology of, say, *a Rocinha* (a favela in Rio), one reads books and essays in Portuguese, but to *think* its poverty, resistance, sex, or violence, one reads Homi Bhabha or Žižek. Finally, there is the temptation to translate the undeniable violence of urban marginality into Latin American code, idealizing it through an appeal to ethnic, cultural, or political authenticity, resistance, or utopianism.[20]

ᥴᖆ

In the discipline of history, Latin America remains an assumed category: *el credo y la cruz del historiador* (the historian's creed and burden). We, US-centered historians working on countries known as Latin America, have embraced the term. We have written the textbooks that furnish the concept with its lasting materialization. But in fact each US-based Latin Americanist historian is nothing more than a digger in the archives of a single nation, an expert in one, or at most two countries. But despite the narrowness of her work, the historian ought to know, either by conviction or by decree, the history of more than thirty countries, for they are all Latin, and presumably part of the same history. She would have to teach Latin America. And yet, historians, like anthropologists—and unlike economists and literary critics—are forced to experience the category Latin America by living and researching in situ, if only to realize that Latin America is not to be found at the sites of fieldwork. As a scholar and as a person, the historian learns and experiences the history of, say, Mexico City, or Puebla, or Cuzco, and only then, as professor and teacher, does he or she frame his or her work in a Latin American format. For, unlike political scientists, economists, or anthropologists, historians in the United States are still hired as Latin Americanists, in charge of teaching this entire "civilizational" track.

I have said it before: very few so-called Latin American intellectuals were truly so; that is, Latin American. I can mention only a few: Andrés Bello, Rufino José Cuervo, Rubén Darío, Pedro Henríquez Ureña, and Alfonso Reyes—all of them were Latin American by knowing a lot about the rest of the Spanish- and Portuguese-speaking worlds, and a lot about the rest of the world. In the same way, very few US Latin Americanist historians have truly been Latin American. But I think it is time to include some of them in the "Order of Reyes and Henríquez Ureña," as it were. They were truly Latin American. I am thinking of the twentieth-century historians who actually knew the continent in full and thus not only told but also influenced its history—all of them also by being knowledgeable about something else besides Latin America (which was and is the only way to be truly knowledgeable about the past). So there were the experts in classics and medieval or modern European history who can rightly claim that citizenship (Latin American): H. E. Bolton, Irving Leonard, J. L. Phelan, Robert Ricard, François Chevalier, John Elliot, John Lynch, Lewis Hanke, Edmundo O'Gorman, Tulio Halperín, Sabine MacCormack, and Benjamin Keen, to mention but a few. There are not many current US-centered Latin Americanist historians who could hold this citizenship. We are almost always historians of one or two nations. But we are all the keepers of the idea of Latin America.[21]

By and large, we do so by assuming, of course, the textbook category, Latin America, but more in our teaching than in our research. What we do in our research is to subject the category to the universal kingdom of the comma. That is, US Latin Americanist historians are national historians of Mexico, Brazil, or Guatemala; but then, no matter whether we deal with the colonial or the modern period, we rely on a common rhetorical device, an automatism. Thus we argue: "in Mexico and in Brazil," then a comma, "as in the rest of Latin America," and then the complement, "love is in the air," "modernity is entangled," "capitalism is crony," "mestizaje prevailed." Of course, if one were to stop and think, one would have to wonder where in the world love is not in the air, modernity has not been entangled, capitalism is not crony, and mestizaje did not prevail.

The kingdom of the comma can be seen as a rather nonsensical but apparently benign slip of the tongue. For instance, urban historians and political historians deal with issues like liberalism or the public sphere in Mexico and Argentina. But then articles and edited volumes are published with the concept Latin America as the grouping criterion: liberalism in Latin America, the public sphere in Latin America. This is another version of the kingdom of the comma, for indeed the topics are more and less than Latin American, but Latin America serves as a mandatory, spatial/temporal/racial demarcation in the current structure of US history departments.[22]

Nevertheless, the kingdom of the comma is disturbing when it is not just a little parenthetical phrase, but it becomes the entire story. For instance, in writing about some Colombian and Mexican liberal thinkers—as a real expression of popular, radical, antiracist 1850s republicanism—historian James E. Sanders wondered, "So why use the term Latin America if the focus is primarily in those societies [Mexico and Colombia]?" The author is adamant: "for convenience: Latin America is simply more pleasing to write than 'Mexico and Colombia.'" But it is more than convenience. It is as if by speaking of Latin America, historical actors would embody their own authenticity and embrace the right history: "Yet Latin America was [then] beginning to emerge as a self-described entity in this period. Most of the time our protagonists employed a more catholic sense of being part of the Americas or the New World, but they did occasionally refer to Latin America or Spanish America—sensing, correctly, that their visions of republicanism, international fraternity, and racial equality were not shared in the United States."[23] So Latin America is not a convenience but the true source of knowledge.

Or think of the following statement and its intellectual assumptions and consequences: "Over the course of the last century, millions of Latin Americans have lived some part of their lives in revolutionary times."[24] Here Latin America is not a parenthetical phrase that complements some concrete story, but inherent in the subject of the sentence, and the consequences are significant: Latin America = Revolution, and vice versa. And no historian would dare to challenge the empirical basis of the statement. Thus the argument is strong; it both proves and reinforces Latin America as the reality it has been assumed to be, and as the necessary analytical category. Yet from a different point of view, that of the twentieth century as a century of world revolutions, the statement becomes either nonsensical or dissolves the idea of Latin America in its own broth. For to which part of the world would the axiom not apply? Of course, it would for Spain, France, Italy, Germany, China, or any part of Africa—they seem to have been like Latin America. Then it seems that maybe it is only the unspecified comparison to the United States that can keep the validity of the argument alive—as is the case with everything derived from the concept of Latin America. But then again, it would work only if we were to exclude the American 1930s, or the 1960s, or the consequences of World Wars I and II in the United States from the notion of "revolutionary times." This simple analytical exercise with a statement—unfairly extracted from an otherwise fine account of the effects of the Cold War in the other America—only seeks to show how consequential these deep-rooted assumptions can be. Without them, the story would be a fragment, unintelligible without the whole, of the history of the Cold War *tout court*.

Used as a textbook entity, thus, Latin America distorts the historian's or the social scientist's findings. Here is another example: Miguel Ángel Centeno explains the weakness of state formation in Latin America not through "Latin America" in the kingdom of the comma, but by using it as an explanatory category. Thus Europe and "by extension North America," the argument goes, were able to build modern states through massive wars of defense against neighbor enemies. Latin America, Centeno finds, did not; the colonial borders were maintained, and Latin America rarely made war preparation the main goal of institutions—thus the weakness of the state. Hence it can be argued that "Latin American states did not have the organizational or ideological capacity to go to war with one another." Except of course, when they did have, and they indeed fought. But in order not only to see this—Centeno, of course, acknowledged those wars—but also to consider them in their real historical importance, one has to diminish the explanatory power of the category Latin America. Only Brazil maintained the colonial structure somehow intact; the rest of the continent became immersed in massive wars that produced many states out of the original viceroyalties and local *audiencias*. And Brazil was not the weakest but the most stable of the states in the nineteenth century, if compared to the rest of the continent, including the United States—but together with Canada. Moreover, there were such important wars as Mexico vs. the United States; Brazil, Argentina, and Uruguay vs. Paraguay; Peru vs. Chile; many bloody wars between different states in Central America; not to mention the constant preparation for wars that never happened but were about to happen between Brazil and Argentina, Mexico and Guatemala, Chile and Peru, Bolivia and Brazil. But Latin America is such a powerful category that Centeno can confidently maintain, "Why have the dogs of war rarely barked in Latin America? It is not that Latin Americans have not tried to kill one another—they have—but that they have generally not attempted to organize their societies with such a goal in mind." This is axiomatic, since "Latin American state power has always been shallow and contested," and this regardless of vast difference between a stable (more than the United States or France in the nineteenth century) Brazilian state and the complicated history of the Guatemalan state; or the vast divergence of the postrevolutionary, twentieth-century Mexican state and the Chilean state. It is not that Centeno's thesis has no interesting insights to contribute; it is that the use of Latin America—not only as unit of geographical analysis but as a governing principle—obscures the potential contributions of the thesis, which, from Hegel to Weber, has been articulated in different fashions: violence against other states was vital for state formation.[25]

I believe that in writing and teaching history in the United States, the idea of Latin America survives in this tricky kingdom of the comma of variegated consequences, and that the strong, recent transnational trends in the discipline have not yet affected the very idea of Latin America. In a way, US Latin Americanist historians have always been transnational; they have written the textbooks that have made it possible—for generations of students, officials, and scholars from other disciplines—to conceive not only of a nation, but a civilization. Comparative, or transnational, or more than national or global histories, however, are now advanced like Catalan chef Ferran Adrià advances his molecular food; that is, as vanguard, as a sign of progress, as an optimal alternative in our discipline, history, which so much needs to overcome its addiction to nations and nationalism. But one could say of history what Josep Pla, another Catalan, said of food: "To speak of progress in the culinary arts is a joke [*irrisió*]. . . . In terms of food, progress is behind us; we have surpassed it [*Ja l'hem superat*]." For history, from Aristotle to Giambattista Vico, from Hegel to Benedetto Croce, from José de Acosta to Father Vieira, had always been universal. It was consciously constructed as covering all that was human, each geographical and cultural specificity constituting a version either of divine history or of reason evolving in time. It is thus rather ironic that, as of late, the discipline assumes that it is cool, hip, and alternative just because it deals with two or three national histories or just because it examines the interconnections of the concept of race in Brazil and the United States. In fact, in doing so, history is merely attempting to return to its pre-nineteenth-century stage; it simply aspires to be post-nineteenth-century. So whatever *transnational* means can only refer to two hundred years of history, and to no more than a decade or so as an academic trend. I wait for the trans-civilizational fashion to emerge in my discipline.

The newness of globalization has become a myth. It has become the sudden discovery that in history everything has to do with everything, a fact that historians had known for centuries, before the term *globalization* was even coined. Historians of the sixteenth or of the eighteenth century had already realized that everything had to do with everything.[26] New Spanish Indian caciques in the seventeenth century defended their privileges, in Nahuatl, through stories full of references to Jerusalem, Rome, and the Palestinian Jew whom they knew as Jesus, thanks to teachings in Nahuatl, Spanish, and Latin, and representations made in local artistic traditions blended with Dutch styles or even Japanese forms through the Namba art that the Portuguese brought from China and Japan. What could be more global than all that? The newness of current talk of globalization is not its scale or comprehensiveness, but its immediateness and its irremediability—that is, the Internet and the centuries-long, accumulative ecological devastation that have made us realize the inexistence of *longues durées*. But here is the historian's practical problem: not only how to notice the connections between everything and everything, but how to narrate such simultaneity in words, which are not simultaneous but sequential. Thus the historian's problem is practical and really troublesome: how to capture, in language, through empirical evidence, how a particular everything-that-has-to-do-with-everything could affect the simultaneity of the present.

It is silly, but I say it nonetheless: The historian's dilemma is synthesis. That dilemma cannot be solved through volumes of philosophy, nor through the nice aphorisms provided by the current scholarly prophets of our contemporaneity. To be sure, no historical synthesis can be achieved without some philosophical point of view, but all philosophical points of view already come from established historical syntheses. Álvaro Coelho de Athayde, the fourteenth Baron of Teive (Fernando Pessoa), put it in this way: "If the systematizing power of thought were sufficient for the work to create itself, if the system were something that could be made from an intensity of emotion, . . . then my work would certainly have been written, since it really would have created itself, within me, rather than myself writing it. . . . Only he who has more will than intelligence, or more impulse than reason, takes part in the real life of the world."[27] Thus my full disclosure: historians are made of little more than will, that of the Mexican saying: "Todo cabe en un jarrito sabiéndolo acomodar" (Everything finds its proper place when you know how to arrange it). This is an odd will, though it does not even start without a minimum spark of intelligence so as to conceive not only the "*jarrito*," but the "*todo*" that, because it is in the past, it is not something waiting there to be known and synthesized; it is something gone, lost, yet to be imagined.

The problem is thus that synthesis, or "transnationalism," vis-à-vis Latin America has often only been able to tango to the Latin tune or the US tune. Both are self-referential academic tunes, in English, citing the theoreticians in vogue (read only in English in US universities), and unable to influence broader historical thought. This of course is an academic problem that does not only occur in English, and does not only apply to US universities. But one cannot exaggerate the influence of knowledge made in the United States.[28] Race, for example, has been a pioneering topic in comparative history, more than in Latin American history, above all because of the importance of race in US history. In the 1940s, Frank Tannenbaum understood that there was no way to fully comprehend the problem of race in US history without a comparative perspective. It was clear then and is today that race stands for evil world interactions between Africa, Europe, and America. Thus Tannenbaum studied US slavery, and also slavery in

Hispanic America and Brazil, creating the myth of the good Iberian master. Carl Degler did the same, without command of Portuguese, and found different systems of slavery in Brazil and the United States based on the number of women and the closeness of masters and slaves. And the last decades have seen the emergence of an industry of histories of race in Brazil and the United States. The comparison, however, does not necessarily imply a true transnationalization of history, I mean a real denationalization, and de-Latin-Americanization, of our histories. Often these comparative histories, if written in English, are about race à l'américaine, although focused on Brazil. That is, they are profoundly domestic histories that assume a blind capacity for universalization of US race relations. Of course, it is rather hard to denationalize histories that are at the core of important national historiographies. No one denies prevailing racism, either in Brazil or the United States, but a more than national history does not necessarily result in anti-racism à l'américaine, or in a US-style African American history of Brazil.[29]

Transnational topics played in a Latin key, together with the kingdom of the comma, have lately created a gap between the interests and approaches of US Latin American historiography and those of Mexican, Brazilian, or Argentinean historiographies—in Spanish and Portuguese. For instance, Spanish-language political history of the Independence period has been concerned with legal history, political cultures, the formation of public opinion, and realpolitik at a very local level. Often this historiography covers more and less than Latin America: it has created strong links with Spanish and Portuguese legal scholars and histories—including the telling cases of the Basque country and Catalonia—with their European connotations; but it often ignores the important counterfactuals: Brazil and Canada—the only successful and relatively stable monarchies in the Americas.[30] In turn, US Latin Americanism has not had much use for these approaches, perhaps, as Pablo Piccato has argued, because it considers them to be histories of elite enlightenment ideas—the fake layer of Latin America.[31] I would add that the kingdom of the comma and transnationalism in a Latin key, which derive from the deep-rooted implications of the term Latin America (in English), also explain this gap, along with the simple fact that a historian writing in Spanish or Portuguese could not afford not to read historiography, theories, and ideas in English. The other way around is not only possible; it is customary in our "Anglo-Globalism," which Carlo Ginzburg has summarized as "the unintentionally imperialistic privileging of studies in comparative literature written in English, based on studies mostly written in English, dealing with literary texts mostly written in languages other than English."[32]

CR

Latin America, as a strong category, has taken refuge in what used to be philology departments, which have been transformed, as a consequence of minorities' struggles in the United States, as a result of the challenges to literary canons, of the discursive turn, and similar phenomena, into all sorts of cultural analyses, full of post-this and post-that agendas. US Hispanism in the style of William Prescott, George Ticknor, and Aurelio Espinoza gave rise to a small, older generation of philologists, who then received the input of the great Spanish and Catalan philological and philosophical schools that came to the United States, escaping the defeat of the Second Republic: Américo Castro, Amado Alonso, Joan Coromines, Juan Marichal, José Ferrater Mora, Francisco Ayala, Pedro Salinas. Then came the exiles from the Southern Cone and Cuba, great philologists, literary critics, and writers who finally consolidated the study of literature in the Spanish and Portuguese of the Americas, going beyond the great masters from the peninsula. Sometime in the second half of the twentieth century, the old projects of philology, literary history, and new criticism experienced a major makeover. The old projects were simultaneously an obsession with aesthetic hierarchy, an example of erudition, a genealogy, a history, and a philosophy par excellence. But the old Hispanism, or what German philologists called *Romanische Sprachen und Literaturen*, became a marginal approach, as much as literary analysis of texts or literary history. What gradually became mainstream in what came to be known as Spanish and Portuguese or Romance language departments—today Iberian, Latin American, and Latino/a studies departments—was a disciplinary flimsiness that was only possible in such departments. That is, art history and criticism light, epistemology light, very light history, zero essayism, philosophy on a diet, and, lightest of all, poetry. Old canonical hierarchies were thankfully challenged, and new voices were heard. There, the Latinness of Latin America found a fertile ground for its existence and reproduction within identity politics—and other sorts of institutional politics—and within the trendy paradigm shifts of these departments.

Literature and language departments' struggles over paradigms and politics, thus, had gone full circle in US institutions. H. W. Longfellow and George Ticknor institutionalized the study of Spanish Golden Age literature as a derivation of *latinité* (starting with Latin, moving on to French and Italian, and then Spanish). From A. M. Espinosa to philologists-in-exile like Leo Spitzer, Joan Coromines, or Raimundo and María Rosa Lida, Spanish was institutionalized more as an Iberian matrix than as part of the tradition of *Romanische Philologie*. By the 1950s, such scholars as Renato Rosaldo, Américo Paredes, and Luis Leal started their careers with a timid Hispanism—only Spanish Golden Age literature—but fulfilling their teaching demands in French and Italian, and gradually smuggling their teaching of Spanish American literature and even Spanish-language Texan and New Mexican literature into the curricula. The increasing demand for Spanish as a second language, US Cold War language policies, as well as the Argentinean, Cuban, Chilean, and Uruguayan exiles consolidated the Spanish and Portuguese departments in the 1970s and 1980s. For the first time, more than just Spanish Golden Age literature, or more than Mexican literature, was taught, including Brazilian literature. There were then many theoretical wars—new criticism vs. traditional essayism, Marxism vs. structuralism, *dependencia*—and subfields were clearly demarcated: peninsular literatures vs. Latin American literatures. Starting in the 1990s, the boom of Spanish and Portuguese departments began a transformation, both institutional (marked by universities' budget cuts) and ideological. Textual literature and philology themselves were challenged. Entities such as Latin American and Latino/a cultural studies departments came into existence. *Latinité,* divorced from its Iberian, French, and Italian connotations, returned. As of late, *iberismo* is back—Iberian and Iberian American cultural studies departments. The idea is to further defeat the imperial notion of the term "Hispanic," of Spain in America vis-à-vis indigenous languages and cultures, and Castile in the peninsula vis-à-vis, above all, Catalonia, but also Portugal and Portuguese-speaking Africa.

Thus, on the one hand, some of these departments have become centers of neo-indigenism, but in English and separated from the long and lasting linguistic study of the indigenous languages of the Americas—which is by and large done in linguistics and anthropology departments. This constitutes a Latin Americanism obsessed with the lasting undertones of the term—authenticity, identity, race, otherness. On the other hand, today's *iberismo* in US language departments is, like the old *iberismo*, a cultural and political defense of "marginalized" Iberian languages (above all Catalan) against what is believed to be the overwhelming power of *hispanismo*. In a way, today's *iberismo* in US institutions has sanitized the old *iberismo* of its intrinsic imperial connotations in favor of "singularities" that have mostly been ignored in US language departments. J. R. Resina, a Catalan scholar at Stanford, has headed the movement: "Iberianism arose from the understanding that the deep-seated commonality of Iberian life manifests itself authentically only in modalities which cannot be identified with the subjacent unity without attacking its very essence." In this talk of authenticities and essences, Latin America becomes, as Resina shows, a North American construction that is "happy to erase the mark of the Spanish master from their identity while espousing the Castilian ideology of the single common language. And yet that commonality on which the Latin America identity is founded dissimulates and silences a great cultural diversity that waits on the wings for a looping of the loop of Longfellow's Law, whereby the circuitous path taken by 19th-century US Hispanists to promote useful knowledge for dealing with the South American continent would curl back through an Iberian studies paradigm to re-open the Hispanic enclosure [sic]." Indeed, somehow, this new *iberismo* challenges traditional US Latin Americanism, through weak but constant references to Quechua, Nahuatl, or Portuguese literature (from Portugal). So far, however, it is only a form of US Catalanism that has yet to come to terms with the imperial connotations of historical Catalanism in a rigorous manner, a movement that was indeed *iberista* but no less imperial than *hispanismo*, in theory and practice.

Vis-à-vis the notion of Latin America, the current US *iberismo* does not do much to dismantle the deep-rooted philosophical and political connotations of the term. It maintains in fact, a rhetorical Latin American-style oppression, as it were, but in this case in reference to Catalonia—a reservoir of endless real, natural authenticity and resistance. Whether the conceptual enclosure that Latin America has implied would be overcome by considering the Spanish spoken in the continent for five centuries as an unreconstructed, quasi-"cosmic" (Resina's adjective) Castilian oppression remains to be seen. It is undeniable that Hernán Cortés and Francisco Franco were the Spanish language with weapons; it is also true and felicitous that Spanish was the language of Rubén Darío, José Martí, J. M Arguedas, Leopoldo Lugones, Antonio and Manuel Machado, J. L. Borges, or Juan Rulfo—and for that matter of Eugeni d'Ors and Josep Pla. And it was also, thank God, the language of the Mexican or New Mexican *Romancero* or of Agustín Lara, Enrique Santos Discépolo, and Felipe Pinglio. Nevertheless, the new *iberismo* has also been advanced as a defense of literature against the excesses of all sorts of cultural studies.[33] This is good news.

ଓ

In sum, in language departments, US Latin Americanism often, if perhaps without meaning to, obeys what the concept demands: it is antidemocratic in the form of the vague antiestablishment populism of authenticity, and antiliberal, either in defense of the legal and moral exceptionality of a sanctioned collectivity (the authentic town, the ethnia, the assumed sexual, racial, or cultural "community"), or through a bizarre antielitism that becomes a heroic patrol of the border between what is assumed to be "popular" and what is "elitist." Mainstream US literary Latin Americanism abhors Latin American elites—they are Westernized, white, criollo, or consumerist urban mestizos—thus its antielitism, its persistent plea for the popular and authentic—the more ethnic, the better. And yet its populist plea is expressed in the most elitist fashion possible: in the language of US academic theory. The theme under consideration might be graffiti, or a narco novel, or some performance, or painting, or social movement in Latin America. But in fact what is being said is about Žižek, or Badiou, or Agamben, or Foucault, or Derrida, or Butler, or Heidegger, or Peter Sloterdijk—or, as the soccer lottery used to say in Mexico: *"lo que se acumule esta semana"* (whatever is added on this week). This antielitism is comprehensible only to its own initiates.

This is a challenging Latin Americanism that seems not to take anything for granted, not text, not gender, not authorship, not power, not hegemony, and of course, not aesthetics. It is nevertheless a Latin Americanism that takes the textbook version of Latin America for granted. My professional duties, and my own curiosity, recently led me to read 260 dissertations from mainstream Spanish and Portuguese/Romance Language/Iberian-Latin American/Cultural Studies departments. I know this is not a representative sample, but it is close. Overall, these works showed, sometimes successfully, others not so much, a will to question, "theorize," and "problematize" the most basic assumptions about aesthetics, literature, the arts, philosophy of knowledge, race, gender, politics, and sexuality. Almost all were companions in disbelief: nothing is what it actually seems to be; any product of human creativity, theoretically read, is a Rosetta stone awaiting its Champollion. I welcome the culture of disbelief, but for all their skepticism and all of their deciphering powers, it seemed to me this scholarship would be unable to think without the textbook category Latin America. Many works in fact included a textbook reconstruction of Latin America and of the country they dealt with—actually too often basing their "theorizing" on US Latin American history textbooks. At times all of their theorizing and doubting seemed to be footnotes to the essential lasting connotations of Latin America. Other times, the theorizing and doubting indeed seriously jeopardized the textbook version of Latin America. And yet, even in the latter cases, the works managed to rescue the concept from its agony, consciously or not, by framing their findings in a historical context, which inevitably becomes that of US Latin American history textbooks—not because they needed the facts and dates, but because they needed a mold to make their cake.

Much of what is called theorizing is historicizing—thus the inevitable and unstoppable need for a convenient and nicely packaged history: history of a specific period, of a place, of a chunk of culture. That is, more than history itself, what is used and abused is textbook history. Unbounded, historicism indeed works as an acid to dissolve any absolute truth . . . except two, historizing itself and the need for historical evidence. Thus the need to "theorize" through the more controlled form of historicism. "We study change," wrote A. Momigliano in a succinct definition of a tame historicism, "*because* we are changeable. . . . Because of change our knowledge of change will never be final: the unexpected is infinite. But our knowledge of change is real enough. At least we know what we are talking about." The only possible thing to do, said Momigliano, was to produce the facts that can illuminate not only our interpretations but those that are to come. Hectic theorizing cum historicizing, applied to Latin latitudes, often implies both a moral position and a disregard of facts. Deconstructing narratives, as it were, is a moral act, especially in regard to such a moral lesson as Latin America. "What history-writing without a moral judgment would be it is hard for me to envisage," said Momigliano. Recent "theorizing" of Latin America can indeed be extremely historicist and nevertheless assume a moral position, often derived from the values of authenticity and resistance implied in the very category of Latin America. Thus the need for the textbook: that is, not the producing of facts about the past but the consuming of facts with a clear moral order—Latin America.[34]

In reading this material, I often wondered why, instead of any national or Latin American history, they did not use the entire flow of, say, the Spanish language (a real archive) as a frame for their theorizing. But invariably they used history. Not being an initiate, I cannot fairly judge the quality of these dissertations. What I can confidently state is that they all used and reproduced the main connotations of that old idea: Latin America/the textbook.

In a way, this kind of Latin Americanism exists, as Neil Larsen has put it, without Latin America; it relies on the idea without requiring that any doubt be cast on the idea itself, or on its real specificities: "It has become a form of 'study' that, over the last couple of decades, has succeeded in inventing for itself a theoretically 'regional' object with almost no remaining connection to any real place."[35] A theoretical region that has not only lost the sense of the reality of the region—which is hard to prove, *pace* Larsen—but also of the very existence of the languages, the peoples that it seems to study, and their lives. Thus the proliferation of theories that tend to reify "Latin America" in sophisticated and new ways (which is very important for academics) rather than to reveal the problems with the term: postmodern Latin America, postcolonial Latin America, Latin American cultural studies, queer Latin America, and so on. Here is Larsen again:

> The further one descends down the ladder from the general trend to the sub- disciplinary *cenâcle* to the individual academic theoretician with cult following, the more arcane and idiosyncratic the designation becomes: Dussel's "philosophy of liberation," or one of Walter Mignolo's many coinages, say "border gnoseology" or "post-occidentalism." The more general designations inhabit and cut across Latin-Americanism the way they do virtually all areas of literary and cultural studies in the US, even if Latin-Americanism—though perhaps here, after all, "Hispanism" is the better word—has typically been "the last to know." Witness the endless and caricatured "debates," continuing to this day, over the possible contours of a "Latin-American Cultural Studies," a "Latin-American post-colonialism," etc.[36]

To be sure, the moment one experiences the cultural production of a city in the Latin part of the Americas, Latin America, as a unit and as a telling category of analysis, disappears—*pace* Larsen. Things become what real things are: so vivid as to be unintelligible. Hence cultural commentary, cultural comprehension, becomes what it can be: an attempt at understanding that both participates in a current of reality and fails in its attempts to fully understand it. In such a way, cultural and political life continues with lots of risks and dangers, lots of enjoyment of the human capability for social and personal introjection.

Often some trend in this post-philological US Latin Americanism appropriates as founders (and thus translates into English) some works (not that many) of such cultural icons of their respective cities and languages as Carlos Monsiváis, Ángel Rama, Beatriz Sarlo, or Roberto Schwarz. One finds them quoted, in English, as *chilaquiles*, in small pieces blended with lots of chunks from the theoretical academic gurus in use—here the use of "Readers" is essential. The quotations reify Latin America, but the Monsiváises, the Ramas, seem to be fish out of water there; their ironic gazes unblinking; their erudite local scales dry.

Politically, of course, the Latin America of these academic disciplines seems as radical as it could possibly be. It is as post-Marxist, *más faltaba*, and post-Western, as it is anti-erudite and anti-objective knowledge. It is postliberal, postdemocratic, and anticapitalist. But these approaches can only do so much politically since they lack practical political engagement. A pro-Kirchnerista and a pro-Chávez intellectual, in Argentina and Venezuela, has to deal with the good and bad consequences of his or her ideas. Beatriz Sarlo, a strong critic of Argentina's neo-populist government, faced the mockery, danger, and the economic disadvantages that resulted from her ideas in her daily life. But nothing good or bad actually happens when a US-based professor of Latin American culture or literature supports, in the name of Žižek or Badiou, antiestablishment violence, or takes an antidemocratic stand based on an unexplained epistemic utopia, or in favor of an "epistemic otherness." Much ado about nothing.

This political criticism lacks what Gérard de Nerval (*Le carnet de Dolbreuse*) tellingly called *hypocondrie mélancolique*: "C'est un terrible mal, elle fait voir les choses telles qu'elles sont" (It is a terrible illness, for it makes one see things as they are). Not that anyone can actually find a single reality for Latin America, but these approaches seem allergic to minimal empirical accountability. Latin America is not a real place, but Latin American reality is often a generic term, in English, for what happens in Mexico City, or in Tlaxcala, or in San Pedro de Macorís. Expressed in the language of Romance, Spanish and Portuguese, cultural, Latin, Iberian studies, however, Latin America becomes a self-referential genealogy. Once more, a real account of the cultural life of Latin America cannot be achieved. That is why the term is only a pseudo-racial/spatial name for a human condition: the unstoppable and yet always unfinished struggle for self-understanding.

CR

In sum, current US Latin Americanism faces three challenges in different disciplines: its own insignificance, the kingdom of the comma, and a textbook category summed up by the model "south of Nogales Arizona everything is Nogales Sonora," or in the style of "epistemic otherness" that nevertheless respect the commands of the old term "Latin America." Thus the term endures as an unchallenged, almost unconscious assumption; a cultural landscape that serves as a place for the projection of new and old utopias and dystopias.

SEVEN

US-Centered Latin America—Part 2: More on one of the forms of survival of Latin Americanism and its proud lack of historiographical accountability, including an exploration of the endurance of the exotic in the term Latin America

The Orient, however, couldn't be authentic anywhere, even in its grave.

—Mümtaz, *character in Ahmet Hamdi Tanpinar's A Mind at Peace (1949), trans. Erdag Göknar (New York: Archipelago Books, 2011), 43*

Think of this genealogy: late nineteenth-century Spain's humanities were connected to German philosophy and social thought thanks to the efforts of the *Junta para Ampliación de Estudios e Investigaciones Científicas*—which sought to professionalize academic disciplines. These links gave rise to such a flamboyant and influential thinker as José Ortega y Gasset, who in turn trained such German-inspired philosophers as Julián Marías, José Gaos, and María Zambrano. The Spanish Civil War made it tragically possible for one branch of this genealogy to end up in Mexico City, embodied by José Gaos, a philosopher and translator of Husserl and Heidegger. (By the way, as philosophical genealogies go, the other branch, that represented by María Zambrano, seems to me more interesting: from Zambrano to José Ángel Valente and thus new views of poetry as knowledge, history, and philology, again very Spanish, rooted in the literature of the entire Spanish-speaking world, and also very German.) Gaos's phenomenological teachings gave rise to two very different intellectual trajectories: on one hand, that of the philosopher (in Spanish) of the Latin American condition par excellence, Leopoldo Zea; on the other, that of the most prominent twentieth-century Mexican historian, Edmundo O'Gorman—

a fully English-Spanish bilingual lawyer cum historian who studied Heidegger under Gaos.

Throughout his life, Zea fostered the most accepted twentieth-century philosophy of an identity, that of Latin America. For decades, Zea's ideas were echoed in the continent, as well as in the United States—for instance, by Louis Hartz, Howard Wiarda, Richard M. Morse, and Claudio Veliz. Something as fleeting as "Latin American identity" became thus a philosophical school, a network of scholars and cultural bureaucrats, and a UNESCO desk. Identities, said Evaldo Cabral de Mello, hardly survive the flow of history, "historicizá-las é, pois, exorcizá-las" (to historicize them is, thus, to exorcize them). But the "Latin American identity" seemed immune to history. Moreover, the Zea-like obsession with identity, in the Latin latitudes, carried over a sense of intellectuals' guilt feeling. "When it is praised by scholars and intellectuals," said Fernando Escalante,

> identity is taken to mean *that something* that the *others* have and makes them *others* (it is fairly common the complaint, by otherwise well-satisfied urban people, about all that *we have lost* by the fact of being urban, half-baked Europeans—but that I count as a simple, shameless bad faith). As it happens, those who do have a true identity are usually poor, oppressed, backward, underdeveloped, etc., and so "identity" becomes a sort of richness of the poor, their sole possession, and claims to be protected as such because it is under siege, threatened by the market, the State, the globalization process, even Civil Rights and, of course, those alienated, self-centered Indians who refuse to live by traditional customs.[1]

To be sure, for long, Zea's influential understanding of "Latin American identity," allergic to Escalante-like views of identity, was considered nevertheless "progressive" because of its anti-Americanism.

Unlike Zea, O'Gorman cannot be said to have founded a school. His erudition, his superb prose, his blend of phenomenology and jurisprudence, and his sarcasm made him unreachable. But as of late, his only book accessible in English (thanks to O'Gorman's own translation), *La invención de América* (1958), has made him into a speaker of a language he could not have spoken (among other reasons, because of his thick, posh English accent and wit)—US trendy academic prose.[2] Indeed, O'Gorman told the behind-the-scenes stories of many of Mexico's nationalist, liberal myths by seeing Mexico in an un-Mexican way; he reshaped the world's conventions about Columbus's trips, and all through readings of pre-Hispanic, Spanish, French, German, US, classic, and English histories. But he had no use for the uniqueness of Latin America or for any sense of the indigenous global south. O'Gorman was an acerbic lawyer/historian fascinated with philosophy of history, Heidegger, and the universality of Mexican history. He endured long-lasting lessons with Gaos in order to learn Heidegger and was also influenced by another Spanish exile, the German-trained philosopher Juan David García Bacca. O'Gorman, however, did not fully command Nahuatl, as did Ángel María Garibay, a priest, who truly knew Otomi and Nahuatl cosmology, but whose philosophical approach seemed closer to idealism and Catholic social thought than to Heidegger or to 1930s Mexican indigenism or twenty-first-century US neo-indigenism.

Gaos's existential philosophy sounded like this in the 1940s: "Because what is it to be I, if not this thinking—which cannot be shared, which cannot be understood; this love—without spiritual fusion; this being in my time—out of time; this being—in the sole reality of this *Augenblick* [moment], from the point of view of this moment?" [*sic*][3] During the Second Republic, he occupied high cultural bureaucracy positions, but the terrible lessons of the Spanish Civil War, exile, his hate-love relationship with Ortega, and the 1940s world's addiction to identities (Freud, existentialism, Erik Erikson) made Gaos articulate his anguish in a self-genealogy of Mexico, sometimes as shorthand for Latin America, and sometimes as a pocket edition of the Hispanic condition.[4] Thus he echoed the lasting commonplaces of Latinity, the search for a nonbeing in relentless pursuit of being: in the Hispanic world, said Gaos, "thinkers propose a politics which, *lato sensu*, introduces foreign ways," mostly from Europe, but there was also "*un Sarmiento norteamericanizante.*" Thus the real unit of *Hispanoamérica* becomes a matter of a Nietzschean minority of educators who can both process and teach the authenticity that lies at the end of all "*extranjerizante*" exercises. That genuineness was, in Gaos, the Spanish language, though his prose was the worst homage to such authenticity:

> The radical quality of Spanish-American thought, that on which its highest meaning rests, . . . can be formulated as follows: A political pedagogy through ethics and even more through aesthetics; an educational endeavor, or more profoundly and broadly, a "formative" endeavor—to create or reform [our] independence, whether constituent or constitutional, for the reconstruction, regeneration, or renovation of the Spanish American peoples, by means of the formation of minorities who can act on the people, and by means of the direct education of the latter; and in turn, principally by means of specifically beautiful themes and ideas, if not specifically beautiful,

exposed as such, in beautiful forms, peaceful and beautiful themes, among which the theme of the intimate spoken word, the theme of conversation, will play an important role.[5]

Incidentally, Gaos's journey from Ortega-Heidegger to the Spanish Civil War and a "Hispanic" *Dasein* was in a way echoed by another philosopher in Spanish America, Italian Ernesto Grassi. He journeyed too from Heidegger and World War II to humanism and then to Chile and Brazil, which he saw as overwhelming nature, an ahistorical ontology that had not realized that Europe was over—so he argued in the book resulting from his 1950s teachings in Chile. For him, Brazil and Chile were imitating what Europe had done long ago, not realizing that 1945 had shown Europe's mistaken historical track. Grassi grew up bilingual, German-Italian (his mother was German), and studied under Heidegger; he taught in Germany for many years, but also in Chile and Italy. However, unlike Gaos, he was not interested in developing a Hispanic or a Latin American ontology, but instead a new humanism based on a critique of Heidegger's antihumanism. He recalled having found in Ortega y Gasset, who at times attended Heidegger's lectures, a Latin friend against Heidegger's very German anti-Latinism (anti–Renaissance humanism).[6]

All in all, Gaos's student, Zea, in due time, translated this kind of approach from a Mexican/Hispanic humanism based on language into a specifically Latin American being, based on the very anguish of trying to be: "In all cases we attempt to deduce what the philosophy of liberation should be from what we call the philosophy of dependence. Like the biblical Jacob, we must always fight against the angel. The angel who is also a part of the fighter. It is this permanent battle against himself which seems to characterize the Latin American who again and again contradicts himself. [This is] the expression of a man between two worlds, that of the conquered and that of the conqueror."[7] This philosophy, good or bad, nicely furnished an ontology phrased in the acceptable languages of identities and ethoses.

O'Gorman was not as nice. He brought with his Heideggerian reading of Columbus's adventures, via Gaos, a European/American self-criticism of imperial prides and naïve philosophical empiricism and idealism. He, however, did not submit a unique and sublime Latin American ontology: "Let us cast aside the fiction that America has a historical individuality. Since the sixteenth century, the fortune of the new world was linked to the culture of the West in the painful state of disintegration in which it then found itself, which is now so exacerbated; but the union was mystical, 'for better or for worse,' and there is no pulling back [from it]. There is no union more fundamental to America than that which is derived from its common culture with Europe."[8]

So, by the 1950s, the Latin American condition, at least in Mexico, had friends and enemies. And yet, ironically, the 1958 "invention of America" has become, in twenty-first-century coloniality approaches to Latin America, as Walter Mignolo put it, commenting on O'Gorman, an example "of how things may look from the varied experiences of coloniality."[9] Thus, what was a very Mexican, very Western, attempt at critical philosophy and history became, in a Quixote-like fashion, a total end of alienation: a final de-Westernization of the Latin American self. In a way, keeping a sense of proportion, O'Gorman could be seen as a Guamán Poma de Ayala: a local voice that is able to speak the universal language. Of course, both could be exoticized, made into alternative ontologies. O'Gorman speaks coloniality, and Guamán Poma is no longer the nobleman who, in the sixteenth century, legally fought for his lands and privileges, asking his king to recognize the injustices committed by local governments; no longer the faithful subject of his Catholic majesty and of God, for, as Mignolo also put it, he was Catholic because he could not be Marxist or Freudian or, for that matter, postcolonial. What were, at the turn of the sixteenth century or in the 1950s, Enlightenment critiques of Enlightenment become non-Westernness vs. Westernness. Universals became Western impositions. Or perhaps not, as it all depends on the current need to save the otherness of the idea of Latin America: "At the end of the sixteenth century and the beginning of the seventeenth," said Walter Mignolo,

> there was no Diderot, no Rousseau, no Kant, no Spinoza, no Marx, no Freud. In other words, secularist enlightenment critique did not exist yet. Waman [sic] Poma assumes Christianity historically and ethically, to the extent that he defends the Christianity of the Andes before the arrival of the Castilians. But at the logical level of epistemology, Christianity in Europe would be nothing more than a regional version of certain principles that affect human conduct and which establish criteria for coexistence, for the good life. . . . The first-level reading is Eurocentric . . . Christianity in Waman Poma is equivalent to democracy in the pen and the word of the Zapatistas: democracy is not the private property of Western thought or political theory, but rather a principle of coexistence, of the good life, which cannot be owned by anyone.[10]

Thus Gaos- or Zea-like Latin Americanism, filtered through decades of academic experimentation after the crisis of Marxism, is finally able to play these axiological games, for at the end of all theorizing, Christian values and democracy turn out to be universal. There are many variations of this new trend, but they share the same conceptual acrobatics. Listen to this (from Enrique Dussell, now a popular theoretician for US Latin Americanists through various translations into English): "The Latin American erotics of liberation is much more complex than that of the European Oedipus. The masculinity of the conqueror (whose symbol is Hernán Cortés) rapes the Indian woman (Malinche); Oedipus is their mestizo Latin American son. Phallocracy becomes conquest, plutocracy, social domination. The *machista* culture of hypocrisy and the mystification of the name of woman. Because of this, the women's liberation was one of the first and central themes of the philosophy of liberation from the beginning of the 1970s."[11]

Of course these are merely examples, which I can be accused of citing out of context. But the point I want to make is precisely about the unimportance of context. None of these recently influential forms of Latin Americanism can be subjected to historiographical scrutiny—not because there is not enough research to examine these statements vis-à-vis what is known of the past, but because their nature is historicist and yet a-historiographical: they consciously dismiss the very idea of any sort of historiographical accountability. They appropriate the textbook version of Latin America—including commonplaces like the colonial legacy, Malinche, Cortés, mestizaje—but they are beyond any historiographical accountability. They can make Guamán Poma or O'Gorman ideologues of whatever, for, as Walter Mignolo stated clearly: "The problem is that 'rigorous historiography' is more often than not complicit with modernity (since the current conceptualization and practice of historiography, as a discipline, are modern articulations of a practice dating back to—again—Greek philosophy). In that respect, the argument for disciplinary rigor turns out to be a maneuver that perpetuates the myth of modernity as something separate from coloniality."[12] Well, I could go on and on about the inaccuracy of this or similar previously cited statements, but only their authors can claim to speak un-modernly, and yet be politically and empirically right. As a historian, I would like to speak so virtuously and so revealingly, but my need for rigor is complicit with modernity. "I would sacrifice a great deal to be a Saint Augustine," said that unreconstructed modernist, Wallace Stevens, "but modernity is so Chicagoan, so plain, so unmeditative. . . . I believe, as unhesitatingly as I believe in anything, in the efficacy and necessity of fact meeting fact—with a background of the ideal."[13] Me too.

ℭℜ

At the beginning of the twentieth century, poet, traveler, physician, and ethnologist Victor Sagalen wrote notes for an essay on exoticism, which was to be "*une esthétique du divers*" (an aesthetics of diversity). He never completed the piece, but his notes are telling in understanding the current survival of the idea of Latin America. In a way, current US Latin Americanism still mirrors what Sagalen called the "parallelism between stepping back in time (historicism) and moving out in space (exoticism)."[14]

Latin America à la Vasconcelos, or à la Rodó, or à la Zea, it needs to be said, could be a case of assumed Western consciousness on the part of people who either ignored or denied their own non-Western being. These, perhaps, were forms of social guilt but not expressions of self-exoticism. Whatever they did was part of their political and personal existence as intellectuals, politicians, and men, not the ecstasy of their own circumstances. In sharp contrast, US Latin Americanism has often been the work of *exotes* (Sagalen). The region became a nearby paradise of exotic desires, of the ability to conceive "otherwise," as Sagalen put it: "Le pouvoir de l'exotisme, qui n'est que le pouvoir de concevoir autre."[15] Thus "I conceive otherwise [*concevoir autre*] and, immediately the vision is tempting." Even in recent critiques, in English, of the very notion of Latin América, the power of exoticism to *concevoir autre* is alive: coloniality, says Walter Mignolo in explaining his approach to the idea of Latin America, "is the theory arising from the project for decolonization of knowledge and being that will lead to the imagining of economy and politics otherwise . . . an attempt to rewrite history following an-other logic, an-other language, an-other thinking."[16]

Sagalen was more direct and faithful to his personal and cognitive desires than certain current, US-centered Latin Americanism (either an involuntary or a dishonest form of exoticism). For him, exoticism was "nothing other than the notion of difference, the perception of the diverse, the knowledge that something is other than one's self." In order for this to exist, in Sagalen or in some US Latin Americanism, one needed to have a love-hate relationship with profound otherness. Ironically this was only possible through familiarity, though never reaching—as in Sagalen's desire for exotic bodies—full possession. Hence the enchantment of unintelligibility, if not real, then manufactured: "Exoticism is thus not an adaptation; it is not the perfect comprehension of something outside one's self that one has managed to embrace fully, but the keen and immediate perception of an eternal incomprehensibility." Like part of US Latin Americanism, Sagalen's real *exotes* are anticolonial, for Spanish, or Portuguese, or American, or English colonialisms aimed at conversion, at exploitation, seeking to end that which fascinates. For him "colonial bureaucrats" were not real "*exotes.*" A kind of US Latin Americanism emerges, thus, like Sagalen's desire, out of the fact that "diversity is in decline. Therein lies the great earthly threat." To maintain difference becomes vital, especially regarding "indigenous identity," as Fernando Escalante has argued: indigenous identity mandates the "defense of *difference* as something valuable in itself (the difference, that is, between *us* and *them*, and not the possible obvious differences *among them*)." This has been the crusade of an influential US Latin Americanism; that is, to preserve exotic diversity, like the Canon Corporation's campaign: "Capture nature, but leave it untouched."[17]

All sorts of academic fashions have declared the old term Latin America obsolete; yet the fashions only make it more alive: still the product of profound *exotes*. Now the old Latin anti-Saxonism becomes just another expression of Western power, in the name of a more solid exoticism, of real diversity, to which everyone is alien, both the Europeans and the local criollos and mestizos; only the indigenous people are real—and, of course, their US interpreters. Latin America becomes a "real" reality, so to speak, that of postcoloniality with all fake historical layers finally removed. Criollo, mestizo, or Western Latin America does not exist, but the exotic home of otherwise-ness, for some US-centered Latin Americanism, does. And it is certainly as full as ever of redemptive violence and unintelligible *esperanza*.

Exotes produced a unique form of diversity within the idea of Latin America. They constructed it out of the undeniable indigenous component of the term, advancing a radically different historical, cultural, moral, and, of course, racial ontology—no matter whether one is talking about Mexico City, Cuzco, or Santiago in the sixteenth or the twenty-first century. This was a strong trend in late twentieth-century Brazilian, Mexican, and Peruvian neo-indigenism, whether in Bonfil Batalla's notion of *México profundo* (1987) or in Darcy Ribeiro's unmistakable assessment of the authenticity of Latin America: Latin America "always existed under the sign of utopia. I myself am convinced that utopia has a site and place. It is here [in Latin America]." And its content is clear: "Meditate with me, reader, on this unfortunate Christian utopian epic in the tropics. More than a tragedy, [it was] a terrible mistake. What [they] wanted to plant here, in the name of Christ, was what had always been here, as nowhere else: a society [based on the] solidarity of free men."[18]

But the new *exotes* are not like the old. They believe in a radically different, both ancient and new, ontology and utopia. It used to be that radical
indigenistas believed in, if not loved, mestizaje, a human inevitability. In
1950, Luis Villoro—twisting Gaos's and Zea's old phenomenology—created an alternative ontology for the real Mexico, if only as a provisional
stage before reaching humans' common universality (just as Octavio Paz
did around the same year with *El laberinto de la soledad*). For Villoro, the
recovery of the true *Gemeinschaft* was indeed the final destiny for all, but
it had to be raceless, a status that only mestizaje could advance: ". . . in a
community without racial inequality, there will be no 'Indians,' or 'whites,'
or 'mestizos,' but rather men who reciprocally recognize themselves in their
freedom. . . . Indigenism should be postulated to perish; it should only be
a way, an indispensable, but passing moment along the path. It will only
achieve its goals when it is able to deny itself; because this act will be the
signal that the specificity of racial elements and the distinction between
them has given way to true community."[19] By the 1990s, however, Luis
Villoro and the new indigenism of US Latin Americanism sustained the
endurance of an ancient and yet endless indigenous being, and projected
that being into the future, into a radically different future. Thus, for these
trends, mestizaje has become a bête noire, an imposed phenomenon that
is almost the equivalent of cultural genocide.

Ironically, five centuries of Christianity, the massive biological and social destruction of pre-Hispanic worlds, nearly one hundred and fifty years
of existence as mass consumer societies in the region, and centuries of
painstaking philological work with many indigenous languages seem to
have made the real, generic, "indigenous" ontology more reachable, not
less. However, as has happened with historiography itself, centuries of the
philology of indigenous languages do not really play a role in this new *indigenista* US Latin Americanism. The vast literature on the structure, changes,
and nuances of the various Totonac, Maya, Nahuatl, Quechua, or Aymara
languages has been the product of five centuries of interaction among *letrado* speakers of European and indigenous languages. Until very recently,
domination and conquest were the goals of the interaction, but the process
has been so complex and lasted so long that all resulting and surviving languages are simultaneously colonial and noncolonial. Latin, Spanish, the
Catholic doctrine, and two "imperial" indigenous languages (Nahuatl and
Quechua) formed for long the code that Spanish friars, indigenous *letrados* and *principales* studied, used, and transformed in indigenous languages
and in Spanish itself. Early Spanish grammars and "*artes de hablar*" became
part of anonymous Maya, Nahuatl, or Mixteco dictionaries and texts.

Over time, many languages disappear, many versions of surviving languages too, but the most lasting effect has been that all languages became something else, including Spanish. Even secret, subversive Maya texts, like the books of *Chilam Balam*, spoke what William Hanks has called "colonial Maya." Documents from the Maya Caste War in the 1850s also spoke of the Holy Trinity and Israel; the text was in Maya and it was subversive, but it was not the expression of an *illo tempore* identity. "The theologies found in the Book of Chilam Balam," said Hanks, "are often exotic and possibly subversive in intent. Yet the linguistic forms are identical to those of the missionaries." In Yucatan, *reducciones*—which sought simultaneously to protect and to convert and exploit Maya Indians—conclusively transformed Maya existence, making preexisting conditions not only unattainable, but soon inconceivable. Thus, the *Chilam Balam* was "*lengua reducida* that is being voiced by Indian authors." This was not mere syncretism, borrowing of terms or beliefs; it was a new, inevitably reciprocal ontological remaking: "Just as missionary *lengua* courted subversion by transposing *doctrina* into Maya, the *indio ladino* and the Indian elites more generally ran the risk of undercutting themselves even as they sought to defend their own interest." In the same way, in the *Manuscrito de Jilotepec* (1589), a letrado Indian tells the story of the town; according to the transcription by Ángel María Garibay, the document tells of the emergence of the Aztec or Otomí dynasties in the town, making use of the "*estatua que fabricó el rey de Babilonia*" (the statue made by the King of Babylon,), which "*esta gentilidad*" (these pagans) called Jupiter. And the discoverer and interpreter of this and many other documents and oral traditions—in Spanish, Otomí, Nahuatl and other languages—was Garibay, a priest, one the most important *nahuatlistas* of the twentieth century, who, like his peers in the nineteenth century, spoke Latin and translated Latin classics, and who said, on reaching the parish of an Otomí town, "Me imagino ser Platón entre sus atenienses" (I imagine that I am Plato among his Athenians).[20]

Of course, in all transcriptions of Maya or Nahuatl texts and oral traditions, there were many nuances unintelligible for non-Maya or non-Nahuatl speakers—maybe not for the many bilingual priests, mestizo authorities, and for the Indian nobility and *literati*. But those uncanny silences are by and large also silences today for speakers of Maya or Nahuatl. Those old texts are full of local, biblical, and classical references that do not have a basis in a common, living language in the present, neither in Spanish nor any other language. No doubt indigenous languages are unique *Weltanschauungen*, reducible neither to a generic, homogenous, "indigenous" being nor to *indigenista* Latin America. An eighteenth-century mestizo letrado, as Hanks shows, Pedro Beltrán de Santa Rosa María, in his *Arte de el idioma maya*, realized the difficulties of fully comprehending the nuances of language. And yet, in Spanish, in his dedication to the Gloriosa Indiana Santa Rosa de Lima (the "Glorious American," not the "glorious Indian," as Hanks translates it), he enigmatically put it as follows—a true poetic monument to both the possibilities and the impossibilities of language comprehension:

> Aunque paresca silencio, el silencio no paresca y,
> aunque se aparesca la espina, la espina se desvanesca
> haciéndose lenguas del Arte
> con este Arte de Lenguas
> los que juzgan que es la Lengua un Arte de espinas lleno [*sic*].

> (Even if it appear to be silence, may silence not appear, and
> even if there appear a thorn, may that thorn disappear,
> making their tongues Artful
> with this Art of tongues,
> those who judge that it is—the tongue—an Art full of thorns.)[21]
> ["appear" here is the subjunctive form, as in the Spanish]

☙

For every version of every indigenous language, an entire philological trajectory could be reconstructed, leading to serious debates about meaning, cosmology, and politics. Among those fully devoted to the language dimension of things, however, the recent work of *indigenista* US Latin Americanists is an uninteresting fashion. And all this work has affected neither the assumption of cultural incompatibility between indigenous and non-indigenous languages, nor the belief in an indigenous Latin America. At the beginning of the twenty-first century, we have returned to ontologies derived from living indigenous languages as if they had existed in a vacuum and not as part of centuries of radical interactions. Therefore, for some, the Nahuatl term *alteptl* is not a city-state, but a mystic notion of ethnic democracy and solidarity, inexpressible in European languages. There were other common Nahuatl words, as Alfredo López Austin has shown, that were hard to understand in Spanish: *yaoyotl* (war) and *tlacotli* (something like slave).[22] "Pachakuti," explains Alberto Flores Galindo, was "for some a character, but for Guamán Poma it is a telluric force, a cataclysm . . . or to be transformed into earth according to José Imbelloni."[23] In the twenty-first century, Pachakuti has become nothing more than the realization of the incompatibility of the current indigenous worldview and modern societies. But, as Flores Galindo explained, "The men of the Andes have not spent [all of] history trapped in an impossible museum."[24] All of these terms are used locally and abused by all, indigenous or not; the words are indigenous, indeed, but not unintelligibly, not exclusively.

Diversity is therefore the key. Sagalen was right. But what is ontologically different from what? The historian deals with this question in more than "us versus them" or "here versus there" terms. And the lesson is simple: diversity cannot easily be demarcated in historical terms, because any past, regardless of place, race, and culture, is diverse, so to speak, unintelligible in some way. There is much talk of various forms of diversity, beyond multiculturalism, either in the name of *interculturalidad*—a Bolivian trend that owes a lot to the interaction of Quebecois and Catalan priests in indigenous towns in Bolivia (the *iberismo* and *latinité* connection once again)—or in the name of a new Tahuantinsuyo—Inca rule and empire. Thus indigenous people, for instance, are seen as essentially different from mestizos, and Latinos are just what Anglos are not, regardless of time and space. Like love and reason, differences and diversity change over time, and after almost five centuries of wars, miscegenation (cultural, sexual, political, economic), adaptation, genocide, or *melcocha*, diversity cannot be an ontological, epistemic, or atavistic past that is always present.

History is often invoked to explain differences. But in writing history, the essential conflict is not between tradition and modernity, or tradition as postmodernity, nor between West and non-West, but simply between the past (gone, alien, incomprehensible) and the present and possible future. Western or not, the past is alien. To decipher it would entail, depending on the case, a command of Nahuatl, Maya, or German, but the very fact of making a past somewhat intelligible to the present transforms it into doubt, conflict, comprehension and incomprehension in the present. That is what history does; it does not serve to create endless essentialities that come floating down from the past whenever the bonds of fakeness or inauthenticity are loosened.

To be sure, to think in terms of radical others, of alternative epistemologies, coming out of the centuries of history in the Americas makes the historian's task much easier. It makes it possible to believe in pasts that are ironically quite translatable to the present, either because they are us or because they are them. That is, they are those ethnic or cultural alternatives that we defend precisely because we have made them intelligible for the present. But the radical otherness of Latin America also makes the historian's task harder than it need be: time and time again it forces us to find the non-Westernness in Latin America; that is, historians are in charge of the intellectual maintenance of that other way of being that allows *exotes* to endlessly renew their stories.

The past is alien to the present everywhere. Therefore either every historical subject is a Martian, unintelligible to us in the present, or else we can, to some degree, understand the Martians through research and imagination, if only partially. And if one wants to grasp them, one ought to assume that they are capable of supreme evil and supreme goodness (regardless of their authenticity).

But there is good news: diversity par excellence, the past, reveals signs of wisdom when treated with empirical respect and erudition. For instance, the late Sabine MacCormack (*On the Wings of Time: Rome, the Incas, Spain, and Peru*, 2006) showed that to understand the Inca past in cultural terms, Plato does not hurt, medieval Spanish thought is quite useful, and both are indispensable to grasp the Inca's notion of an Atlantis. MacCormack's revealing story was written with full knowledge of Latin, Greek, German, English, Spanish, and Quechua.[25] And her image of the Incas does not diminish the cruelty of Spanish conquest a single bit. But neither does it make the Incas into a homogenous group of saints or of alternative epistemologists. In a way, in reading the extraordinary historiography on New Spain and Peru from the sixteenth to the early twentieth centuries, I have sometimes come to think that what that past wants to transmit to us in the present is indeed a justice-seeking *"reclamo"* (to the West, to the ugly things that the entire Americas are), but not the ethereal *reclamo* that simply states: "We were and are what you are not; we have been forced to look like you." But instead it is a bigger *reclamo*, best expressed in Juan Gabriel's lyrics, "Te pareces tanto a mí, que no puedes engañarme" (You are so much like me that you can't fool me).

⚬

Historians are often complacent in this search for the deep Latin America. We look for self-contained cultures, which we assume are untranslatable to the present, to Western mentalities, although we translate them. We search, for instance, for the nineteenth-century indigenous culture of the Bajío, and we find it to be antagonistic and untranslatable to that of the criollos. In the same way, cultural-studies scholars examine *mole* as a non-European ontology, a sign of Mexican hybridity. Or they look for the performativity of gay culture in nineteenth-century Buenos Aires, as something alternative, opposed to, and incompatible with what is considered the city's straight culture. An incompatibility that, within the inevitable idea of Latin America, is invariably supported by traces of race and ethnicity. Of course, the mere naming of a culture as indigenous, or popular, or alternative, in Argentina, Mexico, or India, in the sixteenth or twenty-first centuries, means that such a culture is already a mixture of many recognizable and translatable things. Otherwise these cultures would simply be invisible to our historians' eyes. As the many fine studies about the spiritual conquest of Mesoamerica have shown, it is rather hard to speak of total incompatibility, and when such a thing is truly found, it means that the very discovery of an ontological incompatibility is already the translated form of a past, which makes it usable for grasping the present.

But if Latin America implies the possibility of different ontologies, it is because of what recent studies have called an epistemic gap—that is, because of the historical relativity of truth. In this way Latin America's otherness becomes a political argument, maybe an interesting and devastating one, but there is no need to bring history to the table. Historicizing the power structures behind truths demonstrates that truths are relative, that they have been used and abused. And yet, this political argument cannot logically be made on empirical grounds. For in that case, the truth of historicism—that which states that history can show the relativity and power structures of all truths—would not be relative. It would be *"la mera neta"* (the real deal). This is not only a logical contradiction, but a revelation: Latin America as encompassing a totally alternative ontology is indeed a current progressive political agenda that destroys "hegemonic" truths—a claim that could be politically desirable. But it does so by seeking authority in an unaccountable (empirical or philosophical) knowledge vis-à-vis the past. So there is no need to engage in debates about facts, interpretations, trends, or discoveries in the past. Otherness is claimed to be obscure, mostly incomprehensible, but real. That is why they can project any past, present, or any utopia into the future.[26]

Yes, I am asking for the undertones of utopia and diversity in the term Latin America to be devalued. Not because I lack respect for the equalitarian nature of the social agenda that supports a lot of this utopianism. No. On the contrary, I ask for the end of these connotations because I have too much respect for this agenda. Certain current US Latin Americanisms embrace the present by means of the utopia, but not without limiting, through the very dependence on the term Latin America, the promises of the utopia and the possibilities of conceiving a new one. Today's golden utopia is tomorrow's cheap nickel dystopia. The utopian notion of diversity prevalent in some influential, US-centered Latin Americanism cheapens politics. It makes academic statements new—which is important for academics—but useless. A Latin America that is still capable of grand political utopias based on its intrinsic otherness is condemned not to be able to specify that utopia—for then some kind of empirical and political accountability would be needed. Instead, it has become an academic industry to denounce the historical crime of oppression. And the important thing in this industry is the novelty of the denunciation, not the crime (too old and too long to bother with so much history), nor the victim (so vaguely described as subalterns, indigenous people in all places at all times), nor even the murderer (very well known, huge and comprehensive, but easily captured with such terms as the West, or capitalism, or neoliberalism). As with the latest jacket from Massimo Dutti, originality, academically sanctioned originality, is what counts.[27] Not the utopia.

EIGHT

"Latin America" Abides: But How Should Historians Speak It? On the author's final embrace of Latin America, or a rationale for his defeat and his simpleminded resignation

Por lo demás, la esdrújula esencial
sigue en veremos.

—Gerardo Deniz, *"El consuelo es indeciso; apreciable la paciencia,"* in *Erdera* (Mexico City: Fondo de Cultura Económica, 2005)

Over time the imperial and racial idea, Latin America, attained the silhouette of an epic poem, either in a verse by José Martí or one by Rubén Darío; in Eduardo Galeano's *Las venas abiertas* or in the lyrics of the 1970s "*canción de protesta*" that my cohort sang. And so we sang Latin America, the revolution, as if *"matando canallas"* with our *"cañón de futuro"* (killing the bad guys with our future cannon) (Silvio Rodríguez). "Latin America"/the poem, however, despite epic efforts by twenty-first-century, neo-indigenista scholars, or academia's "epistemological" guerrillas, or the widespread belief in endemic backwardness, wore off. Poetry wears off, said Carlos Vaz Ferreira, in two ways: first, through rationalization; too much theorizing "vampirizes," "washes out" (*decolora*), "holds back" (*inhibe*) poetry; poets become *"pensadores"* or *"moralistas"* (thinkers or moralists). "Latin America"/the poem has not lacked theorizing; does it still hold any poetic power in itself? The other way for poetry to fade, said Vaz Ferreira, is through what actually makes poetry sublime: "the hypertension of sincerity and . . . pain": "Pain and sincerity sometimes result in another 'way of finishing off poets,' which is to shut up."[1] I am keen on this last ending for "Latin America"/the poem: with pain and sincerity, let us accept the inevitability of its institutional and symbolic existence, making the best possible *practical* use of the term as such an academic and political institution, and let the poetics of utopia, ethnicity, and authenticity fade away.

Therefore, I speak *sotto voce*, as a mere historian and educator in US universities, and I accept my own defeat. The term "Latin America" will endure for the foreseeable future. But what should we do with it in historical analysis?

CR

The concept is an institution in all sorts of international governance bodies, in the US government, and in the structure of knowledge of US universities. Furthermore, unlike Slavism, Teutonicism, or Anglo-Saxonism, Latinism still retains its romantic appeal, like a violet that got withered, as says the Mexican bolero, *"en el libro de recuerdos del ayer"* (in the book of yesterday's memories). And yet, for all its problems, this insurmountable institution offers some practical advantages in researching and teaching the past, any past. This is especially so when what still prevails throughout the world is the teaching of national/ist histories—sadly even in today's Europe, the only serious twentieth-century experiment in the institutionalization of a more-than-national writing and teaching of history.

The prevalence of nationalism has been intellectually wearying. It has also been dangerous. In the midst of the economic and human integration of a world of profound inequality, "us/them" endures as a duo addicted to history; the more it gets, the more real wonder at the past becomes irrelevant. However, fighting national myths with historical facts, I am convinced after decades in the task, makes no sense. "Refuting a myth," wrote historian Timothy Snyder, "is dancing with skeletons: one finds it hard to disengage from the deceptively lithe embrace and the music has begun, and one soon realizes that one's own steps are what is keeping the old bones in motion."[2] Realizing this, recently the discipline of history in US universities has prized international, global, transnational, or more than national approaches to the past. Needless to say, there are many obstacles to these kinds of approaches in a milieu that favors monolingüism, identity politics, and neat, self-contained, civilizational tracks—America, the West, Latin America, Africa. Training and placing truly more-than-national historians has proved to be a challenging conundrum. This is where an unconventional use of the established category of Latin America comes in handy. But . . .

CR

Latin America constitutes a long-in-the-making conceptual and moral pres-tidigitation that suitably rhymes with similar intellectual and moral tricks. Thus we find the term used with renewed vigor in twenty-first-century aca-demic discussions of global, Atlantic, or transnational histories, or in histo-ries of the "global south." These academic trends—in English, *comme il faut* —almost instinctually call as witness of their respective crusades the very idea of Latin America. More than any Mexican, Brazilian, or Nicaraguan peculiarity—in pre-Hispanic, colonial, or modern times—every new trend appeals to the old tangle: Latin America. The concept seems like a reser-voir of old and new, hybrid and alternative, auspicious and revolutionary bricks—always there, there awaiting to be discovered time and time again in order to erect new, "big" theoretical or political structures.

In the 1950s Louis Hartz made a call for comparative civilizations ap-proaches in order to grasp American history—as Herbert E. Bolton had done before and C. Vann Woodward did later. Hartz found an equalitarian, John Locke–centered American ethos that had not known a feudal mo-ment. Thus the marvel of Tocquevillian *l'Amérique*: born equal, modern, and liberal. Hartz's conclusion, however, was closer to melancholy than to pride. As Albert O. Hirschman put it commenting on Hartz: "Having been 'born equal,' without any sustained struggle against the 'father'—that is, the feudal past—America is deprived of what Europe has in abundance: social and ideological diversity." Hartz seemed melancholic about genuine diver-sity in views of the US past. Thus the need for comparative history, which led to the inevitable certainty: the existence of another America, one with a full feudal past that was the natural antimatter of the United States. Hence the conceptualization of an anti-Locke, Latin American ethos inspired in the sixteenth-century Spanish political thinker Francisco Suárez—an ap-proach masterfully crafted by Richard M. Morse for Hartz's *The Founding of New Societies* (1964).[3] Latin America, the concept, like Ruth Benedict's de-piction of Japan as an endless "culture of shame" (*The Chrysanthemum and the Sword*, 1946), was music to the ears of the 1950s speakers of the "big" language of civilizations and ethoses. "What truly amazes," wrote historian Harry Harootunian, commenting on 1950s US social science paradigms, "is how so much nonsense could command the time and energies of so many thoughtful people for so long." Indeed, it is truly staggering.[4]

The booming 1950s US social science, in its Modernization Theory version, only reinforced the validity of such a thing as a Latin American ethos. In the same way, Latin America is mandatory in any new volume of transnational, Atlantic, international, global histories, or in histories of the global south. But other than (and recently) the Haitian Revolution, no real specific theme or idea from Haiti, Mexico, Venezuela, or Brazil has made it into old and new, "big," English-speaking academic trends, unless it comes packaged as Latin America—which is always evoked as a handy way to avoid command of any explicit history. Within such new mountings, it is believed, Latin America overcomes its marginality, participating in global trends or partaking of the global south. And yet, such mainstream, English-speaking addiction to the term Latin America only reinforces the marginality of the Spanish- and Portuguese-speaking worlds, because thus speaking Latin America often has meant "*ningunear*" knowledge produced in Spanish and Portuguese.[5] To put it bluntly: if John Rawls had written in Mexican Spanish, his *A Theory of Justice* (1971) would be, first, mere parochial echoes of a local tradition (as it may in fact be in English); second, it would not be philosophy but, by some means, a treatise on Latin American identity; and, finally, it would be unknown to mainstream philosophy.

Hyper-specialization in academic history has always coexisted, nevertheless, with "big" histories, implicitly or explicitly. To be sure, there have been many nationalistic monographs dealing with one battle or with two heroes, but only because such narrow stories were echoes of that larger, lasting, cosmopolitan, and important history and moral: the nation. And there have been such concepts as civilization, modernity vs. tradition, progress, Latin America, Europe, Africa, or development that, regardless of the narrowness of historians' perspectives, have been engines of historical writing. After decades of case studies, community studies, regional history, micro-history, and middle-range theories (always wontedly or unwantedly parts or echoes of "big" histories and theories), "bigness" revived in scholars as a self-assigned task. Thus civilization reemerged in such scholars as Samuel Huntington, and the notion of the global became epidemic. Hence, for some, "civilization" itself and the Third World are dead; long live the "global south." Latin America, however, not only survives within one or another "big" theory, but actually makes possible the "bigness" of the theories.

The global south is a "fuzzily delimited sector of the planet, above all, the place where another way of life is burgeoning," in order precisely "to save us all, including the elite of the G7 nations" (Walter Mignolo). Thus the global south allows us to say, "What if we posit that in the present moment, it is the global south that affords privileged insights into the workings of the world at large?" (J. and J. Comaroff). Africa, South Asia, and Latin America seem, in many respects, to be "running slightly ahead of the Euromodern world, harbingers of its history-in-the making" (J. and J. Comaroff). Latin America regains thus a post–modernization theory, post-Iberian ethos, post–Marxist revolution, and post–Third World happy existence. And it does so as a well-defined cloister: "The closest thing to a common denominator among them is that many were once colonies, protectorates, or overseas possessions" (J. and J. Comaroff).[6] That is, Latin America exists because it is postcolonial, just like, but somehow not like, the United States, Canada, Australia, Italy, Portugal, Poland, or Greece.

Speaking "Latin America" in these new approaches is not merely a convention, an accepted empirical vagueness (is Portugal the global north or south? is Guatemala as global south as India or Brazil?); it is not only a slip of the tongue, an imprecision about which we all understand its pros and cons. This new Latin America of the global this and that, or the post- or trans-, is neither a mere theoretical inconsistency nor an innovative historiographical position. It is simply a necessity. Otherwise ideas of the trans- or global become hard to conjecture. These are mental routines that require each other to exist. But the moment Latin America is used as the category to speak global south or north, or global or crossing histories, the newness and utility of the approaches become dubious: what is newly global or alternative about approaches that still believe in "Latinness"? Are mainstream academic globalizers aware of how much they must chew when they bite the concept of Latin America? Is it not the case that the term Latin America already includes enough old philosophical and moral certainties to truly conceive new historical or political questionings?

I know—we cannot think the world outside such spatial and cultural categories as Latin America. But, as Martin W. Lewis argued about the ideas of Asia and the Pacific, we at least could admit that "none of the main spatial units that we use to think about the world are foundational in any sense."[7] And I think historical and conceptual specificity is required, taking advantage of but also going beyond academic fashions and, above all, questioning the concept of Latin America. Not because historical phenomena in Mexico or Brazil ought to be solely understood as Brazilian (or Paulista) or as Mexican (or Chilango) themes, but because in order to truly understand "*lo mexicano*," "*o brasileiro*," and the global, the historian has to construct a specificity that does not count on a ready-made concept, geography or chronology. Such a specificity especially cannot be found within the conceptual confines of the term Latin America. In a way, each historical topic needs to imagine its localness and its globalness, as well as the peculiarities of the power struggles they involve. The uses of the global south or north, or of Latin America, are ways of avoiding demarcation of such specific localness and globalness, under the undeniable belief in a well-known, all-encompassing, and seemingly absolute power structure.

☙

One can appropriate the term Latin America as an entrance point to more-than-national, thought-provoking, presently relevant, and challenging stories. Not simply by repeating the Latin American history textbook, but by using it as a de facto, long-lasting, fixed idea whose many and large consequences have yet to be fully explored. For, treated with care and modesty, the term yields interesting connections and points out views that can potentially change our experience of the present and our possibilities for the future.

For this to be possible, "Latin America"—the portentous idea, the presumed place, feeling, people, and time—needs to be approached with plebeian specificity. That is, meek specificity in the consideration of time, space, evidence, and language kills the Latin America of the kingdom of the comma, or that of the great utopias and alternative epistemologies, or that presumed *Weltanschauung* caught in the allure of the local vs. the imposition of the global. It reduces those odd historical subjects, the Latin Americans, to obsolescence. In effect, the strategic use of the category of Latin America can grant access to well-documented, disciplined, imaginative readings of specific historical circumstances, with their many more than local implications—beyond the belief that every individual example is a bonsai version of the larger textbook Latin America.

The concept has been more than national all along, though often thanks to the equalizers of exoticism or cultural and racial atavism. When speaking Spanish or Portuguese, the more-than-national connotations of the term tend to be mere rhetorical figures, often linked to another larger national history—that of the United States. In English, however, Latin America is a well-established institution that, though for long it was Mexico-centric, encompasses more-than-national phenomena. Its more-than-national nature can thus bring historical connections and interactions that are unreachable through mere national histories. Hence Latin America becomes the inviting entrance to specific ways of telling stories that echo in many ways and whose final conclusions may not return to the idea of Latin America—but who cares.

Sanjay Subrahmanyam, in his studies of early modern Eurasia, with its Iberian connotations, and Sheldon Pollock, in his studies of Sanskrit, can serve as emblematic of the construction of specific space and time, local-ness and globalness that can hardly fit trendy concepts of global this or trans- that, alas these approaches would have been unthinkable without the last three decades of academic trends. Each approach is, to be sure, a peculiar digestion of decades of academic debates but at the same time an exercise in disbelief. A global imagination, an early modernity, says Sub-rahmanyam, emerged between the late fifteenth and the eighteenth cen-turies, in which notions of one or another centrality turn out to be hard to maintain: "a more or less global shift, with many different sources and roots, and—inevitably—many different forms and meanings, depending on which society we look at it from." In turn, a poetic and political Sanskrit tradition, which occupied a vast and growing space over time, as Pollock shows, created, as Latin did, a premodern (chronologically), cosmopoli-tanism vis-à-vis which all local expressions were simultaneously vernacular versions and transformations of that cosmopolitanism. Unlike Latin, Pol-lock argues, Sanskrit never had an imperial center. Both Sanskrit and Latin, however, were made by their respective multiple connectivities.[8]

It is not a coincidence that in both Subrahmanyam and Pollock, lan-guages are vital for their delimiting of specificity. Only through the com-mand of those many languages, those many repositories of localness and globalness, can real historical specificity, global and local, be imagined. And yet, it is not surprising that the most avant-garde studies of the global south, or of Latin America as global south, or as postcolonial, or as At-lantic opt for a high degree of English monolinguism. It is maybe time to conclude that the subaltern in the global south indeed speaks but in English. As do many other recent studies, Jean and John Comaroff's *Theory from the South* (2012), for instance, makes a strong case of speaking from a global south by using ideas from the "others." But that means utilizing the star-system of Indian, Nigerian, South African, Mexican, and Chinese scholars, who write in English and thus are already "global north." For all their strong case for a theory from the south, the Comaroff's approximately 480 bibliographical references include only twenty-two translations to English (mostly from French, some from German, and one or two from Italian), and only five are in another language than English (that is, in French). Of course, the book includes plenty of ethnography of different groups in South Africa, but this is an ethnography of "unprocessed data"— as they themselves maintain about the habits of the global north vis-à-vis the global south. The scholars process the data, of course, through English and in English. In turn, Mignolo's manifest-like inclusion of Latin America in the global south includes nearly thirty bibliographical references, all in English except for one. His inclusion of Latin America in the global south, of course, includes an allusion to a "Mexican philosopher" (*sic*), of "Irish descent," Edmundo O'Gorman, as Carl Schmitt's antinomian. Mignolo maintains that Schmitt followed the "rules of reasoning of the European legacies and traditions," while O'Gorman's *La invención de América*—so Mignolo argues—was saying that "those rules are not convenient for me. Let's use something else." And O'Gorman's something else was, I believe, Heidegger via two Spanish philosophers, Gaos and García Bacca. But that is as unimportant as O'Gorman is in Mignolo's global south as new academic utopia.

The localness and globalness of any historical phenomena, I believe, ought to depart from knowledge and engagement with long political, cultural, and social flows, which are inevitably, for the historian, linguistic currents. And they are not there, there to be discovered; they are not necessarily awaiting in the categories we use to examine them (national histories, Latin America, global south, postcolonial). Like other important "big" cosmopolitan ideas, such as the nation-state, Latin America is an idea that decrees a clear meaning for the local in the name of a known and established global story.

In history writing, hence, Latin America ought not to delineate our historiographical topics. The topic ought to define whether we speak of Latin America or not, and if so, how. If one studies, say, liberalism in Cuba, the conceptual, geographical, and chronological coordinates of the study will be dictated by the topic under consideration. Hence one could use the category and the historiography of Latin America just as another frame of reference, together with lots of French, Mexican, Spanish, US, German, and Cuban histories. The fact is that Latin America as an historiographical framework is often inapplicable for a well-defined historical topic—it turns out to be unrevealing, either too narrow or too broad, or simply irrelevant. For instance, not even in historical questions about US imperialism have I found the term very useful. To assume unspecifically that the United States that acted through the nineteenth and twentieth centuries in the Caribbean and Mexico (until 1914) is the same empire that acted in Mexico in the 1940s, or before and after in Brazil or Argentina, is far-fetched. Of course the United States acted imperially, but if that explains every case at every moment, then long live Latin American anti-imperialism and let the last one out turn off the lights of history. Neither US imperialism nor the various anti-imperialisms of the rest of the continent can be explained historically through the category of Latin America considered as the generic laboratory of US imperialism. Where would we locate the most important pre-1914 case, which is that of the Philippines, which echoed the imperial concerns of the era that went from the Paraguayan War to the era of the "Eastern question" in Europe and the Boer Wars in South Africa?

Because the idea of Latin America is so attached to a peculiar notion of anti-imperialism, the very mentioning of its name becomes the end of questioning; the problem is solved. Examining specific circumstances—the Philippines in the 1900s, Mexico in the 1940s, Guatemala in the 1950s—with the automatism Latin America in pause, reveals different and important histories of imperialism that may or may not return to the idea of Latin America. For the term itself is not always useful—especially not, for instance, in terms of ideas and intellectuals. José Rizal, that lucid, Spanish- and Tagalog-speaking, Filipino anti-imperialist, can be understood only in the intersections of the histories of the post-1898 Philippines, of the intellectual and political life of the Spain of la Restauración (including its lasting local autonomist movements), and of the strong political and intellectual contradictions of the United States at the end of Radical Reconstruction. The idea of Latin America is of not much use in this examination of the quintessential example of both US imperialism and "Hispanic" anti-imperialism (José Rizal). In turn, José Martí, the great "modernist" of the Spanish language, the hero of Cuban anti-imperialism and Rizal's friend and model, makes sense only in the intersections among Cuba, Spain, the United States, the Caribbean, Guatemala, and Mexico. Touches of Latin America would only add an epic quality to the story, at the cost of obscuring it. Eduardo Prado's anti-Americanism makes sense only in relation to Brazil, the United States, late nineteenth-century iberismo, and the defense of monarchical pacts in Austria-Hungary, Russia, unified Italy, and Germany. In the 1890s no Spanish American intellectual was anti-American in order to defend monarchical arrangements (except, maybe, flamboyant Carlos Pereyra). Prado was monarchical, and in interesting and nuanced ways.

The same can be said about imperialism within the United States. Between, say, 1898 and 1980 the most prominent anti-imperialist intellectuals were not "Latin" but simply Americans responding to a peculiar intellectual history: thus Williams James and his campaign in favor of Filipino Washingtons, Frank Tannenbaum and Ernest Gruening's support of the Mexican Revolution, Waldo Frank's continental mystic Hispanism, C. Wright Mills and the Cuban Revolution, Noam Chomsky and revolutions in Central America. And of course to "historize" this anti-imperialism would require not a Latin American but a US framework with all its cosmopolitan connections. The generic use of the term Latin America hides these details, which, I believe, are the story to tell.[9]

☙

Another example of specificity could be the treatment of that very Latin American thing, mestizaje. The term Latin America commands a clear mestizo trajectory, which often goes back to fifteenth-century Spain's *limpieza de sangre*, clear-cut distinctions between racial subjects, including slavery and *castas*; then nineteenth-century liberal lies, the destruction of "ethnic communities," and the myth of mestizaje as either the end of racism or the whitening of a liberal citizenship—either the presumed world example of hybrid culture or the name of a world cultural genocide. The story is well known; any US Latin American history textbook echoes the plot, from the overused *castas* paintings on the books' covers to exhausting racial typologies doggedly reproduced as a very, very Latin American phenomenon. But this cacophony can be used as the entry point to a *specific* story that can then serve to tell other non–Latin American stories. Simply by reading more than the textbook, just the minimum of literature on, say, the specific social history of seventeenth-century central New Spain, the story becomes both a test for what Latin America ought to mean and a more-than–Latin American narrative. A mere immersion in the vast literature reveals facts, interpretations, connections, and doubts that cry out for freedom from the tight Latin American corset. It brings a lot more European medieval history into the discussion, as well as Jewish history, a serious command of what is known of pre-Hispanic social hierarchies, and the indispensable contrast of British America as part of the same colonial contacts, to mention but a few necessary connections.

In this way, New Spain reveals itself to be a late scenario of an older story; the old manuals of horse breeding, the Jew, and Israel enter the scene, either in legal Spanish formulations of honor and reputation or in central New Spain's Indians' strategies for the defense of their lands and privileges. Mestizaje as a Latin American thing evaporates and becomes a story of social inequality and human promiscuity staged once more, but now in American scenarios with demographic imbalances, wars, imperial needs, defenses of local lands, autonomies, rights, and the omnipresence of God and human lust.

The story goes beyond the conventional Latin American racial plot. For instance, promiscuity, made into legitimate mestizaje, goes back to the idea of the lesser evil, of minimal compensation vis-à-vis the horrible temptation of the flesh—as in medieval ideas of tolerance (mestizaje, prostitution). By contrast, promiscuity can be shown to mean something different historically: miscegenation—a more recent conceptualization. In seventeenth-century Virginia, to be sure, masters slept with their slaves, and Europeans with natives, and everybody with everybody, and in essence there were not many religious differences (at least when it was about Indians and Europeans) from the lesser evil, compensation-like, conception of mestizaje in seventeenth-century New Spain. Marriage was an institution that soon, in the late seventeenth century, acquired legal and even racial restrictions in New England, if not in French North America. Marriage between blacks and whites in Virginia was not conceived of as miscegenation, but as a legal and religious monstrosity.

However, in nineteenth-century British North America (Canada), as in New Spain and Mexico, antimiscegenation was never phrased in jurisprudence; for long (until the 1867 Constitutional Act) "Indians" dealt as nations with the state, and those nations were already assumed *métis*. But, as Debra Thompson has shown, the 1876 Indian Act functioned both as an odd antimiscegenation law and as disenfranchisement of large populations that for long had the status and rights of nations. The 1876 Indian Act, says Thompson, established that "Indian women who married non-Indian men would lose status, as would their offspring. Indian men who married non-Indian women, however, would not only retain status for themselves and their progeny, but their wives would gain status as well." Thus, through these un–Latin American avenues, it could be thought that independent Mexico's removal of the old legal category of "Indian" meant also a dispossession not of "identity" but of citizenship. "Indian" during the Catholic monarchy was charged with so many rights and duties that the *"mexicanización"* of indigenous peoples by, first, Mexican constitutions, and later by the *Leyes de Reforma* could be seen not as granting but as withdrawing rights, especially land and fiscal rights. And yet, it would be far-fetched to argue that, for instance, the *Leyes de Reforma* had the sexual and gender consequences of the Canadian Indian Acts.[10]

Miscegenation, a mid-nineteenth-century concept, first came into being as a legal tool, of a biological nature, to attempt to control not an empirical reality—an impossibility—but the accepted legal reality. Miscegenation thus came to mean illegal forms of existence, and gradually, by the twentieth century, the belief that "nonexistent" by decree meant that it was indeed not real, unlike in New Spain or Mexico, for instance. Thus there is nothing particularly Latin American about promiscuity and mixing; *mesti-*

zaje—cultural, institutional, racial—was a fact everywhere. But New Spain dealt with this fact in different institutional ways than, say, seventeenth-century Virginia. Though we came to this conclusion through a specific treatment of the idea of Latin America, its strong racial and cultural connotations are already starting to dissolve into thin air.[11]

Specific treatments of power and empire can also make use of Latin America and thus reveal un–Latin American conclusions. Since antiquity, imperial adventures have often included forced miscegenation. Robert de Clari told the story of the thirteenth-century treacherous emperor Andronicus, who murdered Constantinople's noble class and then "took the beautiful women he found and lay with them by force." There is no need to repeat here the similar sexual proclivities of conquistadores or of Apaches, Comanches, Americans, and Mexicans who found the kidnapping of women and children to be a great commercial and biological business. The result: territorial domains in which race is historically unthinkable outside of its global, as it were, imperial imperatives, but in which race—if a real factor of social differentiation—is only visible for the historian as a local occurrence. And race, as an imperial category that only acquires existence locally, constitutes an interpretative dilemma often solved by simply recurring to the term Latin America, preferably in English, because it would already include its strong US denotations. Merely by flattening out a local racial order by calling it Latin American, the dilemma seems clearly delimited, if not solved. Then, there is no problem: *castas*, mestizos, and everybody knows how the song goes. But in its spatial and temporal specificity, race loses the imperial precision that we historians often seek. In the midst of many forms of social differentiation, always in the making at the local level, and in the midst of unstoppable and inevitable miscegenation, race and empire lose their clear-cut mutual causation.

Mestizaje, of course, in Mexico or in US Latin American textbooks, seems to be a product of post-revolutionary Mexico's successful and more or less official way of making sense of promiscuity. In fact, if the global possibilities for making sense of promiscuity are considered throughout the history of New Spain and Mexico, sanctioning the mestizo/mestizaje emerges as the common way of dealing with all sorts of promiscuities since the incorporation of the terms into the Spanish legal, social, and moral prose in the 1530s. Pre-Hispanic forms of mestizaje are part of the story, about which we are starting to learn more. Like the Spanish social hierarchy, Mexica stratification was solidly based on lineage, which often involved mestizaje with other groups as a form of political, military, and cultural alliance. Mexicas claimed to be of the same lineage as the people of Culuaca and Tule (Toltecs) both culturally and by blood. All the city-states in central Mexico claimed different forms of lineage by mestizaje with various groups. But mestizaje was not acceptable in all cases; it all depended on specific circumstances. For noble Mexicans, to mix with *macehuales otomíes* (Otomi commoners) in Mexico-Tenochtitlan was to risk social degradation. When the Spaniards, as a matter of necessity, reconstructed the surviving Indian nobility, they preserved old *linajes*, old ways of making sense of promiscuity. In this way, the Mexican colonial souvenir (*castas* paintings) that we, US teachers, give to our students, reveals precisely its souvenir nature: the paintings were "fashionable for some decades among Spanish bureaucrats" as "New Spanish painters' successful theme," but have never had value as evidence or proof of the "order of New Spain's society."[12]

Specificity in the treatment of the subject would not necessarily lead to Malinche and Cortés, but to something hard to miss: the demographic collapse of Mesoamerica, which is, of course, very much a part of the conventional history of Latin America—sometimes as part of the Black Legend of Spain, and sometimes simply as factual proof of "genocide." But it can also be used—together with the consideration of the terrible demographic history of the peninsula, which was always at the brink of demographic collapse—to explain the local way that promiscuity was made sense of in New Spain. Low numbers of *peninsulares* in New Spain and the 70 or 90 percent decline in Indian population explain a lot. The lasting effects of this factor on social structuring throughout colonial times cannot be exaggerated. It explains the early sanctioning and promotion of mestizaje as a policy for colonization—if it meant unions sanctioned by sacraments. The demographic collapse in New Spain also explains the presence of blacks, and the emergence of a small third republic of *pardos* and free blacks, and thus another challenge in making sense of promiscuity. But it also explains the welcoming of mestizaje by exaggerating the religious and even biological potential for redemption offered by mestizos.

The black component, however, was also negotiated at the local level, depending on the circumstances. There was the institution of slavery, which in New Spain did not exclude baptism. But there were free blacks and *pardos* everywhere, and making sense of this "third republic" in an environment dominated by a large indigenous and mestizo population made the obliteration of the black factor a bit easier. This was not the case in other territories, like Nueva Granada, where *pardos*, as Marixa Lasso has shown, were included and excluded in the tumultuous years from 1809 to 1815, according to the complex use of mestizaje as a way to grant rights to citizens in the midst of inevitable promiscuity and the need for *pardo* soldiers in the royal militias during a decade of wars.[13] By the end of the eighteenth century, and especially soon after independence, mestizaje became the way to deal with blacks in Cartagena.

Also, the doggedly Latin-Americanized notion of *limpieza de sangre* can be de-Latin-Americanized through specificity. *Limpieza de sangre* emerged in the peninsula tightly linked to the exclusion of Marranos and Moriscos. The statute, as the late María Elena Martínez showed, acquired a peculiar translation in New Spain, not because it was widely applied to Marranos there—though it was in some thirty cases between 1571 and 1821—but because it reinforced local obsessions with origins and *linaje*.[14] This resulted in a genealogical fever that, though it included what we would call racial and ethnic components today, was not purely racial or ethnic. It is safe to say that *limpieza de sangre* passed from a policy for the protection of religion (against Moors, Jews, and Protestants) to a contingent policy (always varying depending on moments and circumstances) of assuming political and social positions according to *linaje*, and it led to a society of *linajeros*, of seekers of *linaje* in a baroque, Catholic, and courtesan milieu. But it is important to keep in mind, as Josep María Fradera has suggested, that this did not mean the creation of a *sociedad de castas*; rather, it meant making sense of a *sociedad con castas*.[15] For a long time in New Spain there were mestizo Indians—mestizos who by *linaje* or by choice remained in Indian pueblos or barrios—and mestizo Spaniards—mestizos who by *linaje* could claim to be whites, as these things were established by asking *vecinos*, by *reputación*.

In sum, specificity makes the term Latin America a sort of blinking light that sometimes illuminates contrasts and parallels, but at other times disappears completely in its own overgeneralizations and atavisms. Ultimately, students would not be able to speak of mestizaje as defining Latin America in the conventional way, but would count on a much more interesting idea of the history of race, of the elements and complexity that were part of such an important issue in different times and places. These places still require political and moral discussion in our present, beyond recent Latin Americanism's condemnation of mestizaje as a negation of diversity. What could have started as a Latin American story, mestizaje, through specificity becomes not Latin America = mestizaje, but leads to other kinds of questions: for instance, why has mestizaje been believed to be Latin American? How and why did mestizaje (a fact) lead to different institutional and social scenarios in Mexico City and Virginia?

CR

What needs to be done with the history of the region known as Latin America since the fifteenth century can be expressed with a language metaphor: let us say that local historical phenomena are vernacular occurrences of a larger "Latin," as it were. Every vernacular theme can be considered—because it actually was, or because in interpreting from the present we inevitably make it to be—simultaneously unique and a version of the Latin. In researching and imagining the localness of the vernacular, the Latin both visualizes itself and evaporates. It becomes at once somehow unrecognizable in the vernacular and yet something else, what it actually was: a globalness in the making. For Latins were so because they were no one's mother tongue. Unearthing traces of history in order to defend an ontologically unique Latin American localness—either as a mere diffusion of a Latin or as total antimatter of a moment of a global Latin—is in fact speaking the global Latin. To consider Christendom, civilization, capitalism, the Third World, global north or south as someone's mother tongue, as someone's natural habitat (England, Euro-America, Latin America, the United States) is misleading. Any Latin, any real historical cosmopolitanism, has been no one's mother tongue. Power is, to be sure, involved, and it needs precisely to be explained in its specificity.

I use Latin as the metaphor of changing cosmopolitanisms, which are visible only as vernacular expressions that may or may not fully return to that global Latin.[16] It is fine to prove that a historical phenomenon in, say, seventeenth-century San Juan Chamula somehow addressed or touched global trends (historically defined). It would also be necessary to refer to the *Begriffsgeschichte* in Spanish in order to define a topic's localness and globalness in either Mexico or Nicaragua. But the globalness that such conceptual translations both created and imitated needs to be constructed, first, out of the modest awareness of unfamiliarity (do we really command the "context" of a sixteenth- or seventeenth-century Nahuatl speaker, who was also a Spanish writer, or of the transcription of an Inquisition confession?). And, second, it needs to be elaborated through painfully researched familiarity: the *Indias*, the former domains of the Portuguese and Spanish, empires have never been a mere echo, part, or "*basura*" of what we know as the modern world. The *Indias*, the Americas, have been the modern world. And that is true for the historical subjects of examination as well as for the historian who examines. Naive ethnic empathy and ethnocentrism, in this sense, are two sides of the same coin. "I was cured of any residual faith in the utility of empathy," wrote Inga Clendinnen, "by spending rather more than a decade in company with Aztecs."[17] For there is no way to conceive vernaculars that are not simultaneously echoes, rejections, affirmations, reactions, and expressions of a cosmopolitanism that has no place to call home but its multi-presence in the modern world.

In sum, it all depends on the empirical and conceptual creation of the historical topic, and on the command of the erudition required to read all its locality and globalness. The possibilities of historical revelations and discoveries are many, but not if fully controlled by big package-terms like the "nation," or "Latin America," or "Euro-America" (which almost always excludes the Iberian world). Therefore a topic, say, the history of typhus in Mexico City, creates its own globalness, which circumscribes neither Europe nor Latin America, nor solely Mexico: it is Tunis, New York, Barcelona, the Crimean War, World War I, Mexico City, Hamburg, Rio de Janeiro; and it is scientists' egos, twentieth-century nations in cultural and imperial competition, and ideas expressed in English, French, German, Portuguese, English, and Polish. And the same could be said of such topics as the history of specific social movements, climate change, demography, intellectual or economic history. When the historian happens to be a great thinker and a good writer, she can advance new "big" concepts, big stories, with vital theoretical and practical consequences. These contributions may serve as inspiration for new, "narrow" research and modest imagining of the past, which nevertheless, sooner or later, will make of the courageous historian's big concepts and big stories what we should have made long ago of Latin America: tools for thinking, not instruments for circumventing thought.

CR

Another strategy for historiographically appropriating the term Latin America is the very "*cuidado*" that its intrinsic component, diversity, requires in historical terms. The difficulty of grasping the otherness of the past ought to prevail over any other form of diversity, bearing in mind that things appear to be the same, similar, incompatible, or antagonistic depending on the angle of view. Let us take Latin America as encompassing changing diversities within an undeniable empirical fact: it constitutes a piece of human history that for the last half a millennium has undergone the clash, interaction, and mixing of native groups, demographic collapse, European empires, slavery, the Asian and African presence, modern nation-states, and twentieth-century consumerist societies. The essential sources of otherness (race, ethnicity, religion, culture, genes) can be assumed to be historical by definition, and can thus be subjected to the larger task: trying to comprehend what can never fully be understood, the past, in a rigorously empirical and philosophically imaginative way.

I could take Emilio Kourí's telling, specific, and erudite consideration (as yet unpublished) of the *longue-durée* notion of Indian community and land property in Mexico as an example.[18] It is a story in which communal, solidary possession and cultivation of lands in Indian towns is shown to be a myth, not in twenty-first-century neoliberal Mexico but at least since the seventeenth century. The story destroys the notions of ontological diversity, of indigenous views of, and mystical attachments to, land. It demonstrates the constant struggle between Indian concepts, Catholic ideas, European law, and local political power. Varying versions of ethnic otherness are part of the story, but are not *the* story, not even in the myth of the *ejido* and Zapatismo, which, it turns out, had nothing to do with the figure of the twentieth-century Mexican *ejido*.

Through specificity and research, diversity becomes not the guiding principle of storytelling, but a challenge to face in understanding the past, and a well-established present belief calling for demystification. Kourí's work illustrates a simultaneous demystification of two powerful and inseparable concepts: Mexico/Latin America and community. For, as Fernando Escalante has maintained,

> In the Mexican public language, the idea of a community has undertones of *Ancien Régime*, a kind of moral authority that is almost natural and commands respect. . . . It is almost unavoidable to speak of the "indigenous communities" and just as frequently of the "peasant communities," but no one would speak of the "trade-union community," the "priísta community" or the "Mexico City community," for there are no such things. Every now and then, when there are vital issues at stake, someone might voice the interest or the sentiments of the "business community" or the "academic community"—those two, in particular—by which it is meant that both are corporate bodies, having a number of fundamental values and interests in common that are being threatened. . . . All the complex, interwoven interests and conflicts [. . .] make any human association suddenly disappear when it is labeled as a "community"; . . . anything you say about the "neighbors of San Juan Chamula" or the "inhabitants of San Juan Chamula" can be contested and discussed (it almost begs to be falsified), but if you speak of the "community of San Juan Chamula" you are on another political level, perfectly alien to statistics and hardly open for rational debate.

As Kourí shows, the link of the *ejido* to ideas of "indigenous communities" and their mythical past was mostly a twentieth-century construction. And this simple chronology exposes the constructive side of the conceptual unity "indigenous community/Latin America." Three decades ago, Richard M. Morse suggested that there had been no Narodnichestvo in nineteenth-century Latin America; there had not been that faith in the cultural and communitarian values of peasants sustained by aristocratic Russian populists and Pan-Slavists. According to Morse, it was only in the twentieth century that Latin American intellectuals developed such faith—Kourí's point. But there was Narodnichestvo for Mexico as Latin America in the nineteenth century, articulated in English—from the views of Lewis H. Morgan and A. Bandelier of classless communitarian Indians in Mexico or Peru to the ideas of Robert Redfield, Frank Tannenbaum, or Eyler Simpson. Kourí's very specific demystification, thus, perhaps unwantedly, touches not solely on Mexican history but on the very modern conception of Latin America as communitarian other.[19]

The idea of Latin America would reveal to us the story of the Indian republics vs. the Spanish republics and the endless, pristine survival of the Indian community and its traditional ways of relating to land and politics. But in its particulars, the story is de-Latin-Americanized if, for instance, like the great Peruvian historian Alberto Flores Galindo, we consider the *longue durée* of the struggle for rights and lands, and the return of the Inca myth in the Andes. As Sabine MacCormack had shown, Spanish friars and Quechua-speaking *letrados* studied the Inca past in tandem with medieval European religious thought.[20] In the 1980s, Flores Galindo, departing from this specific background, indeed found the strong sense of otherness intrinsic to the term Latin America—in 1970s anthropological and sociological studies—in people in Cuzco, where "both teachers and students are convinced that the Inca Empire was an equalitarian society in which there was no hunger, no injustice and that it is therefore a paradigm for the world now."[21] He found many local legends about the Inkarri, stating various versions of the idea that the head of the Inca king was separated from his body, and the reunification of the head and body would mean the beginning of a period of turmoil and confusion, the start of a new era. He used popular lyrics and, as it were, highbrow literature (José María Arguedas) to find narratives that absorbed this myth, only to then diminish the ontological otherness argument by historicizing the idea of the Inca utopia. Flores Galindo argued, using Arguedas's conflictive life as a metaphor, that "the history of the Andean utopia is a conflictive one, like the soul of

Arguedas."[22] But then this local history becomes something else, more than Peru, and more than "Latin America"; it becomes the history of popular messianic movements in the world and their interactions with various moments of political, economic, and social conflict.

Thus Joachim of Fiore, or the many millenarian movements in Europe, or the same in the colonial United States, become one with the Andes, diminishing the ontological argument for ethnic uniqueness. Thus the Inca myth becomes more than Indian, yet remains very local, as with the seventeenth-century Franciscan priest Gonzalo Tenorio, who maintained that just before dying, Jesus did not look toward Spain and Europe but toward the "Indias," whose natives were destined to be like Israel in the Old Testament. And the killing of the Inca in 1533, *a garrote*, becomes not an ethnic symbol, but a shared symbol, understood in Europe and in Peru: to kill a king, and in such a way, was to invite disaster. And it did, as Cicero in Rome knew, or as many Indians and non-Indians in Peru knew. For, as Flores Galindo explained, the return of the Inca was an Indian belief that was intelligible for the historian, in its uniqueness and its broader ramifications:

> The idea of the return of the Inca did not appear in Andean culture spontaneously. It wasn't a mechanical reaction to colonial domination. In memory, previously, the Andean past was reconstructed and transformed to make it into an alternative to the present. This is a distinctive feature of the Andean utopia. The ideal city is not outside of history or very distant at the beginning of time. On the contrary, it is an historical event. It has existed. It has a name: Tahuantinsuyo. It has rulers: the Incas. And a Capital: Cuzco. The content that this construction maintains has been modified in order to image a kingdom without hunger, without exploitation, and in which Andean men rule once again. The end of disorder and obscurity. Inca means organizing idea or principle.[23]

This utopia was not to be found in New Spain, regardless of ethnic diversity, precisely because of its specificity, though New Spain had its own share of millenarian movements and Indian revolts. In all cases, Flores Galindo was aware of the conventional connections of Latin America to indigenous alterity, and hence, he said, "It would be absurd to imagine it [the Inka myth] as the unchanged prolongation of pre-Hispanic Andean thought." The revolts' violence itself, their outrageous violence, could then be explained not because of ontological diversity but precisely because of a code that was common to all in Peru: "The Spaniards could have died the way they did because they weren't good Christians; they didn't practice what they preached, and they were heretics: the discourse of the conquest inverted."[24] And thus the Inca myth changed with time, not fixed to any endless notion of indigenous ontology, but constantly transformed as a political weapon, depending on circumstances, until the arrival of modern *indigenistas* like Pedro Zulen and the idea of Gamonalismo, and then, of course, José Carlos Mariátegui and the idea of the very old, the mythical, becoming the very new, the revolutionary socialist utopia. This new idea produced local criticism of the idealization of the myth (like that articulated against Mariátegui by Luis Alberto Sánchez), and thus of the myth as a broader factor, more than indigenous and yet fully rooted in the life of Indians, in politics, in Peruvian politics. Hence the call from progressive intellectuals like Flores Galindo in the 1980s, not in defense of ontological otherness, but for united forces exemplified in a *socialismo democrático* that could translate into real governing the end of one of Arguedas's stories, "Tayta que se mueran los principales de todas partes" (Tayta, let the important people everywhere die).[25] Maybe this was a bit naive, maybe this was the wrong politics, but it was certainly a more telling, specific, approach to the assumed diversity of Latin America. And, of course, it was much more and much less than a Latin American story.

⟨⟩

Another strategy is to use the category of Latin America as a starting point to build on what has always been part of the term: another view of the United States. The term has long been an unobserved call for this. The overwhelming anti-American connotations of the idea of Latin America have never, to this day, given rise to solid knowledge about the United States in Spanish, in Portuguese, or in the English of US Latin Americanism. In a way, the idea of Latin America has implied that the United States is somehow already known, that there is no need to learn it. But teaching Latin American history ought to have been a way of teaching US history. We ought to train the new cohort of US Latin Americanists in this ability. Whether the category of Latin America would survive if we managed to do so should not be a matter of concern. Enough of the old-fashioned anti-Americanism that curses the name of the ugly elephant in the room, a monolithic monster, without ever stopping to examine it. For what modern subject or moment in the region can be examined without knowledge of US history, politics, and culture?

Elsewhere I have dealt extensively with this strategy. I only add urgency to the call. US Latin Americanism, in this regard, has certain advantages and an important responsibility. From the language and all the way to the daily lives of US Latin Americanists, it is all an American experience. The only thing that has to be added institutionally is that, as part of the core training of our US Latin Americanist historians, they take as many US as Latin American history courses. Moreover, US Latin Americanism can be the "*avanzada*," assisting in the creation of, say, a Brazilian, Mexican, or Colombian school of experts on the United States. Then, and only then, can a true historiographical dialogue take place, beyond the category of Latin America and beyond parochial US history. Whether mine is an old, Boltonean call for history of the Americas or a mere internationalizing of US history is irrelevant. Latin American history as another US history, and the other way around, is what I see as the paramount intellectual and political experiment for us to undertake. Let us start it, and then we shall see . . .

CR

The term Latin America has included Brazil by mythical treaty, but rarely has it implied knowledge of the Portuguese-speaking world. The institution of Latin America as a form of knowledge offers a handy advantage: it can serve to smoothly expand any historical knowledge by considering the other giant of the Americas, Brazil. Thus Latin America could be used to break the language curtain, fully incorporating into Spanish and English the history, languages, literatures, and thought produced in Portuguese. The term can also help Brazilian scholars, especially of the new generations—less accustomed to use Spanish than the old cohort of scholars—to participate in the Spanish-speaking world.

Moreover, for historians of the Americas, a good use of the knowledge institution Latin America would be to get curious about the history of *las Españas* and Portugal. It could be said that this would be useless for a US Latin Americanist devoted to the study of, say, twentieth-century Peru. But these extra avenues of learning, which are naturally handed over by the very idea of Latin America, constitute an optimal way to throw away the heavy ballast in the discipline—I mean, parochialism, nationalism, ethnocentrism, epistemological biases, naïveté, exoticism. I consider this a good use of a category that so far has seemed to reproduce, on one hand, conventional national histories and, on the other, either the textbook existence of Latin America or Latin America, the engagé poem.[26]

 CR

Another strategy is a consciously unconventional appropriation of what history is: namely, synthesis. Latin America has been, despite all odds, an efficient synthesis, grouping a vast amount of data and anecdotal evidence under deep-rooted cultural and racial assumptions. This can be effective for starting new syntheses, based on relevant and consciously constructed political and cultural criteria. Thus Latin America, the idea, could serve as a point of departure, for instance, for an ecological history that would necessarily bring about a more than Latin American synthesis.[27] The same could be said of such a topic as immigration, citizenship, or language itself— I fantasize about a history of philology in the Spanish-speaking world, which would necessarily cover Latin America but less as a commanding framework and more in the way that Russian philologist Viktor Shklovski spoke of the notion of the avant-garde: "The staircase of literary movements leads to doors that have been sketched in. The staircase exists while you are climbing it." The story would have to involve the United States, Spain, Germany, and France. All in all, any new synthesis could start from Latin America" but only to come out with new syntheses of national histories that could show, say, an un-Mexican Mexican history or an un-Brazilian Brazilian history by going beyond both Latin America and their respective *historias patrias*.[28]

There is also the strategic use of the category of Latin America as a synthesis consisting in embracing the very vagueness of the term. The textbook Latin America ought to be considered as a peculiar collection of useful facts aiming at documenting a long-established, obsolete conception. That in and of itself is a good use of Latin America/the textbooks—to map phenomena in time and space, to introduce students to the multiplicity of potential topics. But it also serves to point out the vagueness, the need to furnish the category, Latin America, with significant empirical, philosophical, and moral content. The very history of the concept ought to be used to show the advantages of vagueness and the risk of assuming "big," utopian, philosophical, or empirical overgeneralizations. For Latinness is such a common assumption that any good use of the term Latin America becomes more an un-teaching than a teaching of the term.

The exercise, if unrepresentative and personal, is telling: over the course of a decade of teaching Latin American history in the United States, and US history in Mexico, I have begun my courses with simple questions: What is Latin America? Why study its history? *¿Qué saben de la historia de Estados Unidos? ¿Para qué estudiarla?* The answers have not varied much over the last decade: Latin America is a clearly defined place, it is its indigenous people, it is where mestizaje took place, unlike the United States, it is Catholicism, the Spanish language, the Inquisition, the expulsion of the Jews, resistance, backwardness, violence, corruption, and the true homeland of US Latinos. . . . . *Estados Unidos no tiene mucha historia, no como nosotros, allá mataron a los indios, aquí el mestizaje, es el imperialismo, es el consenso de Washington, es el imperialismo cultural, es Hollywood y es McDonalds, hay que conocer al enemigo, hay que estudiarlo para entender la manera de vencerlo, es lo que no somos.* (The United States doesn't have much history, not like us, they killed the Indians there, here we had mestizaje, it's imperialism, it's the Washington consensus, cultural imperialism, Hollywood and McDonald's, one has to know one's enemy, one has to study it to understand how to defeat it, it is what we aren't.) Then the course becomes an unlearning of all these deep-rooted beliefs, abusing the vagueness of the term Latin America in a *reductio ad absurdum*, teaching them some historical problems that indeed belong to Mexico or Brazil, but also to the United States, Spain, and Africa . . . and to the students themselves. I end up teaching a version of the same course in both places. The hardest thing is to show my Mexican students how American (United States) they inevitably are, sharing the history they did not believe existed, and to convince my US students that even if they are Chicanas or Latinas, they are as close or as alien to the past I am explaining as any "Anglo," Jew, or Chinese student in the class. In their course evaluations, they often write things like "Professor Tenorio is a . . . man who hates students, especially Americans," or "very knowledgeable but unapproachable, does not think Latin America exists." Over the years, the summer-guerrilleros in Chiapas or the neo-Bolivarians have challenged me with stories of romantic equalitarianism in which the Mexican or the Brazilian state disappears, but not the University of Chicago or the US NGO where they worked during the summer. Conservative students have complained about my mocking religion, and they hate when I ask them questions about US history and they do not know the answer. In sum, I teach the vagueness that Latin America teaches, and I fantasize that students will go on with their lives secretly infected with this methodical disbelief; this is what I consider historical knowledge.

⚬⚬

Some final, simple recommendations are in order, again, in the spirit of acknowledging that "Latin America," the idea, the institution of knowledge, is here to stay. In listing these minutiae, I am aware, I risk unpopularity—

ainda mais—but so be it. First, US or any sort of Latin Americanism should simply mean the full command of Spanish and Portuguese and at least reading competency in other languages (Nahuatl, Quechua, French, Italian, German). This seems to be a no-brainer, but the truth is that rarely in the United States do we train students in the full command of languages. The way to truly engage in a more than US Latin Americanist kind of intellectual dialogue is this: experts on Brazil or Mexico ought to *write* in Portuguese and/or Spanish in addition to English. I do not mean they should seek for their scholarship to be translated; I mean they should be scholars in either or both of those languages. The face of Latin America, as a US-centered category, would radically change if US Latin Americanists wrote in at least one language of the region. "Latin America" sounds very Latin American because it is written in English, even by Mexicans and Brazilians. Let's see what remains of the idea of Latin America once US Latin Americanists have as their paramount duty that other dimension of things: *writing* in Spanish or Portuguese, which is the only way to become part of the cultural and political flow that Latin Americanists seek to grasp.

Finally, since the nineteenth-century historiographical debates about what were called "philosophical" vs. "empirical" (or theoretical vs. narrative) histories, we have exhausted this nonsensical dichotomy. Theory and facts, ideas and narrative, imagination and evidence, all together are what history writing is, no more, no less. US Latin Americanism in history writing, like many other scholarly disciplines, has shown great dependence on sexy academic fashions. If theory is to be a rigorous part of the historian's task, we ought to overcome the vice of the "Reader," the endless reproduction of the two or three recent references in vogue. "Before writing is, reading must be," read a manual of history writing.[29] Indeed, reading—history, philosophy, novels, poems, economic and political treatises—is the historian's craft. US Latin Americanism should mean doing this extensively in English and in the other languages. By reading in other languages, I do not mean that a Brazilianist should read documents in Portuguese; I mean that she should read the novels, poems, essays, and sciences, in sum, the Portuguese milieu in which those documents make sense. Theory is not that ready-made plate on the table, served in English, already cut into pieces and catchy sound bites, just to be used as "theoretical" framework with which to read or organize an array of empirical evidence. True theory or, better said, true tools for the imagination, are not the plate; they are the table. Sitting at the table means joining a long, many-versed, and rich conversation that is almost impossible to follow in its entirety. What can be gained from deep immersion in such conversation is far from a theoretical framework, far from commonly used academic sound bites. What one gains from this time-consuming endeavor is indeed a historical perspective, a historical imagination, which is always in the making. Whether this imagination is or becomes a historiographical school should not be a concern, but experiencing glimpses of the past in the relevance of the present, breeding futures other than death.

CR

In sum, these are the modest strategies of a simple professor. They do not reach the pomposity of the theories, the concepts, and the politics that we, US-centered Latin Americanists, use in crafting our own profile as scholars. But, unable to escape my present, aware of my own limitations, it is all I can do with a term that became *"mi manda"* (my vow). *Ni yo ni el conceptito damos para mucho más.* (Neither I nor the little concept can go much further.)

NOTES

INTRODUCTION

1. Mauricio Tenorio-Trillo, *Argucias de la historia: Siglo XIX, cultura y "América Latina"* (Mexico City: Paidós, 1999). What follows avoids self-referencing; allow me this one only.

2. See Friedrich Nietzsche, "On the Uses and Disadvantages of History in Life," in *Untimely Meditations*, trans. R. J. Hollingdale (Cambridge: Cambridge University Press, 1997), 57–124.

3. Leopold von Ranke, *History of the Latin and Teutonic Nations (1491 to 1514)*, trans. Philip A. Ashworth (London: George Bell and Sons, 1887), 1–2, 56–58.

4. See Andrew Lintott, "What Was the 'Imperium Romanum'?" *Greece & Rome* 28, no. 1 (1981): 53–67.

5. To gain a sense of the numbers, professions, and nationalities of Latin Americans in Paris starting in 1870, see Jens Streckert, *Die Hauptstadt Lateinamerikas: Eine Geschichte der Lateinamerikaner im Paris der Dritten Republik (1870–1940)* (Cologne: Böhlau Verlag, 2013).

6. Francisco Bilbao, *La América en peligro* (Buenos Aires: Impr. de Bernheim y Boneo, 1862), 14, 23.

7. Francisco Bilbao, "Prefacio a los evangelios (Inédito): El libro en América," in *Obras completas de Francisco Bilbao* (Buenos Aires: Impr. de Buenos Aires, 1865–66), 1:72.

8. Bilbao, "Prefacio a los evangelios," 1:72.

9. Ibid., 75. About Mexico, Brazil, and Pan-Slavism, see "Prefacio a los evangelios"; about Latin America as monopoly of spirituality, see "Iniciativa de la América: Idea de un Congreso Federal de las Repúblicas. Post-dictum," both in Bilbao, *Obras completas de Francisco Bilbao*, vol. 1 (Buenos Aires: Impr. de Buenos Aires, 1866–65). For the Eastern European parallel, see Larry Wolff, *Inventing Eastern Europe: The Map of Civilization on the Mind of the Enlightenment* (Stanford, CA: Stanford University Press, 1994). See also Mark J. van Aken, *Pan-Hispanism: Its Origin and Development to 1866* (Berkeley: University of California Press, 1959). On Lamennais, see Carolina Armenteros, *The French Idea of History: Joseph de Maistre and His Heirs, 1794–1854* (Ithaca, NY: Cornell University Press, 2011), 307–11.

10. *Colección de ensayos i documentos relativos a la unión i confederación de los pueblos hispano-americanos. Publicada a espensas de la "Sociedad de la unión americana de Santiago de Chile," por una comisión nombrada por la misma i compuesta de los señores don*

José Victorino Lastarria, don Álvaro Covarrubias, don Domingo Santa María i don Benjamín Vicuña Mackenna (Santiago: Imprenta Chilena, 1862), 69.

11. *Ambas Américas: Revista de educación, bibliografía i agricultura, bajo los auspicios de D. F. Sarmiento* (New York: Imprenta de Hallet y Breen, 1867–68); Ramón Páez, *Ambas Américas: Contrastes* (Mexico City: N. Chávez, 1873); originally published in New York (in Spanish) in 1872. I thank Arturo Taracena; over the years, his immense wisdom guided me to this and many other sources. See also Álvaro Fernández Bravo, "La idea americana de Sarmiento," in *Historia crítica de la literatura argentina*, ed. Noé Jitrik, vol. 4, ed. Adriana Amante (Buenos Aires: Emecé, 2012), 395–420; and Streckert, *Die Hauptstadt Lateinamerikas.*

12. For the history of the study of Romance language and its publications, see Alberto Várvaro, *Storia, problemi e metodi della linguistica romanza* (Naples: Liguari, 1968); Boyd G. Carter, *Las revistas literarias de Hispanoamérica; breve historia y contenido* (Mexico City: Ediciones de Andrea, 1959); Héctor René Lafleur, *Las revistas literarias argentinas, 1893–1960* (Buenos Aires: Ediciones Culturales Argentinas, Ministerio de Educación y Justicia, Dirección General de Cultura, 1962); Jorge Schwartz and Roxana Patiño, *Revistas literarias/culturales latinoamericanas del siglo XX* (Pittsburgh, PA: Instituto Internacional de Literatura Iberoamericana, 2004); Álvaro Fernández Bravo, "Utopías americanistas: La posición de la *Revista Americana* en Brasil (1909–1919)," in *Construcciones impresas: Panfletos, diarios y revistas en la formación de los Estados nacionales en América Latina, 1820–1920* (Buenos Aires: Fondo de Cultura Económica, 2004), 331–38; and Streckert, *Die Hauptstadt Lateinamerikas*, 261–98.

13. Francisco Bilbao, "El evanjelio americano," in *Obras completas de Francisco Bilbao*, 2:449; Eduardo Galeano, *Las venas abiertas de América Latina* (Havana: Casa de las Américas, 1971), 1.

14. Arthur, comte de Gobineau, *Œuvres* (Paris: Gallimard, 1983), 1:1201; José María Eça de Queirós, *Os Maias: Episódios da vida romântica* (Porto, Portugal: Livraria Internacional de Ernesto Chardron, Casa Editora Lugan e Genelioux, 1888), 2:366; Ramiro de Maeztu, quoted in Pedro Carlos González Cuevas, *Maeztu: Biografía de un nacionalista español* (Madrid: Marcial Pons, 2003), 314; Mircea Eliade, *Salazar e a Revolucão em Portugal*, trans. Anca Milu-Vaidesegan (Lisbon: Esfera do Caos Editores, 2011), originally published in Romanian in 1942; Ilan Stavans, *The Hispanic Condition: The Power of a People* (New York: Rayo, 2001), 109.

15. Michel Chevalier, *France, Mexico, and the Confederate States*, trans. Wm. Henry Hurlbut (New York: C. B. Richardson, 1863), 12; and *Society, Manners, and Politics in the United States* (Boston: Weeks, Jordan, 1839), 16. See also Stève Sainlaude, *Le gouvernement impérial et la guerre de Sécession (1861–1965): L'action diplomatique* (Paris: l'Harmattan, 2011).

16. Justo Arosemena, quoted in Octavio Méndez Pereira, "Justo Arosemena y el americanismo," *Revista Lotería* (July–August, 1987): 60.

17. Bilbao, "El evanjelio americano," in *Obras Completas*, 2:311–444.

18. Justo Arosemena, *Estudios constitucionales sobre los gobiernos de la América latina* (Paris: A. Roger and F. Chernoviz, 1888), 2:505; see also Justo Arosemena, *Constituciones políticas de la América meridional* (Havre: Imprenta A. Lemale Ainé, 1870), 1:v–xxxii; and *Estudios sobre la idea de una liga americana* (Lima: Imprenta de Huerta, 1864).

19. Arcadio Díaz Quiñonez, "José Martí (1853–1895): La guerra desde las nubes," in *Sobre los principios: Los intelectuales caribeños y la tradición* (Buenos Aires: Universidad

Nacional de Quilmes, 2006), 255–88; Ariela Schnirmajer, "Minorías sociales y hete-rogeneidad: José Martí y la inmigración europea," *Anclajes* 15, no. 1 (2011): 49–59.

20. José Martí, *Guatemala* (Guatemala City: Universidad de San Carlos de Guatemala, 1998); Arturo Taracena Arriola, *Invención criolla, sueño ladino, pesadilla indígena* (Antigua, Guatemala: Centro de Investigaciones Regionales de Mesoamérica, 1999); Juan Blanco, "Modernidad y metamodernidad en el discurso de José Martí sobre el indígena," *A Parte Rei* no. 60 (November 2008): 1–33 (available online at http:// serbal.pntic.mec.es/AParteRei). I thank Arturo Taracena and J. Ramón González Ponciano for these references. For a view, not mine, of Martí's Latin Americanism, see Julio Ramos, *Desencuentros de la modernidad en América Latina: Literatura y política en el siglo XIX* (Mexico City: Fondo de Cultura Económica, 1989).

21. John Barret, *The Pan-American Union: Peace, Friendship, Commerce* (Washington DC: Pan-American Union, 1911), 110; for an analysis of the building, see Robert Alexander González, *Designing Pan-America: U.S. Architectural Visions for the Western Hemisphere* (Austin: University of Texas Press, 2011), chap. 2; for a history of the many attempts at regional or subregional unions, see Salvador Rivera, *Latin American Unification: A History of Political and Economic Integration Efforts* (London: McFarland, 2014).

22. Centro de Investigación y Docencia Económicas (CIDE), Mexico City, "México, las Américas y el Mundo"; available online from the División de Estudios Internacionales, at www.lasamericasyelmundo.cide.edu. I thank Gerardo Maldonado and Luis Antonio Hernández for access to this survey.

23. Elsewhere I have dealt with the large literature on the idea of Latin America begun by Arturo Ardao and continued by J. L. Phelan in the 1960s. Here I repeat only the basics: see the long trajectory of Ardao's thought from an essay in *Semanario Marcha* (November 25, 1962) to his *Génesis de la idea y el nombre de América Latina* (Caracas: Centro de Estudios Latinoamericanos Rómulo Gallegos, 1980); and, finally, *Romania y América Latina* (Montevideo: Biblioteca Marcha, Universidad de la República Oriental del Uruguay, 1991); see also J. L. Phelan, "Pan-Latinism, French Intervention in Mexico (1861–1867) and the Genesis of the Idea of Latin America," in *Conciencia y autenticidad histórica*, ed. José Ortega y Medina (Mexico City: Universidad Nacional Autónoma de México, 1968), 123–77. Thanks to the incredible labor of Mari Carmen Ramírez, scholars now have digital access to many of the founding documents for the study of the idea of Latin America; see International Center for the Arts of the Americas at the Museum of Fine Arts, Houston, Documents of 20th-Century Latin American and Latino Art, a Digital Archive, online at http://icaadocs .mfah.org/icaadocs/en-us/about/theproject/whatistheicaadocumentsproject.aspx.

See also Pedro L. San Miguel, *Muchos México: Representaciones de México en la historiografía estadounidense* (Mexico City: Ins. José María Luis Mora, forthcoming); Fernando Mires, *El discurso de la miseria, o la crisis de la sociología en América Latina* (Caracas: Nueva Sociedad, 1993); Guy Martinière, "Michel Chevalier et la latinité de l'Amérique," *Revista NEIBA, Cadernos Argentina-Brasil* 3, no. 1 (2014): 1–10; Michel Gobat, "The Invention of Latin America: A Transnational History of Anti-Imperialism, Democracy, and Race," *American Historical Review* 118, no. 5 (2013): 1345–75; Sergio Guerra Vilaboy, *Tres estudios de historiografía latinoamericana* (Morelia, Mexico: Universidad Michoacana de San Nicolás de Hidalgo, 2002); Enrique Ayala Mora, "El origen del nombre América Latina y la tradición católica del siglo XIX," *Anuario Colombiano de Historia Social y de la Cultura* 40, no. 1 (2013): 213–41;

João Feres, *A história do conceito de "Latin America" nos Estados Unidos* (Bauru, Brazil: EDUSC, 2005); Santiago Castro-Gómez and Ramón Grosfoguel, eds., *El giro decolonial: Reflexiones para una diversidad epistémica más allá del capitalism global* (Bogota: Siglo del Hombre Editores, 2007); Santiago Castro-Gómez, *Crítica de la razón latinoamericana* (Barcelona: Puvil Libros, 1996); Mabel Moraña, Enrique Dussel, and Carlos A. Jáuregui, eds., *Coloniality at Large: Latin America and the Postcolonial Debate* (Durham, NC: Duke University Press, 2008); Jussi Pakkasvirta, *Nationalism and Continentalism in Latin American History*, Institute of Development Studies, University of Helsinki, Working Papers (14/96), online at http://www.helsinki.fi/aluejakulttuurintutkimus/tutkimus/xaman/articulos/9701/9701_jup.html; Fabio Moraga Valle, "¿Una nación ibero, latino o indoamericana? Joaquín Edwards Bello y *El nacionalismo continental*," in *Pensar el antiimperialismo. Ensayos de historia intelectual latinoamericana, 1900–1930*, ed. Alexandra Pita González and Carlos Marichal Salinas (Mexico City: El Colegio de México, Universidad de Colima, 2012), 247–82; Neil Larsen, "Latin America as a Historico-Philosophical Relation," *CR: The New Centennial Review* 3, no. 1 (2003): 55–66; Miguel Ángel Centeno and Fernando López-Alves, eds., *The Other Mirror: Grand Theory Through the Lens of Latin America* (Princeton, NJ: Princeton University Press, 2001); Jorge E. Gracia and Elizabeth Millan-Zaibert, eds., *Latin American Philosophy for the 21st Century* (New York: Prometheus Books, 2004); Arleen L. F. Salles and Elizabeth Millán-Zaibert, eds., *The Role of History in Latin American Philosophy: Contemporary Perspectives* (New York: State University of New York Press, 2005); Guillermo Hurtado, *México sin sentido* (Mexico City: Universidad Nacional Autónoma de México/Siglo XXI, 2011); José Moya, "Introduction: Latin America—The Limitations and Meaning of a Historical Category," in *The Oxford Handbook of Latin American History*, ed. José Moya (New York: Oxford University Press, 2010), 1–24; the difficult Román de la Campa, *Latin Americanism* (Minneapolis: University of Minnesota Press, 1999); and John Beverley, *Latinamericanism after 9/11* (Durham, NC: Duke University Press, 2011). See also Miguel Ángel Barrios, *El latinoamericanismo en el pensamiento político de Manuel Ugarte* (Buenos Aires: Editorial Biblos, 2007); Fernand Braudel, "Y a-t-il une Amérique latine?" *Annales ESC* 3 (1948): 467–71; Juan Carlos Torchia Estrada, "'América Latina': Origen de un nombre y una idea," *Inter-American Review of Bibliography* 32, no. 1 (1982): 47–53; Mónica Quijada, "Latinos y anglosajones: El 98 en el fin de siglo sudamericano," *Hispania* 57, no. 196 (1997): 589–609, and "Sobre el origen y difusión del nombre 'América Latina': O una variación heterodoxa en torno al tema de la construcción social de la verdad," *Revista de Indias* 58, no. 214 (1998): 595–616; Miguel Rojas Mix, *Los cien nombres de América, eso que descubrió Colón* (Barcelona: Lumen, 1991); Aims McGuinness, "Searching for 'Latin America': Race and Sovereignty in the Americas in the 1850s," in *Race and Nation in Modern Latin America*, ed. Nancy P. Appelbaum, Anne S. Macpherson, and Karin Alejandra Rosemblatt (Chapel Hill: University of North Carolina Press, 2003), 87–107; Paul Estrade, "Del invento de 'América Latina' en París por latinoamericanos (1856–1889)," in *París y el mundo ibérico e iberoamericano: Actas del XXVIII Congreso de la Sociedad de Hispanistas Franceses, París, 21, 22 y 23 de marzo de 1997*, ed. Jacques Maurice and Marie-Claire Zimmermann (Paris: Université de Paris X, Nanterre, 1998), 179–88; Streckert, *Die Hauptstadt Lateinamerikas*; Rivera, *Latin American Unification*.

24. Jorge Volpi, *El insomnio de Bolívar* (Barcelona: Random House Mondadori, 2009); Juan Villoro, "Iguanas y dinosaurios: América Latina como utopía del atraso," in *Efectos personales* (Mexico City: Era, 2000), 93.

25. Larry Rohter, "Author Changes His Mind on '70s Manifesto," *New York Times*, May 23, 2014, online at http://www.nytimes.com/2014/05/24/books/eduardo -galeano-disavows-his-book-the-open-veins.html.

26. Sarah Pollack, "The Tradditore in the North: The Politics of Mexican Narrative in Translation in the U.S.," unpublished paper. I thank Sarah Pollack for sharing her paper.

27. Carlos Rangel *Del buen salvaje al buen revolucionario* (Caracas: Monte Avila Editores, 1976); Plino Apuleyo Mendoza, Carlos Alberto Montaner, and Álvaro Vargas Llosa, *Manual del perfecto idiota latinoamericano* (Barcelona: Plaza & Janés, 1996).

28. Sérgio Buarque de Holanda, *Raízes do Brasil* (Rio de Janeiro: José Olympio, 1976), originally published in 1936. See also Silviano Santiago's comparison of Octavio Paz's *El laberinto de la soledad* and Buarque de Holanda's *Raízes*, in S. Santiago, *As raízes e o labirinto da América Latina* (Rio de Janeiro: Rocco, 2006).

29. Leandro Narloch and Duda Teixeira, *Guia politicamente incorreto da América Latina* (São Paulo: Leya, 2011), 12.

30. See the interesting case of Francisco Olympio—a Brazilian mulatto who became a slave trader in the 1850s and then a plantation owner in Togo, controlling the commercial routes and facing German imperial attempts—described in Alicione M. Amos, "Afro-Brazilians in Togo: The Case of the Olympio Family, 1882–1945," *Cahiers d'Etudes Africaines*, no. 162 (2001): 293–314.

31. Rojas Mix, *Los cien nombres de América*.

32. César Vallejo, *Crónicas desde Europa*, ed. Jorge Puccinelli (Buenos Aires: Losada, 2015), 41

33. Rojas Mix, *Los cien nombres de América*, 132.

34. Gerardo Mosquera, "Good-bye identidad, welcome diferencia. Del arte latinoamericano al arte desde América Latina: Tránsitos globales" (2000), available online at www.fba.unlp.edu.ar/visuales4/Mosquera.doc.

35. See Antenor Orrego, "¿Cuál es la cultura que creará América? III. Mexicanización y Argentinización," *Amauta* (1928), 8–9; available online at the Web site of the International Center for the Arts of the Americas (ICAA), http://icaadocs.mfah .org/icaadocs/en-us/about/theproject/whatistheicaadocumentsproject.aspx. See also *Third Text*, special issue (Spring 1989); Luis R. Cancel, ed., *The Latin American Spirit: Art and Artists in the United States, 1920–1970* (New York: Bronx Museum of the Arts, Harry N. Abrams, 1988); Gabriela A. Piñero, "Políticas de representación/políticas de inclusión: La actualización del debate de lo latinoamericano en el arte durante la primera etapa de la globalización (1980–1990)," *Anales del Instituto de Investigaciones Estéticas* 36, no. 104 (2014): 157–86.

36. Ernesto Deira, quoted in Mari Carmen Ramírez, Tomas Ybarra-Fraustro, and Hector Olea, *Resisting Categories: Latin American and/or Latino?* vol. 1 (New Haven, CT: Yale University Press, 2012), 664; Shifra M. Goldman "El Espíritu Latinoamericano: La perspectiva desde los Estados Unidos," *Arte en Colombia: Internacional*, no. 41 (September 1989): 48–55; Jacqueline Barnitz, "The Question of Latin American Art: Does It Exist?" *Arts Magazine* 47, no. 3 (1966–1967): 53–55; online at the ICAA Web site, http://icaadocs.mfah.org/icaadocs/en-us/about/theproject/ whatistheicaadocumentsproject.aspx.

37. Jorge A. Manrique, "Invención del Arte Latinoamericano," Primer Encuentro Iberoamericano de Críticos del Arte y Artistas Plásticos, Caracas (June 18–27, 1978), n.p., online at the ICAA Web site, http://icaadocs.mfah.org/icaadocs/en-us/about/ theproject/whatistheicaadocumentsproject.aspx.

38. Ibid., n.p.

39. Jorge A. Manrique, "Identidad o modernidad?" in *América Latina en sus artes*, ed. Damián Bayón (Mexico City: Siglo XXI, 1974), 19–33, and "Invención del Arte Latinoamericano."

40. Graciela Speranza, *Atlas portátil de América Latina* (Barcelona: Anagrama, 2012), 13.

41. Peter Smith, *Talons of the Eagle*, 3rd ed. (New York: Oxford University Press, 2007), 351. For a comprehensive cultural view of the origins of a Latin American *Weltanschauung*, see Richard M. Morse, *New World Soundings: Culture and Ideology in the Americas* (Baltimore, MD: John Hopkins University Press, 1989). For a political science perspective, see John D. Martz, "Political Science and Latin American Studies: A Discipline in Search of a Region," *Latin American Research Review* 6, no. 1 (1971): 73–99, and "Political Science and Latin American Studies: Patterns and Asymmetries of Research and Publications," *Latin American Research Review* 15, no. 1 (1990): 67–86. About the politics of the field, and the field in politics, see Irving Louis Horowitz, ed., *The Rise and Fall of Project Camelot: Studies in the Relationship between Social Science and Practical Politics* (Cambridge, MA: MIT Press, 1967); Robert Packenham, *Liberal America and the Third World: Political Development Ideas in Foreign Aid and Social Science* (Princeton, NJ: Princeton University Press, 1973). See also the "post-structuralist" study of US hegemony in Latin American Studies in Mark T. Berger, *Under Northern Eyes: Latin American Studies and U.S. Hegemony in the Americas* (Bloomington: Indiana University Press, 1995); and the two general histories of US views of Latin America: James William Park, *Latin American Underdevelopment: A History of Perspectives in the United States, 1870–1965* (Baton Rouge: Louisiana State University Press, 1995); and Fredrick B. Pike, *The United States and Latin America: Myths and Stereotypes of Civilization and Nature* (Austin: University of Texas Press, 1992). For a specialized, Foucauldian approach to development and the role of Latin America, see Arturo Escobar, *Encountering Development: The Making and Unmaking of the Third World* (Princeton, NJ: Princeton University Press, 1995); and the more eclectic and policy-oriented view by Gilbert Rist, *Le développement: Histoire d'une croyance occidentale* (Paris: Presses de Sciences Po, 1996); and Javier Elguea, *Las teorías de desarrollo social en América Latina: Una reconstrucción racional* (Mexico City: El Colegio de México, 1989). For an angry view of Latin Americans' poisoning of US scholarship with the *dependencia* affair, see Robert Packenham, *The Dependency Movement: Scholarship and Politics in Development Studies* (Cambridge, MA: Harvard University Press, 1992).

42. Sonia Álvarez, Arturo Arias, and Charles R. Hale, "Re-Visioning Latin American Studies," *Cultural Anthropology* 26, no. 2 (2011): 226.

43. Ibid., 232–33.

44. Walter Mignolo, *The Idea of Latin America* (Malden, MA: Blackwell, 2005), x.

45. See Elías José Palti's criticism of essentialist interpretations of Latin America in *Mito y realidad de la cultura política latinoamericana*, ed. E. J. Palti (Buenos Aires: Prometeo, 2010), 12.

46. Vicente Aleixandre, "Rostro final," in *Obras completas* (Madrid: Aguilar, 1977), 2:37.

47. *Oxford English Dictionary*, 3rd ed., s.v. "epistemology."

48. Moreiras, as quoted in Beverley, *Latinoamericanism after 9/11*, 53.

49. Ibid., 61, 105.

50. Ibid., 20.

51. Ibid., 23; Jon Beasley-Murray, *Posthegemony: Political Theory and Latin America* (Minneapolis: University of Minnesota Press, 2010); Alberto Moreiras, *The Exhaustion of*

Difference: The Politics of Latin American Cultural Studies (Durham, NC: Duke University Press, 2010), and "Irrupción y conservación en las Guerras Culturales," *Revista de Crítica Cultural*, no. 17 (1998): 67–71; Jon Beasley-Murray, ed., "The New Latin Americanism: Cultural Studies Beyond Borders," special issue, *Journal of Latin American Cultural Studies* 11, no. 3 (2002); Santiago Castro-Gómez and Eduardo Mendieta, eds., *Teorías sin disciplina: Latinoamericanismo, poscolonialidad y globalización en debate* (Mexico City: Porrúa, 1998); Román de la Campa, *Latin Americanism*; John Beverley, José Oviedo, and Michael Aronna, eds., *The Postmodernism Debate in Latin America* (Durham, NC: Duke University Press, 1995).

52. Gobat, "Invention of Latin America"; see also James McPherson, *Battle Cry of Freedom: The Civil War Era* (New York: Oxford University Press, 1988), 104–16.

53. Gobat, "Invention of Latin America," 1353–54, 1375.

54. Bilbao, *Obras completas*, 2:408.

55. James E. Sanders, *The Vanguard of the Atlantic World: Creating Modernity, Nation, and Democracy in Nineteenth-Century Latin America* (Durham, NC: Duke University Press, 2014), 8.

56. José Martí, *Los Estados Unidos* (Madrid: Sociedad Española de Librerías, 1915), 156; for Martí and war, the US Civil War, and Emerson, see Díaz Quiñonez, "José Martí (1853–1895)."

57. Bilbao, *Obras completas*, 1:39.

58. Donoso and Alvarado as quoted by Pedro Rújula in, "Fraternité catholique et fraternité révolutionnaire en Espagne, fin du XVIIe–1848," in Gilles Bertrand, Catherine Brice, and Gilles Montègre, eds., *Fraternité, pur une histoire du concept* (Grenoble: Les Cahiers du CRHIPA, 2012), 112, 131.Francesco Viganò, *La fraternité humaine*, trans. J. Favre (Paris: Librairie Guillaumin, 1880). His moral treaty is a reaction to the horrors of the 1871 Franco-Prussian War; thus it goes beyond *latinité*. See also Mukul Asthana, "Fraternity: A Political Ideal," *Indian Journal of Political Science* 53, no. 1 (1992): 118–24; Fernando Escalante Gonzalbo, *In the Eyes of God: A Study on the Culture of Suffering*, trans. Jessica C. Locke (Austin: University of Texas Press, 2006); see the long and enlightening entry "Brüderlichkeit," by Wolfgang Schieder, in *Geschichtliche Grundbegriffe: Historisches Lexikon zur politisch-sozialen Sprache in Deutschland*, vol. 1, ed. R. Koselleck (Stuttgart: E. Klett, 1972); on Lamennais and fraternity, see Marcel David, *Le printemps de la fraternité: Genèse et vicissitudes 1830–1851* (Paris: Aubier, 1992), 129–33.

59. Bernard Williams, *Essays and Reviews* (Princeton, NJ: Princeton University Press, 2014), xv.

60. See Moya, "Introduction: Latin America," 4; Arduino Agnelli, *La genesi dell'idea di Mitteleuropa* (Milan: Dott. A. Giuffrè Editore, 1971); Claudio Magris, *Itaca e oltre* (Milan: Garzanti, 1982), 42.

61. Sanjay Subrahmanyam, "Connected Histories: Notes Towards a Reconfiguration of Early Modern Eurasia," *Modern Asian Studies* 31, no. 3 (1997): 742.

CHAPTER ONE

1. Giambattista Vico, *Principios de una ciencia nueva. En torno a la naturaleza común de las naciones . . .* , trans. Josep Carner, 2 vols. (Mexico City: El Colegio de México, 1941); María Zambrano, *Hacia un saber sobre el alma* (Madrid: Alianza,1987), 60; Hans-Georg Gadamer, *Arte y verdad de la palabra*, trans. Gerard Vilar i Roca (Barcelona: Paidós, 1998); Max Black, *Models and Metaphors: Studies in Language and Philosophy* (Ithaca, NY: Cornell University Press, 1962).

2. Aldo Mazzucchelli, "Julio Herrera y Reissig's Treatise on the Imbecility of the Country . . . An Unknown Source for the Discussion on the Intellectual Self-Image of Latin America . . . ," PhD diss., Stanford University, 2007, 662; M. L. Guzmán, "La tragedia ibero-Americana," *La Prensa* (San Antonio, TX), February 2, 1926, 1 (written in Madrid, 1926).

3. Li Chen, "Law and Sensibility of Empire in the Making of Modern China, 1750–1900," PhD diss., Columbia University, 2009.

4. Juan Villoro, "Iguanas y dinosaurios: América Latina como utopía del atraso," in *Efectos personales* (Mexico City: Era, 2000), 91.

5. Jean Franco, *The Modern Culture of Latin America; Society and the Artist* (New York: F. A. Praeger, 1967); for newer versions of the argument, see Jean Franco, "Latin American Intellectuals and Collective Identity," *Social Identities* 3, no. 2 (1997): 265–74.

6. Jorge de Sena, "O culto do 'autêntico' ou a crítica pelo buraco da fechadura," in his *O reino da estupidez*, vol. 1 (Lisbon: Moraes Editores, 1978), 160; W. Gombrowicz, *Diary*, trans. L. Vallee (New Haven, CT: Yale University Press, 2012), 473–76; Evaldo Cabral de Mello, *A educação pela guerra* (São Paulo: Penguin Classics, Companhia das Letras, 2014), 16.

7. John Beverley, *Latinamericanism after 9/11* (Durham, NC: Duke University Press, 2011).

CHAPTER TWO

1. Enrico Corradini, *L'ora di Tripoli* (Milan: Fratelli Treves, 1911), 101. See, for instance, Carlos Cañete Jiménez, "El origen africano de los íberos: Una perspectiva historiográfica," PhD diss., Universidad de Málaga, 2009; and Gonzalo Álvarez Chillida and Eloy Martín Corrales, "Haciendo patria en África: España en Marrucos y en el Golfo de Guinea," in *Ser españoles: Imaginarios nacionales en el siglo XX*, ed. Javier Moreno Luzón and José M. Núñez Seixas (Barcelona: RBA, 2013). I thank Eloy Martín Corrales for referring me to this literature. See also Fabio Filippi, *Una vita pagana: Enrico Corradini dal superomismo dannunziano a una politica di massa* (Florence: Vallecchi Editore, 1989); August Rafanell, *La il·lusió occitana*, 2 vols. (Barcelona: Quaderns Crema, 2006).

2. José Álvarez Junco, *Mater dolorosa: La idea de España en el siglo XIX* (Madrid: Taurus, 2001).

3. António Manuel Hespanha, *As vésperas do Leviathan: Instituções e poder político, Portugal século XVII* (Coimbra: Livraria Almedina, 1994), 300; John H. Elliott, "Europe of Composite Monarchies," *Past and Present*, no. 137 (1992): 48–71; Anthony Pagden, *The Enlightenment: And Why It Still Matters* (New York: Random House, 2013).

4. E. Prat de la Riba, *La nacionalitat catalana* (Barcelona: L'Anuari de la Exportació, 1906), 128; Maria da Conceição Meireles Pereira, "A questão ibérica: Imprensa e Opinião (1850–1870)," 2 vols., PhD diss., Universidade do Porto, 1995; António Sardinha, *A questão ibérica* (Lisbon: Almeida, Miranda & Sousa, 1916); Aleš Vrbata, "Between Latinité and Aliança Peninsular: Mediterranean Thought in Search of Renewal," *Studia Historica Nitriensia* 17, no. 1 (2013): 93–111; Rafanell, *La il·lusió occitana*. See also Enric Ucelay-Da Cal, *El imperialismo catalán* (Barcelona: Edhasa, 2003); Horst Hina, *Castilla y Cataluña en el debate cultural: 1714–1939* (Barcelona: Ed. Península, 1985); José Enrique Rodó, *El mirador de Próspero*, vol. 1 (Madrid: Editorial América, 1920), 112–13; orig. pub., 1913.

5. F. Alaiz, *Hacia una federación de autonomías ibéricas* (Madrid: Madre Tierra, 1993),

orig. pub. 1945; Antero de Quental, *Causas da decadência dos povos peninsulares* (Lisbon: Cadernos Peninsulares, 1971), orig. pub. 1871. See Rubem Barboza Filho, *Tradição e artifício: Iberismo e barroco na formação americana* (Rio de Janeiro: IUPERJ, 2000), 21–68; F. Pi i Margall, *Guatimozín y Hernán Cortés: Diálogo* (Madrid: Imprenta y Fundición de los Hijos de J. A. García, 1899).

6. Maragall, quoted in Josep Pla, *Joan Maragall: Un assaig* (Barcelona: Ediciones Destino, 1984), 96; Fernando Pessoa, *Iberia: Introducción a un imperialismo futuro*, ed. Antonio Sáez Delgado (Valencia: Pre-Textos, 2013), 99.

7. Valentín Cabero Diéguez, *Iberismo y cooperación: Pasado y futuro de la península ibérica* (Salamanca: Universidad de Salamanca, 2002); Jaume Vicens Vives, *Notícia de Catalunya* (Barcelona: Ediciones Destino, 1962); Sérgio Campos Matos, "Iberismo e identidade nacional (1851–1910)," *Clio*, n.s., nos. 14–15 (2006): 349–400; José Antonio Rocamora, *El nacionalismo ibérico: 1732–1936* (Valladolid: Publicaciones Universidad de Valladolid, 1994); Edmundo González-Blanco, *Iberismo y germanismo: España ante el conflicto europeo (tres estudios)* (Valencia: Editorial Cervantes, 1917); J. Fred Rippy, "Literary Yankeephobia in Hispanic America," *Journal of International Relations* 12, no. 3 (1922): 350–71; "Literary Yankeephobia in Hispanic America (Concluded)," *Journal of International Relations* 12, no. 4 (1922): 524–38; Luiz Werneck Vianna, *A revolução passive: Iberismo e americanismo no Brasil* (Rio de Janeiro: Editora Revan, 1997); Rafanell, *La il·lusió occitana*; and Josep María Fradera, *La nación imperial*, 2 vols. (Barcelona: Edhasa, 2015).

8. Pla, quoted in Gabriel Ferrater, *Tres prosistes: Joaquim Ruyra, Víctor Català i Josep Pla* (Barcelona: Editorial Empúries, 2010), 93.

9. Nicolau María Rubió, *La patrie latine: De la Méditerranée à l'Amérique* (Paris: La Nouvelle Édition, 1945), 87, 199; Claude-François Lallemand, *Le hachych* (Paris: Paulin, 1843), 16, 18; Joan Nogué and Antonio Luna, "Patria Latina, corazón africano: Nicolau María Rubió i Tudurí el viajero," *Boletín de la Sociedad Geográfica Española*, no. 31 (2008): 100–113; and Rafanell, *La il·lusió occitana*, 1345–47.

10. On the origins of French nationalism as a European sense of civilization vs. English barbarism, and as a sense of civilization in the making vis-à-vis peasants, colonies, and immigrants, see David A. Bell, *The Cult of the Nation in France: Inventing Nationalism, 1680–1800* (Cambridge, MA: Harvard University Press, 2001). Prosper Vallerange, *Le panlatinisme, confédération Gallo-Latine et Celto-Gauloise contre-testament de Pierre le Grand et contre-Panslavisme ou . . .* (Paris: Passard, Libraire-Éditeur, 1860), 2. Prosper Vallerange was indeed François Lubin Passard (1817–?), a prolific writer and editor who wrote much on Pan-Latinism. See Hans Kohn, *Pan-Slavism, Its History and Ideology* (Notre Dame, IN: University of Notre Dame Press, 1953); on the emergence of Pan-Latinism in this context, see Lily Litvak, *Latinos y anglosajones: Orígenes de una polémica* (Barcelona: Puvill, 1980); see also Robert Stam and Ella Shohat, *Race in Translation: Culture Wars around the Postcolonial Atlantic* (New York: New York University Press, 2012); Frank Ibold, "Die Erfindung Lateinamerikas: Die Idee der Latinité im Frankreich des 19. Jahrhunderts und ihre Auswirkungen auf die Eigenwahrnehmung des südlichen Amerika," in *Transatlantische Perzeptionen: Lateinamerika-USA-Europa in Geschichte und Gegenwart*, ed. Hans-Joachim König and Stefan Rinke (Stuttgart: Alcademischer Verlag, 1998), 77–98.

11. F. Dostoevsky, *A Writer's Diary*, vol. 1, 1873–1876, trans. Kenneth Lantz (Evanston, IL: Northwestern University Press, 1994), 598.

12. Marie-José Ferreira dos Santos, "La Revue du Monde Latin et le Brésil, 1883–1896," *Cahiers du Brésil Contemporain*, no. 23–24 (1994): 77–92; João Paulo Jeannine An-

drade Carneiro, "O último propagandista do Império: O 'barão' de Santa-Anna Nery (1848–1901) e a divulgação do Brasil na Europa," PhD diss., Universidade de São Paulo, 2013; Alphonse V. Roche, *Provençal Regionalism: A Study of the Movement in the Revue Félibréenne, Le feu, and Other Reviews of Southern France* (Evanston, IL: Northwestern University Press, 1954); Rafanell, *La il·lusió occitana*; Maike Thier, "The View from Paris: 'Latinity,' 'Anglo-Saxonism,' and the Americas, as Discussed in the *Revue des races latines*, 1857–64," *International History Review* 33, no. 4 (2011): 627–44; Käthe Panick, *La race latine: Politischer Romanismus im Frankreich des 19. Jahrhunderts* (Bonn: Röhrscheid, 1978).

13. Napoleone Colajanni, *Latini e anglo-sassoni (Razze inferiori e razze superiori)* (Rome: Revista Popolare, 1906), xiv, 342; Delia Frigessi, *Cesare Lombroso* (Torino: Giulio Einaudi Editore, 2003); Aliza S. Wong, *Race and the Nation in Liberal Italy, 1861–1911: Meridionalism, Empire, and Diaspora* (New York: Palgrave, 2006).

14. About Garibaldi in Uruguay, see Carlos Rama, *Garibaldi y el Uruguay* (Montevideo: Nuestro Tiempo, 1968); for the new Latinizing, as it were, of the hero, see James S. Sanders, *The Vanguard of the Atlantic World: Creating Modernity, Nation, and Democracy in Nineteenth-Century Latin America* (Durham, NC: Duke University Press, 2014), 24–37. François-Lubin Passard also wrote on Pan-Latinism and Garibaldi: a pamphlet that was a letter to the director of the journal *La Presse*, in which he tried to prove that Garibaldi's famous 1860 *Mémorandum alle potenze d'Europa* was indeed inspired by Pan-Latinism; see his *Le panlatinisme et le Mémorandum du général Garibaldi comparés* (Paris: n.p., 1860).

15. Richard H. Davis, *The Bhagavad Gita: A Biography* (Princeton, NJ: Princeton University Press, 2014), 121–22; Arnold Armand del Greco, *Giacomo Leopardi in Hispanic Literature* (New York: S. F. Vanni, 1952).

16. José Ignacio Víctor Eyzaguirre, *Los intereses católicos en América* (Paris: Librería de Garnier Hermanos, 1859) 1:iv–v.

17. Luis Medina Ascensio, *Historia del Colegio Pío Latino Americano (Roma: 1858–1978)* (Mexico City: Jus, 1979); Rafael Rojas, "Plumas que matan: El duelo intelectual entre Gabriel García Moreno y Juan Montalvo en el XIX ecuatoriano," *Istor* 12, no. 50 (2012): 7–37; Enrique Ayala Mora, "El origen del nombre América Latina y la tradición católica del siglo XIX," *Anuario Colombiano de Historia Social y de la Cultura* 40, no. 1 (2013): 213–41; Salvador Méndez Reyes, "José Ignacio Víctor Eyzaguirre y las corrientes intelectuales de su época," in *América Latina: Las caras de la diversidad* (Mexico City: Universidad Nacional Autónoma de México, 2006), 295–309; Carlos Silva Cotapos, *Monseñor José Ignacio Víctor Eyzaguirre Portales* (Santiago: Soc. Imprenta-Litografía Barcelona, 1919); José Ignacio Víctor Eyzaguirre, *Los intereses católicos en América*, 11; "Carta circular del episcopado brasileño (1927)," and the hymn, in *Historia del Colegio Pío*, by Luis Medina Ascencio, 335, 451.

18. Trudel, quoted in Maurice Demers, "Pan-Americanism Re-Invented in Uncle Sam's Backyard: Catholic and Latin Identity in French Canada and Mexico in the First Half of the 20th Century," PhD diss., York University, 2010, 56. This study fully dissects the characteristics and relative impact of the Union des Latins de l'Amerique. See also Victor Armony, "Des Latins du Nord? L'identité culturelle québécoise dans le contexte panaméricain," *Recherches Sociographiques* 43, no. 1 (2002): 19–48; Daniel Gay, *Les élites québécoises et l'Amérique latine* (Montreal: Nouvelle Optique, 1983); José A. de Larrinaga, "L'intervention française au Mexique vue par les principaux journaux canadiens français du Québec (1861–1867)," Master's thesis, Université

d'Ottawa, 1976; Marie Couillard and Patrick Imbert, eds., *Les discours du Nouveau Monde au XIXe siècle au Canada français et en Amérique latine* (New York: Legas, 1995); Michel Lacroix, "Lien social, idéologie et cercles d'appartenance: Le réseau 'latin' des Québécois en France, 1923–1939," *Etudes littéraires* 36, no. 2 (2004): 51–70.

19. *Revue Felibréene* (June 1985), quoted in Alphonse V. Roche, *Provençal Regionalism*, 41.

20. Silvana Patriarca, *Italian Vices: Nation and Character from the Risorgimento to the Republic* (Cambridge: Cambridge University Press, 2010); Bardina and *Som*, quoted in Joan-Lluís Marfany, *La cultura del catalanisme: El nacionalisme en els seus inicis* (Barcelona: Biblioteca Universal Empúries, 1995), 195, 260; Prat de la Riba, "De lluny," *La Veu* (1904), reproduced in Rafanell, *La il·lusió occitana*, 243; José María Portillo Valdés, *Monarquia y gobierno provincial: Poder y constitución en las provincias vascas (1760–1808)* (Madrid: Centro de Estudios Constitucionales, 1991); Antonio Elorza, *Tras la huella de Sabino Arana: Los orígenes totalitarios del nacionalismo vasco* (Madrid: Temas de Hoy, 2005).

21. Herder, quoted in Maurice Olender, *The Language of Paradise*, trans. Arthur Goldhammer (Cambridge, MA: Harvard University Press, 2008), 42.

22. Carlos Badía Malgrida, *El factor geográfico en la política sudamericana* (Madrid: Jaime Rates, 1919); José María Vargas Vila, *Ante los bárbaros (los Estados Unidos y la Guerra): El yanki, he ahí el enemigo* (Barcelona: Casa Editorial Maucci, 1917); Eduardo Prado, *A ilusão americana* (Brasilia: Senado Federal, 2003), orig. pub. 1893; J. M. Torres Caicedo, *Religión, patria, amor: Colección de versos escritos por . . .* (Paris: T. Ducessois, 1860), 55.

23. Luis Cardoza y Aragón, *El río, novelas de caballería* (Mexico City: Fondo de Cultura Económica, 1986), 234.

24. Julio Camba, "Rubén Darío," in *Caricaturas y retratos*, ed. Francisco Fuster (Madrid: Forcola, 2013), 37–46.

25. Josep María Fradera, *La nación imperial*; Ucelay-Da Cal, *El imperialismo catalán*; Horst Hina, *Castilla y Cataluña en el debate cultural: 1714–1939*; Joan-Lluís Marfany, *La llengua maltractada: El castellà i el català a Catalunya del segle XVI al segle XIX* (Barcelona: Editorial Empúries, 2001); *Correspondencia entre Unamuno y Vaz Ferreira* (Montevideo: Cámara de Representantes de la República Oriental del Uruguay, 1957); and Michel Levallois, *Ismaÿl Urbain (1812–1884): Une autre conquête de l'Algérie* (Paris: Maisonneuve et Larose, 2001).

26. Nicolau M. Rubió i Tudurí, *Llatins en servitud, París 1940–1944*, trans. J. M. Quintana (Barcelona: Leonard Muntaner Editor, 2006), 64.

27. Manuel Ugarte, *El porvenir de la América latina: La raza—la integridad territorial y moral; la organización interior* (Valencia: F. Sempere y Compañía, 1911), 73; José Vasconcelos, *La raza cósmica. Misión de la raza iberoamericana: Notas de viajes a la América del Sur* (Paris: Agencia Mundial de Librería, 1925); Justo Sierra, *Viajes en tierra Yankee, en la Europa Latina* (Mexico City: Universidad Nacional Autónoma de México, 1948), orig. pub. 1897.

28. Miomandre, quoted in Roche, *Provençal Regionalism*, 20.

CHAPTER THREE

1. Leslie Bethell, "O Brasil e a ideia de 'América Latina' em perspectiva histórica," *Revista Estudos Históricos* 22, no. 44 (2009): 289–321; Ori Preuss, *Bridging the Island: Brazilians' Views of Spanish America and Themselves, 1865–1912* (Frankfurt: Iberoamericana Vervuert, 2011), and *Transnational South America: Experiences,*

Ideas, and Identities, 1860–1920 (New York: Routledge, 2016); Luís Cláudio Villa-fañe G. Santos, *O Brasil entre a América e a Europa: O Império e o interamericanismo, do Congresso do Panamá à Conferência de Washington* (São Paulo: Editora Unesp, 2004), and *O império e as repúblicas do Pacífico: As relações do Brasil com Chile, Bolívia, Peru, Equador e Colômbia* (Curitiba: Editora UFPR, 2002); António Cândido, "Os brasileiros e a nossa América," in *Recortes* (Rio de Janeiro: Ouro sobre Azul, 2004), 143–55; Kátia Gerab Baggio, "A 'outra' América: A América Latina na visão dos intelectuais brasileiros das primeiras décadas republicanas," PhD diss., Universi-dade de São Paulo, 1998; Gilberto Freyre, *O brasileiro entre os outros hispanos: Afini-dades, contrastes e possíveis futuros nas suas interrelações* (Rio de Janeiro: Livraria José Olympio, 1975); Edson Nery da Fonseca, Gilberto Freyre, *Americanidade e latinidade da América Latina e outros textos afins* (Brasilia: Editora UnB/São Paulo Imprensa Oficial, 2003); Gabriela Pellegrino Soares and Júlio Pimentel Pinto, "A América La-tina no universo das edições brasileiras," *Diálogos* 8, no. 2 (2004): 133–51; Moniz Bandeira, *Brasil, Argentina e Estados Unidos: Conflito e integração na América do Sul (da Triplice Aliança ao Mercosul, 1870–2003)* (Rio de Janeiro: Revan, 2003); Beatriz Co-lombi, *Viaje intelectual: Migraciones y desplazamientos en América Latina, 1880–1915* (Rosario: B. Viterbo Editora, 2004); Georg Wink, *Die Idee von Brasilien: Eine kultur-wissenschaftliche Untersuchung der Erzählung Brasiliens als vorgestellte Gemeinschaft im Kontrast zu Hispanoamerika* (Frankfurt: Peter Lang, 2009) (an informative piece but too influenced by "cultural studies," as if Benedict Anderson really knew something about Brazil as *"vorgestellte Gemeinschaft"*): Richard M. Morse, *El espejo de Próspero*, trans. Stella Mastrangelo (Mexico City: Siglo XXI, 1986) (never published in its original English version); Richard M. Morse "The Heritage of Latin America," in *The Founding of New Societies: Studies in the History of the United States, Latin America, South Africa, Canada, and Australia*, ed. Louis Hartz (New York: Harcourt, Brace & World, 1964), 123–77; Vitória Rodrigues e Silva, "O ensino de história da América no Brasil," *Diálogos* 8, no. 2 (2004): 83–104; António Pedro Tota, *O imperialismo sedutor* (São Paulo: Companhia das Letras, 2000); Luiz Werneck Vianna, *A revolução passiva: Iberismo e americanismo no Brasil* (Rio de Janeiro: Editora Revan, 1997); Ru-bem Barboza Filho, *Tradição e artifício: Iberismo e barroco na formação americana* (Rio de Janeiro: IUPERJ, 2000).

2. Quoted from the 1859 edition of the *Staatslexikon*, in Georg Wink, *Die Idee von Bra-silien*, 161.

3. Ricardo Salles, *Nostalgia imperial*, 2nd ed. (Rio de Janeiro: Ponteio, 2013), 59; for the United States as a Brazilian route for independence, see Eric Nelson, *The Royalist Revolution: Monarchy and the American Founding* (Cambridge, MA: Harvard Univer-sity Press, 2014); Manoel Luiz Lima Salgado Guimarães, "Nação e civilização nos trópicos: O Instituto Histórico Geográfico Brasileiro e o projeto de uma história na-cional," *Revista Estudos Históricos* 1, no. 1 (1988): 5–27. Nabuco is quoted in Salles, *Nostalgia imperial*, 27.

4. Luiz Felipe de Alencastro, "O ocaso dos bacharéis," *Novos Estudos CEBRAP*, no. 50 (March 1998): 55–60.

5. Manuel de Oliveira Lima, *América latina e America ingleza: A evolução brasileira com-parada com a hispano-americana e com a anglo-americana* (Rio de Janeiro: Livraria Gar-nier, 1913).

6. For a view of these interactions as "transnational" "Latin American modernity," see Ori Preuss, *Transnational South America*.

7. Luís Cláudio Villafañe G. Santos, *O Brasil entre a América e a Europa*, 25.

8. Luís Cláudio Villafañe G. Santos, *O império e as repúblicas do Pacífico*; Salvador Rivera, *Latin American Unification: A History of Political and Economic Integration Efforts* (London: McFarland, 2014).

9. Lucas Alamán, *Historia de Méjico desde los primeros movimientos que prepararon su independencia en el año de 1808, hasta la época presente* (Mexico City: Impr. de J. M. Lara, 1849–1852), 1:123.

10. Justo Arosemena, *Constituciones políticas de la América meridional* (Havre: Imprenta A. Lemale Aíné, 1870), 1:58.

11. Among the books from this period were some by Oliveira Lima: see, for example, Manuel de Oliveira Lima, *Formación histórica de la nacionalidad brasileña* (Madrid: Editorial América, 1918); see also Francisco José de Oliveira Vianna, *Evolución del pueblo brasileño*, trans. Julio E. Payró (Buenos Aires: Imprenta Mercatali, 1937), and *La evolución histórica de la América latina: Bosquejo comparativo*, trans. A. C. Rivas (Madrid: Editorial América, 1910); see also Euclides da Cunha, *Los sertones*, trans. B. Garay (Buenos Aires: Imprenta Mercatali, 1938); and a translation of Eduardo Prado's book published in Spain: *La ilusión yanqui*, trans. Carlos Pereyra (Madrid: Editorial América, 1918). J. M. Sagarra's vivid description of Pereyra appears in his *Memòries* (Barcelona: Selecta, 1954), 711–12. Among the Mexican books on Brazil, see Alfonso Reyes, *Introducción al estudio económico del Brasil* (Mexico City: Imprenta mundial, 1938); Vicente Lombardo Toledano, *La revolución del Brasil* (Mexico City: Talleres Gráficos de la Nación, 1931). About Brazil in Argentina, see José León Suárez, *Diplomacia universitaria americana: Argentina en el Brasil; ciclo de conferencias: Derecho internacional, política internacional, historia diplomática* (Buenos Aires: Imprenta Escoffier, Caracciolo y Cía, 1918); Vicente G. Quesada, *Mis memorias diplomáticas: Misión ante el gobierno del Brasil* (Buenos Aires: Impr. de Coni Hermanos, 1907–1908); Manuel Bernárdez, *El Brasil, su vida, su trabajo, su futuro; itinerario periodístico* (Buenos Aires: Talleres Heliográficos de Ortega y Radaelli, 1908), also published in French; Juan Gregorio Beltrán, *Historia del Brasil* (Buenos Aires: Editorial Beltrán, 1935); R. de Carvalho, *Pequeña historia de la literatura brasileña*, trans. Julio E. Payró (Buenos Aires: Imprenta Mercatali, 1943); see also Gustavo Arboleda, *El Brasil a través de su historia* (Bogota: Arboleda & Valencia, 1914); Eduardo Guzmán Esponda, *Bajo el sol del Brasil* (Bogota: Editorial Minerva, S. A., 1931); Juan Bautista Alberdi, *El imperio de Brasil ante la democracia de América: Colección de artículos escritos durante la guerra del Paraguay contra la Triple Alianza* (Asunción: Edición especial de "El Diario," 1919); Mariano Reyes Cardona, *La política imperialista del Brasil* (La Paz: Escuela Tipográfica Salesiana, 1925). See also Paulo Moreira, *Literary and Cultural Relations between Brazil and Mexico: Deep Undercurrents* (New York: Palgrave Macmillan, 2013); Robert P. Newcomb, *Nossa and Nuestra América: Inter-American Dialogues* (West Lafayette, IN: Purdue University Press, 2012).

12. Manuel Ugarte, *El porvenir de la América latina: La raza—la integridad territorial y moral; la organización interior* (Valencia: F. Sempere y Compañía, 1911).

13. Marcelo Mendes de Souza, "Machado de Assis and Jorge Luis Borges as Ironists: National, Universal or Latin American Writers?" PhD diss., University of Auckland, New Zealand, 2014; Adriana Amante, *Poéticas y políticas del destierro: Argentinos en Brasil en la época de Rosas* (Buenos Aires: Fondo de Cultura Económica, 2010), 351. See also, João Paulo Coelho de Souza Rodrigues, "Da revolução à regeneração: Crônicas de Machado de Assis e de Olavo Bilac sobre a Argentina," *Antíteses* 6, no. 11 (2013): 127–48; and Georg Wink, *Die Idee von Brasilien*.

14. José Vasconcelos, *Indología: Una interpretación de la cultura ibero-americana* (Barce-

lona: Agencia Mundial de Librería, 1927), 10, 120; Fred P. Ellison, *Alfonso Reyes e o Brasil: Um mexicano entre os cariocas* (Rio de Janeiro: Topbooks, 2002); Regina Aída Crespo, "Cultura e política: José Vasconcelos e Alfonso Reyes no Brasil (1922–1938)," *Revista Brasileira de História* 23, no 45 (2003): 187–207.

15. J. M. Machado de Assis, *Memorias póstumas de Blas Cubas*, trans. Rafael Mesa y López (Paris: Garnier Hermanos, 1911); *Narraciones escogidas*, trans. Rafael Cansinos-Asséns (Madrid: Editorial América, 1916); *Quincas Borba*, trans. J. de Amber (Paris: Garnier Hermanos, 1913); *Don Casmurro*, trans. Rafael Mesa y López (Paris: Garnier Hermanos, 1910); *Esaú y Jacob. Tomo II* (Buenos Aires: Imprenta de La Nación, 1905); *Las memorias póstumas de Blas Cubas*, trans. Antonio Alatorre (Mexico City: Fondo de Cultura Económica, 1951). See also Carlos Espinosa Domínguez, "Andanzas póstumas: Machado de Assis en español," *Caracol*, no. 1 (2010): 65–85; Moreira, *Literary and Cultural Relations between Brazil and Mexico*.

16. Cândido, "Os brasileiros e a nossa América," 145.

17. Nabuco's letter is quoted in Ori Preuss, *Bridging the Island*, 103.

18. Ribeiro Couto, "Epistolario: III. El hombre cordial, producto americano," *Monterrey: Correo Literario de Alfonso Reyes*, no. 8 (March 1932): 169; Prudente de Moraes Neto, "I. La inconexión de América; II. Espacio y tiempo en el alma americana," *Monterrey: Correo literario de Alfonso Reyes*, no. 8 (March 1932): 169; both included at the ICAA Web site, http://icaadocs.mfah.org/icaadocs/en-us/about/theproject/whatistheicaadocumentsproject.aspx; José Veríssimo, *Cultura, literatura e política na América Latina*, ed. J. A. Barbosa (São Paulo: Brasiliense, 1986); Manuel de Oliveira Lima, *América latina e América ingleza*; Cândido, "Os brasileiros e a nossa América"; Eduardo Prado, *A ilusão americana*; about Oliveira Vianna, see Luiz Werneck Vianna, *A revolução passiva*.

19. Richard Blaine McCornack, "Maximilian's Relations with Brazil," *Hispanic American Historical Review* 32, no. 2 (1952): 175–86; Moreira, *Literary and Cultural Relations between Brazil and Mexico*. See also Newcomb, *Nossa and Nuestra América*.

20. Manoel Bomfim, *A América latina: Males de origem* (Rio de Janeiro: H. Garnier, 1905), 14, 87; Ronaldo Conde Aguiar, *O rebelde esquecido: Tempo, vida e obra de Manoel Bomfim* (Rio de Janeiro: Topbooks, 2000); Cândido, "Os brasileiros e a nossa América"; and Roberto Ventura, *Estilo tropical* (São Paulo: Companhia das Letras, 1991).

21. Afrânio Coutinho, "¿Qué es América Latina?" *Mundo Nuevo*, no. 36 (1969): 20.

22. Sérgio Buarque de Holanda, "Ariel" (1920), in *Raízes do Sérgio Buarque de Holanda*, ed. Francisco de Assis Barbosa (Rio de Janeiro: Rocco, 1989), 43–46; Coutinho, "¿Qué es América Latina?" 19–20; Morse, *El espejo de Próspero*; Darcy Ribeiro, *A América latina existe?* (São Paulo: Fundação Darcy Ribeiro, 2010).

23. Mary Anne Junqueiral, Vitória Rodrigues e Silva, "Entrevista com Maria Ligia Coelho Prado," *Diálogos* 8, no. 2 (2004): 65–79.

CHAPTER FOUR

1. Tomás R. Jiménez, *Replenished Ethnicity, Mexican Americans, Immigration, and Identity* (Berkeley: University of California Press, 2010); David Montejano, *Quixote's Soldiers: A Local History of the Chicano Movement, 1966–1981* (Austin: University of Texas Press, 2010); Manuel G. Gonzales, *Mexicanos: A History of Mexicans in the United States* (Bloomington: Indiana University Press, 1999); Francisco Rosales, *Chicano! The History of the Mexican American Civil Rights Movement* (Houston: Arte Público Press, 1996); Arlene Dávila, *Latinos, Inc.: The Marketing and Making of a*

People (Berkeley: University of California Press, 2001); Ramón A. Gutiérrez, "What's in a Name? The History and Politics of Hispanic and Latino Panethnic Identities," in *The Contours of Latino Studies*, ed. by Tomás Almaguer and Ramón A. Gutiérrez (Berkeley: University of California Press, forthcoming); G. Cristina Mora, *Making Hispanics: How Activists, Bureaucrats, and Media Constructed a New American* (Chicago: University of Chicago Press, 2014).

2. Andrés Reséndez, *Changing National Identities at the Frontier: Texas and New Mexico, 1800–1850* (New York: Cambridge University Press, 2004).

3. Gutiérrez, "What's in a Name?"

4. Ibid., n.p.

5. Dávila, *Latinos Inc.,*4

6. Agassiz's letter is quoted in Christoph Irmscher, *Louis Agassiz, Creator of American Science* (Boston: Houghton Mifflin Harcourt, 2013), 248–49; "Mexicanize" is quoted in Louis Menand, *The Methaphysical Club* (New York: Farrar, Straus and Giroux, 2002), 102

7. Nephtalí de León, *Chicano Popcorn* (n.p., N. De León, 1996); Richard Rodriguez, *Brown: The Last Discovery of America* (New York: Viking, 2002), 11, 35.

8. David Hollinger, *Postethnic America: Beyond Multiculturalism* (New York: Basic Books, 1995).

9. *Corrido* "El enganchado," in *Mexican Labor in the United States*, by Paul S. Taylor (Berkeley: University of California Press, 1928–1934), 1:vii.

10. Aurelio M. Espinosa, *Conchita Argüello* (New York: MacMillan, 1938); quotation from *El Nuevo Mexicano*, in *Breve reseña de la literatura hispana de Nuevo México y Colorado*, by José Timoteo López, Edgardo Núñez, and Roberto Lara Vialpando (Juárez: Imprenta Comercial, 1959), 9. See the remarkable digital archive, "Hispanic American Newspapers, 1808–1980," produced by the University of Houston.

11. Carlos Pereda, "Sobre la enseñanza de la filosofía entre nosotros," in *La filosofía en México en el siglo XX* (Mexico City: CONACULTA, 2013), 393.

12. David Wasserstein, "So, What Did the Muslims Do for the Jews?" *Jewish Chronicle Online*, http:/www.thejc.com/comment-and-debate/comment/68082/so-what-did-muslims-do-jews; Peter Novick, *The Holocaust in American Life* (Boston: Houghton Mifflin, 1999).

13. R. A. E. Blanchard, "Les tableaux du métissage au Mexique," *Journal de la Société des Américanistes* 5, no. 1 (1908): 59–66.

14. Mayellen's interrogation quoted in Peggy Pascoe, *What Comes Naturally: Miscegenation Law and the Making of Race in America* (New York: Oxford University Press, 2009), 109–10.

15. Anthony W. Marx, *Making Race and Nation: A Comparison of South Africa, the United States, and Brazil* (New York: Cambridge University Press, 1998); Pascoe, *What Comes Naturally*; Jolie A. Sheffer, *The Romance of Race: Incest, Miscegenation, and Multiculturalism in the United States, 1880–1930* (New Brunswick, NJ: Rutgers University Press, 2012); Taylor, *Mexican Labor in the United States*; Mark Brilliant, *The Color of America Has Changed: How Racial Diversity Shaped Civil Rights Reform in California, 1941–1978* (New York: Oxford University Press, 2010).

16. William D. Carrigan and Clive Webb, *Forgotten Dead: Mob Violence Against Mexicans in the United States, 1848–1928* (New York: Oxford University Press, 2013).

17. Richard Kagan, "Prescott's Paradigm: American Historical Scholarship and the Decline of Spain," *American Historical Review* 101, no. 2 (1996): 423–46. James D. Fernández, "'Longfellow's Law': The Place of Latin America and Spain in U.S. His-

panism, circa 1915," in *Spain in America: The Origins of Hispanism in the United States*, ed. Richard Kagan (Chicago: University of Illinois Press, 2002), 122–41; see also Fredrick B. Pike, *The United States and Latin America: Myths and Stereotypes of Civilization and Nature* (Austin: University of Texas Press, 1992); Iván Jaksić, *Ven conmigo a la España lejana: Los intelectuales norteamericanos ante el mundo hispano, 1820–1880* (Santiago: Fondo de Cultura Económica, 2007); Miguel Romera Navarro, *El hispanismo en Norte América: Exposición y crítica* (Madrid: Renacimiento, 1917).

18. George Ticknor, *Life, Letters, and Journals of George Ticknor* (London: Sampson Low, Marston, Searle and Rivingtion, 1876), 1:188.

19. Miguel Ángel Puig-Samper, Consuelo Naranjo, and María Dolores Luque, "Hacia una amistad triangular: Las Relaciones entre España, Estados Unidos y Puerto Rico," in *Los lazos de la cultura: El Centro de Estudios Históricos de Madrid y la Universidad de Puerto Rico (1916–1939)*, ed. Consuelo Naranjo, María Dolores Luque de Sánchez, Miguel Ángel Puig-Samper, et al. (Madrid: CSIC, 2002), 121–52.

20. Lawrence Wilkins, "Spanish as a Substitute for German for Training and Culture," *Hispania* 1, no. 4 (1918): 210.

21. Aurelio M. Espinosa's article was originally published in *Hispania* 1, no. 3 (1918) and later published as *América española o hispano América: El término América latina es erróneo*, trans. Felipe M. de Septién (Madrid: Comisaría Regia del Turismo, 1919); see also Aurelio M. Espinosa, *The Spanish Language in New Mexico and Southern Colorado* (Santa Fe: New Mexican Printing Company, 1911), and *The Folklore of Spain in the American Southwest*, ed. J. Manuel Espinosa (Norman: University of Oklahoma Press, 1985), 102.

22. José Timoteo López, Edgardo Núñez, and Roberto Lara Vialpando, *Breve reseña de la literatura hispana de Nuevo México y Colorado*, 12.

23. Translation based on Espinosa, *Folklore of Spain in the American Southwest*, quoted in Mary C. Montaño, *Tradiciones Nuevomexicanas: Hispano Arts and Culture of New Mexico* (Albuquerque: University of New Mexico Press, 2001), 319.

24. Neil Foley, *The White Scourge: Mexicans, Blacks, and Poor Whites in Texas Cotton Culture* (Berkeley: University of California Press, 1997); Craig Kaplowitz, *LULAC, Mexican Americans and National Policy* (College Station: Texas A & M University Press, 2005); George I. Sánchez, *Forgotten People: A Study of New Mexicans* (Albuquerque: University of New Mexico Press, 1940), 32. See also Carlos Kevin Blanton, *George I. Sanchez: The Long Fight for Mexican American Integration* (New Haven, CT: Yale University Press, 2014); for how Sánchez was inspired by both Moisés Sáenz and John Dewey, see Ruben Flores, *Backroads Pragmatists: Mexico's Melting Pot and Civil Rights in the United States* (Philadelphia: University of Pennsylvania Press, 2014).

25. Doris Meyer, "Reading Early Neomexicano Newspapers: Yesterday and Today," in *Recovering the U. S. Hispanic Literary Heritage*, ed. Ramón Gutiérrez et al., vol. 3 (Houston: Arte Público Press, 2000); Michael A. Morrison, *Slavery and the American West: The Eclipse of Manifest Destiny and the Coming of the Civil War* (Chapel Hill: University of North Carolina Press, 1997); Jerry Thompson, *Civil War in the Southwest: Recollections of the Sibley Brigade* (College Station: Texas A & M University Press, 2001); James A. Irby, *Backdoor at Bagdad: The Civil War on the Rio Grande* (El Paso: Texas Western Press, 1977); William Randolph Howell, *Westward the Texans* (El Paso: Texas Western Press, 1990); Henry Davies Wallen, *New Mexico Territory During the Civil War* (Albuquerque: University of New Mexico Press, 2008); Henry Hopkins Sibley, *The Civil War in West Texas and New Mexico* (El Paso: Texas Western Press, 2001); William Clarke Whitford, *Colorado Volunteers in the Civil War: The New*

Mexico Campaign in 1862 (Glorieta, NM: Rio Grande Press, 1971), orig. pub. in 1906; Harry Thayer Mahoney, *Mexico and the Confederacy, 1860–1867* (San Francisco: Austin & Winfield, 1998); F. Stanley, *The Civil War in New Mexico* (Denver: World Press, 1960); Walter E. Pittman, *New Mexico and the Civil War* (Charleston, SC: History Press, 2011); T. William Wahlstrom, "A Vision for Colonization: The Southern Migration Movement to Mexico after the U.S. Civil War," *Southern Historian* 30 (Spring 2009): 50–66; Deren Earl Kellogg, "The Lincoln Administration and the Southwestern Territories," PhD diss., University of Illinois, Urbana-Champaign, 1998; Carl Coke Rister, "Carlota, a Confederate Colony in Mexico," *Journal of Southern History* 11, no.1 (1945): 33–50; Richard Blaine McCornack, "Los Estados Confederados y México," *Historia Mexicana* 4, no. 3 (1955): 337–52, and "Juárez y la armada norteamericana," *Historia Mexicana* 6, no. 4 (1957): 493–509.

26. María Camacho, "Cinco de Mayo NOT FOR SALE," *Hispanic* 13, no. 3 (2000): 30–32; Alvar W. Carlson, "America's Growing Observance of Cinco de Mayo," *Journal of American Culture* 21, no. 2 (1998): 7–16; Robert Davis-Undiano "Cinco de Mayo: Reinventing a Mexican Holiday," *Hispanic* 13, no. 3 (2000): 100; Maudi Gomez Schneide, "Reflections on Cinco de Mayo: Bridging Two Cultures," *Hispanic* 9, no. 5 (1996): 66; Liliana Castañeda Rossmann, "Cinco de Mayo: Stories, Rituals, and Transcendence in Celebration," *Text* 25, no. 5 (2005): 665–89.

27. Sonia Álvarez, Arturo Arias, and Charles R. Hale, "Re-Visioning Latin American Studies," *Cultural Anthropology* 26, no. 2 (2011): 225–46; Jonathan Fox, "Bridging Latin American and Latino Studies: Juntos Pero No Revueltos," *LASA Forum* 33, no. 4 (2003): 112; Pedro Cabán and Frances Aparicio, "The Latino in Latin American Studies," *LASA Forum* 33, no. 4 (2003): 10–11.

28. Ilan Stavans, ed., *The Norton Anthology of Latino Literature* (New York: W. W. Norton, 2011).

29. Raúl Coronado, *A World Not to Come: A History of Latino Writing and Print Culture* (Cambridge, MA: Harvard University Press, 2013).

30. Guillermo Gómez-Peña and Coco Fusco, "Nationalism and Latinos, North and South: A Dialogue," in *Las relaciones culturales entre América Latina y Estados Unidos después de la Guerra Fría* (Berlin: Gaudig und Veit, 2000), 186–94, included on the ICAA Web site, http://icaadocs.mfah.org/icaadocs/en-us/about/theproject/whatistheicaadocumentsproject.aspx.

CHAPTER FIVE

1. In the following analysis of popular music, I save the reader from dense footnotes, reducing references to a minimum and instead basing my argument on memory, for the very act of recollecting—despite errors—is part of the argument I am making.

2. Alejo Carpentier, *La novela latinoamericana en vísperas del nuevo siglo y otros ensayos* (Mexico City: Siglo XXI, 1981), 18; Natalio Galán, *Cuba y sus sones*, prologue by Guillermo Cabreara Infante (Valencia: Pre-textos, 1997), 250. I read Alexander Lernet-Holenia's novel in Spanish translation: *El estandarte*, trans. A. R. Glücksmann (Barcelona: Libros del Asteroide, 2013).

3. About Mexican countercultural music, see Eric Zolov, *Refried Elvis: The Rise of the Mexican Counterculture* (Berkeley: University of California Press, 1999); Juan Pablo González, *Pensar la música desde América Latina* (Buenos Aires: Gourmet Musical Ediciones, 2013), 84.

4. João Ribeiro, *O folk-lore (estudos de literatura popular)* (Rio de Janeiro: J. Ribeiro dos Santos, 1919), 29.

5. See, for instance, Eleanor Hague, *Spanish-American Folk-Songs, as Sung and Played by Mrs. Francisca de la Guerra Dibblee* . . . (Lancaster, PA: American Folk-Lore Society, 1917); or Julio Vicuña Cifuentes, *Mitos y supersticiones recogidos de la tradición oral chilena con referencias comparativas a los de otros países latinos* (Santiago: Imprenta Universitaria, 1915).

6. "Jesus Christ is depicted as brown, as is Magdalena; brown is the one I love: long live brown people. The brown color was made by God, the white by a silversmith: white is for God, brown for me." Antonio Machado y Álvares, *Poesía popular; postscriptum á la obra Cantos populares españoles, (de F. R. Marín) por Demófilo* (Seville: F. Álvarez, 1883).

7. *Poesía Popular de España: Romances tradicionales de Asturias por D. José Amador de los Ríos, Publicado en la Revista Ibérica* (Madrid: Imprenta de Manuel Galiano, 1861), 22.

8. John Donald Robb, *Hispanic Folk Music of New Mexico and the Southwest* (Albuquerque: University of New Mexico Press, 2014), 31; José Pérez Ballesteros, *Cancionero popular gallego: Y en particular de la provincia de la Coruña* . . . *con un prólogo del ilustre mitógrafo portugués Theóphilo Braga y concordancias por Antonio Machado y Álvarez* (Madrid: Fé, 1886); Carlos A. Castellanos, "El tema de Delgadina en el folk-lore de Santiago de Cuba," *Journal of American Folklore* 33, no. 127 (1920): 43–46.

9. Carlos Monsiváis, "De los lectores de poesía y sus metamorfosis," in *Modernidad, vanguardia y revolución en la poesía mexicana (1919–1930)*, ed. Anthony Stanton (Mexico City: El Colegio de México, Centro Katz de Estudios Mexicanos, 2015), 45–58..

10. In the original version the lyrics talk about a man saying goodbye to his "buddies," recalling the good old partying times; the German version refers to a toast for Tarragona, a better city than Barcelona. Conversations: Marco A. Torres; Pablo Palomino. Francisco de Assis Barbosa, ed., *Raízes do Sérgio Buarque de Holanda* (Rio de Janeiro: Rocco, 1989), 120; Pablo Palomino, "Nationalist, Hemispheric, and Global: 'Latin American Music' and the Music Division of the Pan American Union, 1939–1947," *Nouveaux mondes, mondes nouveaux—Novo Mundo, Mundos Novos—New World, New Worlds* (2015), http://nuevomundo.revues.org/68062.

11. This is Pablo Palomino's idea (conversation, January 2016).

12. Conversations: Palomino and Marco A. Torres (January 2016).

CHAPTER SIX

1. Daniel Rodgers, *Age of Fracture* (Cambridge, MA: Harvard University Press, 2011).

2. Edward Shils, quoted in Nils Gilman, *Mandarins of the Future: Modernization Theory in Cold War America* (Baltimore, MD: John Hopkins University Press, 2003), 2.

3. Debraj Ray, *Development Economics* (Princeton, NJ: Princeton University Press, 1998); see also his "What's New in Development Economics?" (January 2000), online at http://www.econ.nyu.edu/user/debraj/Papers/AmerEcon.pdf

4. Fernando Escalante Gonzalbo, *Historia mínima del neoliberalismo* (Mexico City: El Colegio de México, 2015).

5. Thomas Holt, *The Problem of Race in the Twenty-First Century* (Cambridge, MA: Harvard University Press, 2002), 17.

6. Adam Przeworski, *Democracy and the Limits of Self-Government* (New York: Cambridge University Press, 2010), xiii; Wanderley Guilherme dos Santos, "Poliarquia em 3D," *Dados* 41, no.2 (1998): 207; see also Fernando Escalante Gonzalbo, *Estampas de Liliput* (Mexico City: Fondo de Cultura Económica, 2004); Fernando Escalante Gonzalbo, *Ciudadanos imaginarios* (Mexico City: El Colegio de México, 1992).

7. Edmund S. Morgan, *Inventing the People: The Rise of Popular Sovereignty in England and America* (New York: W. W. Norton, 1988).

8. Pablo Iglesias, "Understanding Podemos," *New Left Review*, May–June 2015, 14.

9. See Guillermo O'Donnell, Philippe C. Schmitter, and Laurence Whitehead, eds., *Transitions from Authoritarian Rule: Latin America* (Baltimore, MD: Johns Hopkins University Press, 1986).

10. Patrick W. Kelly, "Sovereignty and Salvation: Transnational Human Rights Activism in the Americas in the Long 1970s," PhD diss., University of Chicago, 2015. For the relations of violence and democracy, see Enrique D. Arias and Daniel M. Goldstein, eds., *Violent Democracies in Latin America* (Durham, NC: Duke University Press, 2010).

11. See Fernando Escalante Gonzalbo, *El crimen como realidad y representación* (Mexico City: El Colegio de México, 2012); Bernard E. Harcourt, *The Illusion of Free Markets* (Cambridge, MA: Harvard University Press, 2011).

12. Harcourt, *Illusion of Free Markets*.

13. Gilbert Rist, *Le développement: Histoire d'une croyance occidentale* (Paris: Presses de Sciences Po, 1996); Arturo Escobar, *Encountering Development: The Making and Unmaking of the Third World* (Princeton, NJ: Princeton University Press, 1995); see also Ray, "What's New in Development Economics?"

14. Daron Acemoglu and James A. Robinson, *Why Nations Fall: Origins of Power, Prosperity and Poverty* (New York: Crown, 2012), 3. The book is an interesting political twist on the various institutionalist views, see Stephen Haber, ed., *Political Institutions and Economic Growth in Latin America* (Stanford, CA: Hoover Institution Press, 2000).

15. John Coatsworth, "Notes on the Comparative Economic History of Latin America and the United States," in *Development and Underdevelopment in America: Contrast of Economic Growth in North and Latin America in Historical Perspective*, ed. Walther L. Bernecker and Hans Werner Tobler (Berlin: Walter de Gruyter, 1993). See also John Coatsworth and G. Tortella Casares, *Institutions and Long-Run Economic Performance in Mexico and Spain, 1800–2000*, Working Paper (Cambridge, MA: David Rockefeller Center for Latin American Studies, Harvard University, 2003); and John Coatsworth and Alan M. Taylor, eds., *Latin America and the World Economy Since 1800* (Cambridge, MA: Harvard University Press, 1998).

16. Adam Przeworski and Carolina Curvale, "Does Politics Explain the Economic Gap between the United States and Latin America?" in *Falling Behind: Explaining the Development Gap between Latin America and the United States*, ed. Francis Fukuyama (New York: Oxford University Press, 2008), 99–133; Adam Przeworski, "The Last Instance: Are Institutions a Deeper Cause of Economic Development?" *European Archives of Sociology* 45, no. 2 (2004): 165–88; Wanderley Guilherme dos Santos, *Kantianas brasileiras: A dual-ética da razão política nacional* (Rio de Janeiro: Paz e Terra, 1984), "Poliarquia em 3D," and *Paradoxos do liberalismo* (Rio de Janeiro: Revan, 1999).

17. For a nostalgic view of these paradigmatic changes in academic politics, see Philippe C. Schmitter, "The Nature and Future of Comparative Politics," *European Political Science* 1, no. 1 (2009): 33–61; and "Seven (Disputable) Theses Concerning the Future of 'Transatlanticised' or 'Globalised' Political Science," *European Political Science* 1, no. 2 (2002): 23–40.

18. Adam Przeworski and Henry Teune, *The Logic of Comparative Social Inquiry* (New York: Wiley-Interscience, 1970). For a specific treatment of recent developments in the discipline, see Carles Boix and Susan C. Stokes, eds., *The Oxford Handbook of Comparative Politics* (New York: Oxford University Press, 2007).

19. Eduardo Viveiros de Castro, *The Relative Native: Essays on Indigenous Conceptual Worlds* (Chicago: Hau Books, 2015), 42 (orig. pub. 2003).

20. See Brodwyn Fischer's critique of various approaches to urban poverty in her *A Poverty of Rights: Citizenship and Inequality in Twentieth-Century Rio de Janeiro* (Stanford, CA: Stanford University Press, 2008); and "A Century in the Present Tense: Crisis, Politics, and the Intellectual History of Brazil's Informal Cities," in *Cities from Scratch: Poverty and Informality in Latin America*, ed. B. Fischer, Bryan McCann, and Javier Auyero (Durham, NC: Duke University Press, 2014), 9–67.

21. See José Moya, "Introduction: Latin America."

22. See, for instance, the discussion of the importance of Habermas's "Öffentlichkeit" as a new political and cultural history, mapped onto the study of the historiographical subfield, Latin America, in Pablo Piccato, "Public Sphere in Latin America: A Map of the Historiography," *Social History* 35, no. 2 (2010): 165–92.

23. James E. Sanders, *The Vanguard of the Atlantic World: Creating Modernity, Nation, and Democracy in Nineteenth-Century Latin America* (Durham, NC: Duke University Press, 2014), 19–20.

24. Greg Grandin, "Living in Revolutionary Time: Coming to Terms with the Violence of Latin America's Long Cold War," in *A Century of Revolution: Insurgent and Counterinsurgent Violence during Latin America's Long Cold War*, ed. Greg Grandin and Gil Joseph (Durham, NC: Duke University Press, 2010), 1–44, quotation, 1.

25. Miguel Ángel Centeno, *Blood and Debt: War and the Nation-State in Latin America* (University Park: Pennsylvania State University Press, 2002), 15, 16, 66.

26. Sanjay Subrahmanyam, *Aux origines de l'histoire globale*, Leçons Inaugurals du Collège de France (Paris: Collège de France, Fayard, 2015).

27. Barão de Teive (Fernando Pessoa), *A educação do estóico* (Lisbon: Assírio & Alvim, 1999), 32.

28. Laura Briggs, Gladys McCormick, and J. T. Way, "Transnationalism: A Category of Analysis," *American Quarterly* 60, no. 3 (2008): 625–48; Frederick Cooper, "What Is the Concept of Globalization Good For? An African Historian's Perspective," *African Affairs* 100, no. 399 (2001): 189–213; Anna Tsing, "The Global Situation," *Cultural Anthropology* 15, no. 3 (2000): 327–60; see the telling review of Thomas Bender, ed., *Rethinking American History in a Global Age*, in Louis A. Perez, "We Are the World: Internationalizing the National, Nationalizing the International," *Journal of American History* 89 (2002): 558–66; Antoinette Burton, "Not Even Remotely Global? Method and Scale in World History," *History Workshop Journal* 64 (2007): 323–28; Sanjay Krishnan, *Reading the Global: Troubling Perspectives on Britain's Empire in Asia* (New York: Columbia University Press, 2007); Graham Murdock and Michael Pickering, "The Birth of Distance: Communications and Changing Conceptions of Elsewhere," in *Narrating Media History*, ed. Michael Bailey (London: Routledge, 2009), 171–83; Lauren Benton, "No Longer Odd Region Out: Repositioning Latin America in World History," *Hispanic American Historical Review* 84 (2004): 423–30; Micol Seigel, "World History's Narrative Problem," *Hispanic American Historical Review* 84 (2004): 431–46; David Sartorius and Micol Seigel, "Introduction: Dislocations Across the Americas," *Social Text* 28, no. 3 (2010): 1–10; Ramón Gutiérrez and Elliott Young, "Transnationalizing Borderlands History," *Western Historical Quarterly* 41, no. 1 (2010): 26–53.

29. Frank Tannenbaum, *Slave and Citizen: The Negro in the Americas* (New York: A. A. Knopf, 1947); Carl Degler, *Neither Black nor White: Slavery and Race Relations in Brazil and the United States* (New York: Macmillan, 1971); Edward E. Telles, *Race in*

Another America (Princeton, NJ: Princeton University Press, 2004); Peter Fry, *A persistência da raça: Ensaios antropológicos sobre o Brasil e a Africa austral* (Rio de Janeiro: Civilização Brasileira, 2005); and Micol Seigel, *Uneven Encounters: Making Race and Nation in Brazil and the United States* (Durham, NC: Duke University Press, 2009).

30. For instance, see François-Xavier Guerra, *Modernidad e independencias: Ensayos sobre las revoluciones hispánicas* (Madrid: Mapfre, 1992); José María Portillo Valdés, *Crisis atlántica: Autonomía e independencia en la crisis de la monarquía hispana* (Madrid: Marcial Pons, 2006); Rafael Rojas, *Las repúblicas de aire: Utopía y desencanto en la revolución de Hispanoamérica* (Madrid: Taurus, 2009).

31. Piccato, "Public Sphere in Latin America."

32. Carlo Ginzburg, "Our Words, and Theirs: A Reflection on the Historian's Craft, Today," *Cromohs* 18 (2013): 115; Jonathan Arac, "Anglo-Globalism?" *New Left Review* (July–August 2002): 35–45.

33. *Iberian Modalities: A Relational Approach to the Study of Culture in the Iberian Peninsula*, ed. J. R. Resina (Liverpool: Liverpool University Press, 2013), 14, 17; for the cosmic power of Castile and for a critique of cultural studies, see J. R. Resina, *Del hispanismo a los estudios ibéricos: Una propuesta federativa para el ámbito cultural* (Madrid: Editorial Biblioteca Nueva, 2009), 127–65.

34. Arnaldo Momigliano, "Historicism Revisited" (1974), in *Essays in Ancient and Modern Historiography* (Chicago: University of Chicago Press, 2012), 368, 370.

35. N. Larsen, "Latin-Americanism without Latin America: 'Theory' as Surrogate Periphery in the Metropolitan University," *A Contracorriente* 3, no 3 (2006): 37–46

36. Ibid., 39, 40.

CHAPTER SEVEN

1. Roger Bartra, ed., *Anatomía del mexicano* (Mexico City: Plaza y Janés, 2002); Jordi Gracia, *La resistencia silenciosa: Fascismo y cultura en España* (Barcelona: Anagrama, 2004); Javier Varela, *La novela de España* (Madrid: Taurus, 1999); Pio Colonnello, *Entre fenomenología y filosofía de la existencia: Ensayo sobre José Gaos* (Mexico City: Analogía Filosófica, 1998); Andrés Lira, "Historia de nuestra idea del mundo en la obra de José Gaos" (Monterrey: Universidad Autónoma de Nuevo), Conferencia presentada el día 23 de septiembre de 2009 en el Centro Cultural Universitario Colegio Civil, 2010; Aurelia Valero Pie, *José Gaos en México: Una biografía intelectual, 1938–1969* (Mexico City: El Colegio de México, 2015); Evaldo Cabral de Mello, *A educação pela guerra* (São Paulo: Penguin Classics, Companhia das Letras, 2014), 17; Fernando Escalante Gonzalbo, in "Identidad, nuestra preclara obsesión: Un diálogo y algo más" (original English version), dialogue with Roger Bartra, Partha Chatterjee, Robin Kelley, Fernando Escalante Gonzalbo, and Sanjay Subrahmanyam, *Istor* 3, no. 11 (2002): 4–29.

2. The final version of *La invención de América* was O'Gorman's reelaboration—in English—of some of his previous works, taking advantage of a six-week stay at Indiana University in 1958—thanks to a grant from the William T. Patten Foundation, which before had brought to Indiana Gilberto Freyre (1944) and later sponsored Jorge Luis Borges (1979). See http://patten.indiana.edu/lecturers2/index.html.

3. José Gaos, *Confesiones profesionales* (Mexico City: Fondo de Cultura Económica, 1958), 163.

4. On the odd trajectory of "identity," see Philip Gleason, "Identifying Identity: A Semantic History," *Journal of American History* 69, no. 4 (1983): 910–31; and Vincent Descombes, *Les embarras de l'identité* (Paris: Gallimard, 2013).

5. José Gaos, *Pensamiento de lengua española* (Mexico City: Editorial Stylo, 1945), 12.

6. Joaquín Barceló, "La confrontación de Ernesto Grassi con Sudamérica," *Revista de Humanidades* 7 (2000): 25–36; on Grassi's criticism of Heidegger and his encounter with Ortega, see Ernesto Grassi, *El poder de la fantasía: Observaciones sobre la historia del pensamiento occidental*, trans. Jorge Navarro Pérez (Rubí: Anthropos, 2013); on Grassi's views of South America, see his *Viajar sin llegar: Un encuentro filosófico con Iberoamérica*, trans. Joaquín Barceló (Rubí: Anthropos; Mexico City: Universidad Autónoma Metropolitana-Iztapalapa, 2008).

7. Leopoldo Zea, *Filosofía de la historia americana* (Mexico City: Fondo de Cultura Económica, 1978), 24.

8. Edmundo O'Gorman, "Hegel y el moderno panamericanismo," *Letras de México*, no. 11 (1939): 14–15.

9. Walter Mignolo, *The Idea of Latin America* (Malden, MA: Blackwell, 2005), 5.

10. Walter Mignolo, "El pensamiento decolonial: Desprendimiento y apertura. Un manifiesto," in *El giro decolonial: Reflexiones para una diversidad epistémica más allá del capitalism global*, ed. Santiago Castro-Gómez and Ramón Grosfoguel (Bogota: Siglo del Hombre Editores, 2007), 37.

11. Enrique Dussel, *Historia de la filosofía latinoamericana y filosofía de la liberación* (Bogota: Editorial Nueva América, 1994), 171.

12. Mignolo, *Idea of Latin America*, 14.

13. Wallace Stevens, from his journal, August 1891, in *The Letters of Wallace Stevens*, ed. H. Stevens (Berkeley: University of California Press, 1966), 32.

14. Victor Sagalen, *Essai sur l'exotisme: Une esthétique du divers* (Paris: Fata Morgana, 1978), 20.

15. Ibid., 41

16. Mignolo, *Idea of Latin America*, xx.

17. Sagalen, *Essai sur l'exotisme*, 44; Fernando Escalante Gonzalbo, in "Identidad, nuestra preclara obsesión" (original English version), 11.

18. See Ribeiro's various Latin American essays in *A América latina existe?* (São Paulo: Fundação Darcy Ribeiro, 2010), 45; see also Helena Maria Bousquet Bomeny, *Darcy Ribeiro: Sociologia de um indisciplinado* (Belo Horizonte: Editora UFMG, 2001).

19. Luis Villoro, *Los grandes momentos del indigenismo en México*, 3rd ed. (Mexico City: El Colegio de México, 1996), 278.

20. William F. Hanks, *Converting Words: Maya in the Age of the Cross* (Berkeley: University of California Press, 2010), 13, 21; Rosa Brambila Paz, ed., *Los otomíes en la mirada de Ángel María Garibay* (Toluca: Instituto Mexiquense de Cultura, 2006), 62; Miguel León Portilla and Patrick Johansson, *Ángel María Garibay: La rueda y el río* (Mexico City: Espejo de Obsidiana Ediciones, 1993), 43.

21. Beltrán, as quoted in Hanks, *Converting Words*, 232.

22. Alfredo López Austin, *La constitución real de México Tenochtitlán* (Mexico City: Universidad Nacional Autónoma de México, 1961).

23. Alberto Flores Galindo, *Buscando un inca* (Lima: Instituto de Apoyo Agrario, 1987), 46.

24. Ibid., 18.

25. Sabine MacCormack, *On the Wings of Time: Rome, the Incas, Spain, and Peru* (Princeton, NJ: Princeton University Press, 2007).

26. Hilary Putnam, *Reason, Truth, and History* (Cambridge: Cambridge University Press, 1981).

27. See Boris Groys, *Sobre lo nuevo*, trans. M. Fontán del Junco (Valencia: Pre-Textos, 2005).

CHAPTER EIGHT

1. Carlos Vaz Ferreira, *Fermentario* (Montivedeo: Cámara de Representantes de la República Oriental del Uruguay, 1957), 104.

2. Timothy Snyder, *The Reconstruction of Nations: Poland, Ukraine, Lithuania, Belarus, 1569–1999* (New Haven, CT: Yale University Press, 2003), 10.

3. Louis Hartz, ed., *The Founding of New Societies: Studies in the History of the United States, Latin America, South Africa, Canada, and Australia* (New York: Harcourt, Brace & World, 1964); Louis Hartz, *The Liberal Tradition in America: An Interpretation of American Political Thought Since the Revolution* (New York: Harcourt, Brace, 1955); Albert O. Hirschman, *Rival Views of Market Society and other Recent Essays* (Cambridge, MA: Harvard University Press, 1992), 133.

4. Harry Harootunian, *The Empire's New Clothes. Paradigm Lost and Regained* (Chicago: Prickly Paradigm Press, 2004), 35.

5. Samuel Moyn and Andrew Sartori, editors, *Global Intellectual History* (New York: Columbia University Press, 2013); C. A. Bayly et al., "AHA Conversation: On Transnational History," *American Historical Review* 111, no. 5 (2006): 1440–64; Sanjay Subrahmanyam, "Historicizing the Global, or Labouring for Invention," *History Workshop Journal* 64, no. 1 (2007): 329–34, and *Aux origines de l'histoire globale*, Leçons Inaugurals du Collège de France (Paris: Collège de France, Fayard, 2015); David Armitage, "The International Turn in Intellectual History," in *Rethinking Modern European Intellectual History*, ed. Darrin M. McMahon and Samuel Moyn (New York: Oxford University Press, 2014), 232–52; Sebastian Conrad, *What Is Global History?* (Princeton, NJ: Princeton University Press, 2016); Jean and John Comaroff, *Theory from the South; or, How Euro-America Is Evolving Toward Africa* (Boulder, CO: Paradigm, 2012); Walter D. Mignolo, "The Global South and World Dis/Order," *Journal of Anthropological Research* 67, no. 2 (2011): 165–88; C. A. Bayly, *The Birth of the Modern World, 1780–1914: Global Connections and Comparisons* (Oxford: Blackwell, 2004); Josep María Fradera, "The West and the Rest en el basurero de la historia," *Revista de libros de la Fundación Caja Madrid*, no. 110 (February 2006): 3–6.

6. Mignolo, "The Global South," 165; J. and J. Comaroff, *Theory from the South*, 45.

7. Martin W. Lewis, "Locating Asia Pacific: The Politics and Practice of Global Division," in *Remaking Area Studies: Teaching and Learning Across Asia and the Pacific*, ed. Terence Wesley-Smith and Jon Gross (Honolulu: University of Hawai'i Press, 2010), 41.

8. Sanjay Subrahmanyam, "Connected Histories: Notes Towards a Reconfiguration of Early Modern Eurasia," *Modern Asian Studies* 31, no. 3 (1997): 737, and *Aux origines de l'histoire globale*; S. Pollock, *The Language of the Gods in the World of Men: Sanskrit, Culture, and Power in Premodern India* (Berkeley: University of California Press, 2006).

9. Greg Grandin, *Empire's Workshop* (New York: Metropolitan Books, 2006); Alan Knight, *U.S.-Mexican Relations, 1910–1940: An Interpretation* (San Diego: Center for U.S.-Mexican Studies, University of California, San Diego, 1987); Amy Kaplan and Donald E. Pease, eds., *Cultures of United States Imperialism* (Durham, NC: Duke University Press, 1993); Paul A. Kramer, *The Blood of Government: Race, Empire, the United States, and the Philippines* (Chapel Hill: University of North Carolina Press, 2006); Vicente Rafael, *White Love and Other Events in Filipino History* (Durham, NC: Duke University Press, 2000); Augusto Fauni Espiritu, *Five Faces of Exile: The Nation and Filipino American Intellectuals* (Stanford, CA: Stanford University Press, 2005); José Luis Ramos, "Diplomacy, Social Politics, and United States-Mexico Relations

After the Mexican Revolution, 1919–1930," PhD diss., University of Chicago, 2014. On the nuances of the Cold War among intellectuals, see Patrick Iber, *Neither Peace nor Freedom: The Cultural Cold War in Latin America* (Cambridge, MA: Harvard University Press, 2015).

10. Debra Thompson, "Nation and Miscegenation: Comparing Anti-Miscegenation Regulations in North America," online at https://www.cpsa-acsp.ca/papers-2008/Thompson.pdf, 11.

11. Marixa Lasso, *Myths of Harmony: Race and Republicanism During the Age of Revolution: Colombia, 1795–1831* (Pittsburgh, PA: University of Pittsburgh Press, 2007); David Nirenberg, "Was There Race before Modernity? The Example of 'Jewish' Blood in Late Medieval Spain," in *The Origins of Racism in the West*, ed. Miriam Eliav-Feldon, Benjamin Isaac, and Joseph Ziegler (Cambridge: Cambridge University Press, 2009), 232–64; Enric Ucelay-Da Cal, "The Influence of Animal Breeding on Political Racism," *History of European Ideas* 15, nos. 4–6 (1992): 717–25; Colin Kidd, *The Forging of Races: Race and Scripture in the Protestant Atlantic World, 1600–2000* (Cambridge: Cambridge University Press, 2006); Robert C. Young, *Colonial Desire: Hybridity in Theory, Culture and Race* (London: Routledge, 1995); Edward E. Telles, *Race in Another America* (Princeton, NJ: Princeton University Press, 2004); María Elena Martínez, *Genealogical Fictions: Limpieza de Sangre, Religion, and Gender in Colonial Mexico* (Stanford, CA: Stanford University Press, 2008); Brian Owensby, *Empire of Law and Indian Justice in Colonial Mexico* (Stanford, CA: Stanford University Press, 2008); Roger M. Smith, *Civic Ideals: Conflicting Visions of Citizenship in U.S. History* (New Haven, CT: Yale University Press, 1997); Joyce E. Chaplin, *Subject Matter: Technology, the Body, and Science on the Anglo-American Frontier, 1500–1676* (Cambridge, MA: Harvard University Press, 2001); Sarah Carter, "Aboriginal People of Canada and the British Empire," in *The Oxford History of the British Empire: Canada and the British Empire*, ed., Phillip Buckner (Oxford: Oxford University Press, 2008), 200–219; Victoria Freeman, "Attitudes Toward 'Miscegenation' in Canada, the United States, New Zealand, and Australia, 1860–1914," *Native Studies Review* 16, no. 1 (2005): 41–69; Charles Taylor, "The Politics of Recognition," in *Philosophical Arguments* (Cambridge, MA: Harvard University Press, 1995), 225–56; Lucy Eldersveld Murphy, *A Gathering of Rivers: Indians, Métis, and Mining in the Western Great Lakes, 1737–1832* (Lincoln: University of Nebraska Press, 2000); Emmanuelle Saada, *Les enfants de la colonie: Les métis de l'empire français entre sujétion et citoyenneté* (Paris: Découverte, 2007); David A. Hollinger, *Cosmopolitanism and Solidarity: Studies in Ethnoracial, Religious, and Professional Affiliation in the United States* (Madison: University of Wisconsin Press, 2006); Peggy Pascoe, *What Comes Naturally: Miscegenation Law and the Making of Race in America* (New York: Oxford University Press, 2009); Ariela J. Gross, *What Blood Won't Tell: A History of Race on Trial in America* (Cambridge: Harvard University Press, 2008); Joanne Rappaport, *The Disappearing Mestizo: Configuring Difference in the Colonial New Kingdom of Granada* (Durham, NC: Duke University Press, 2014); Josep María Fradera, "A cultura de 'castas' e a formação do cidadão moderno (Um ensaio sobre a particularidade do Império espanhol)," in *A experiência constitucional de Cádiz: Espanha, Portugal e Brasil*, ed. Márcia Regina Berbel and Cécilia Helena de Salles de Oliveira (São Paulo: Alameda, 2013), 77–108.

12. Solange Alberro and Pilar Gonzalbo, *La sociedad novohispana: Estereotipos y realidades* (Mexico City: El Colegio de México, 2013), 27.

13. Lasso, *Myths of Harmony.*

14. Martínez, *Genealogical Fictions.*

15. Fradera, "A cultura de 'castas' e a formação do cidadão moderno."

16. See Jürgen Leonhardt, *Latin: Story of a World Language*, trans. Kenneth Kronenberg (Cambridge, MA: The Belknap Press of Harvard University Press, 2013).

17. Inga Clendinnen, "The History Question: Who Owns the Past?" *Quarterly Essay*, no. 23 (2007): 12.

18. Emilio Kourí, *The Making of the Ejido*, unpublished MS. I thank Emilio Kourí for sharing his manuscript.

19. Fernando Escalante Gonzalbo in "Identidad, nuestra preclara obsesión: Un diálogo y algo más" (original English version), dialogue with Roger Bartra, Partha Chatterjee, Robin Kelley, Fernando Escalante Gonzalbo, and Sanjay Subrahmanyam, *Istor* 3, no. 11 (2002): 4–29; Kourí, *Making of the Ejido*; Richard M. Morse, *El espejo de Próspero*, trans. Stella Mastrangelo (Mexico City: Siglo XXI, 1986).

20. Sabine MacCormack, *On the Wings of Time: Rome, the Incas, Spain, and Peru* (Princeton, NJ: Princeton University Press, 2007).

21. Alberto Flores Galindo, *Buscando un inca* (Lima: Instituto de Apoyo Agrario, 1987), 411.

22. Ibid., 24.

23. Ibid., 49.

24. Ibid., 138.

25. Arguedas, quoted in ibid., 282.

26. See P. Moreira, *Literary and Cultural Relations between Brazil and Mexico: Deep Undercurrents* (New York: Palgrave Macmillan, 2013); Robert P. Newcomb, *Nossa and Nuestra América: Inter-American Dialogues* (West Lafayette, IN: Purdue University Press, 2012); and a nice example of a historian of Brazil able to understand and contribute to the history of Spanish-American independences: Richard Graham, *Independence in Latin America: A Comparative Approach*, 2nd ed. (New York: McGraw-Hill, 1994); or the example of historians of Spain contributing simultaneously to Latin American history: José María Portillo Valdés, *Crisis atlántica*, and *Revolución de nación: Orígenes de la cultura constitucional en España, 1780–1812* (Madrid: Centro de Estudios Políticos y Constitucionales, 2000); Josep María Fradera, *Colonias para después de un imperio* (Barcelona: Ediciones Bellaterra, 2005); Josep María Fradera, *Gobernar colonias* (Barcelona: Ediciones Península, 1999); Josep María Fradera, *La nación imperial*, 2 vols. (Barcelona: Edhasa, 2015).

27. For a recent example, see Gregory T. Cushman, *Guano and the Opening of the Pacific World: A Global Ecological History* (Cambridge: Cambridge University Press, 2013).

28. Viktor Shklovski, *La tercera fábrica: Érase una vez* (1926), trans. Irina Bogdaschevski (Buenos Aires: Fondo de Cultura Económica, 2012), 43. For US history, this synthesis has been at least attempted, and one hopes that the attempt continues; see David Thelen, "Of Audiences, Borderlands, and Comparisons: Toward the Internationalization of American History," *Journal of American History* 79 (1992): 432–62; D. Thelen and Roy Rosenzweig, *The Presence of the Past: Popular Uses of History in American Life* (New York: Columbia University Press, 1998); Ian Tyrell, "American Exceptionalism in an Age of International History," *American Historical Review* 96, no. 4 (1991): 1031–55; Thomas Bender, ed., *Rethinking American History in a Global Age* (Berkeley: University of California Press, 2002), and *A Nation Among Nations: America's Place in World History* (New York: Hill & Wang, 2006).

29. Savoie Lottinville, *The Rhetoric of History* (Norman: University of Oklahoma Press, 1976), 6.

BIBLIOGRAPHY

Acemoglu, Daron, and James A. Robinson. *Why Nations Fall: Origins of Power, Prosperity and Poverty*. New York: Crown, 2012.

Agnelli, Arduino. *La genesi dell'idea di Mitteleuropa*. Milan: Dott. A. Giuffrè Editore, 1971.

Aken, Mark J. van. *Pan-Hispanism: Its Origin and Development to 1866*. Berkeley: University of California Press, 1959.

Aleixandre, Vicente. "Rostro final." In *Obras completas*, vol. 2. Madrid: Aguilar, 1977.

Álvarez Junco, José. *Mater dolorosa: La idea de España en el siglo XIX*. Madrid: Taurus, 2001.

Álvarez, Sonia, Arturo Arias, and Charles R. Hale. "Re-Visioning Latin American Studies." *Cultural Anthropology* 26, no. 2 (2011): 225–46.

Amante, Adriana. *Poéticas y políticas del destierro: Argentinos en Brasil en la época de Rosas*. Buenos Aires: Fondo de Cultura Económica, 2010.

Ardao, Arturo. *Génesis de la idea y el nombre de América Latina*. Caracas: Centro de Estudios Latinoamericanos Rómulo Gallegos, 1980.

———. *Romania y América Latina*. Montevideo: Biblioteca Marcha, Universidad de la República Oriental del Uruguay, 1991.

Armony, Victor. "Des Latins du Nord? L'identité culturelle québécoise dans le contexte panaméricain." *Recherches Sociographiques* 43, no. 1 (2002): 19–48.

Arosemena, Justo. *Constituciones políticas de la América meridional*, 2 vols. Havre: Imprenta A. Lemale Ainé, 1870.

———. *Estudios constitucionales sobre los gobiernos de la América latina*. Paris: A. Roger and F. Chernoviz, 1888.

———. *Estudios sobre la idea de una liga americana*. Lima: Imprenta de Huerta, 1864.

Ayala Mora, Enrique. "El origen del nombre América Latina y la tradición católica del siglo XIX." *Anuario Colombiano de Historia Social y de la Cultura* 40, no. 1 (2013): 213–41.

Bandeira, Moniz. *Brasil, Argentina e Estados Unidos: Conflito e integração na América do Sul (da Tríplice Aliança ao Mercosul, 1870–2003)*. Rio de Janeiro: Revan, 2003.

Barbosa, Francisco de Assis, ed. *Raízes do Sérgio Buarque de Holanda*. Rio de Janeiro: Rocco, 1989.

Barboza Filho, Rubem. *Tradicão e artifício: Iberismo e barroco na formação americana*. Rio de Janeiro: IUPERJ, 2000.

Barrios, Miguel Ángel. *El latinoamericanismo en el pensamiento político de Manuel Ugarte.* Buenos Aires: Editorial Biblos, 2007.

Bartra, Roger, ed. *Anatomía del mexicano.* Mexico City: Plaza y Janés, 2002.

Bartra, Roger. *La jaula de la melancolía: Identidad y metamorfosis del mexicano.* Mexico City: Grijalbo, 1987.

Bayly, C. A. *The Birth of the Modern World, 1780–1914: Global Connections and Comparisons.* Oxford: Blackwell, 2004.

Beasley-Murray, Jon, ed. "The New Latin Americanism: Cultural Studies Beyond Borders." Special issue, *Journal of Latin American Cultural Studies* 11, no. 3 (2002).

———. *Posthegemony: Political Theory and Latin America.* Minneapolis: University of Minnesota Press, 2010.

Bernecker, Walther L., and Hans Werner Tobler, eds. *Development and Underdevelopment in America: Contrast of Economic Growth in North and Latin America in Historical Perspective.* Berlin: Walter de Gruyter, 1993.

Bethell, Leslie. "O Brasil e a ideia de 'América Latina' em perspectiva histórica." *Revista Estudos Históricos* 22, no. 44 (2009): 289–321.

Beverley, John. *Latinamericanism after 9/11.* Durham, NC: Duke University Press, 2011.

Bilbao, Francisco. *Obras completas de Francisco Bilbao.* 2 vols. Buenos Aires: Impr. de Buenos Aires, 1866–65.

Blanchard, R. A. E. "Les tableaux du métissage au Mexique." *Journal de la Société des Américanistes* 5, no. 1 (1908): 59–66.

Blanton, Carlos Kevin. *George I. Sanchez: The Long Fight for Mexican American Integration.* New Haven, CT: Yale University Press, 2014.

Bomeny, Helena Maria Bousquet. *Darcy Ribeiro: Sociologia de um indisciplinado.* Belo Horizonte: Editora UFMG, 2001.

Bomfim, Manoel. *A América latina: Males de origem.* Rio de Janeiro: H. Garnier, 1905.

Braudel, Fernand. "Y a-t-il une Amérique latine?" *Annales ESC* 3 (1948): 467–71.

Brilliant, Mark. *The Color of America Has Changed: How Racial Diversity Shaped Civil Rights Reform in California, 1941–1978.* New York: Oxford University Press, 2010.

Buarque de Holanda, Sérgio. *O espírito e a letra: Estudos de crítica literária.* Edited by Antonio Arnoni Prado. 2 vols. São Paulo: Companhia das Letras, 1996.

———. *Raízes do Brasil.* Rio de Janeiro: José Olympio, 1976.

Cabral de Mello, Evaldo. *A educação pela guerra.* São Paulo: Penguin Classics, Companhia das Letras, 2014.

Cancel, Luis R., ed. *The Latin American Spirit: Art and Artists in the United States, 1920–1970.* New York: Bronx Museum of the Arts, Harry N. Abrams, 1988.

Cândido, António. *Recortes.* Rio de Janeiro: Ouro sobre Azul, 2004.

Castro-Gómez, Santiago. *Crítica de la razón latinoamericana.* Barcelona: Puvil Libros, 1996.

———, and Ramón Grosfoguel, eds. *El giro decolonial: Reflexiones para una diversidad epistémica más allá del capitalism global.* Bogota: Siglo del Hombre Editores, 2007.

Centeno, Miguel Ángel. *Blood and Debt: War and the Nation-State in Latin America.* University Park: Pennsylvania State University Press, 2002.

———, and Fernando López-Alves, eds. *The Other Mirror: Grand Theory Through the Lens of Latin America.* Princeton, NJ: Princeton University Press, 2001.

Chevalier, Michel. *France, Mexico, and the Confederate States.* Translated by Wm. Henry Hurlbut. New York: C. B. Richardson, 1863.

———. *Society, Manners, and Politics in the United States.* Boston: Weeks, Jordan, 1839.

Coatsworth, John, and Alan M. Taylor, eds. *Latin America and the World Economy Since 1800*. Cambridge, MA: Harvard University Press, 1998.

———, and G. Tortella Casares. *Institutions and Long-Run Economic Performance in Mexico and Spain, 1800–2000*. Working Paper, Cambridge, David Rockefeller Center for Latin American Studies, Harvard University, 2003.

Colajanni, Napoleone. *Latini e anglo-sassoni (Razze inferiori e razze superiori)*. Rome: Revista Popolare, 1906.

Colombi, Beatriz. *Viaje intelectual: Migraciones y desplazamientos en América Latina, 1880–1915*. Rosario: B. Viterbo Editora, 2004.

Comaroff, Jean, and John Comaroff. *Theory from the South; or, How Euro-America Is Evolving Toward Africa*. Boulder, CO: Paradigm, 2012.

Conde Aguiar, Ronaldo. *O rebelde esquecido: Tempo, vida e obra de Manoel Bomfim*. Rio de Janeiro: Topbooks, 2000.

Conrad, Sebastian. *What Is Global History?* Princeton, NJ: Princeton University Press, 2016.

Coronado, Raúl. *A World Not to Come: A History of Latino Writing and Print Culture*. Cambridge, MA: Harvard University Press, 2013.

Couillard, Marie, and Patrick Imbert, eds. *Les discours du Nouveau Monde au XIXe siècle au Canada français et en Amérique latine*. New York: Legas, 1995.

Dávila, Arlene. *Latinos, Inc.: The Marketing and Making of a People*. Berkeley: University of California Press, 2001.

Demers, Maurice. "Pan-Americanism Re-Invented in Uncle Sam's Backyard: Catholic and Latin Identity in French Canada and Mexico in the First Half of the 20th Century." PhD diss., York University, 2010.

Descombes, Vincent. *Les embarras de l'identité*. Paris: Gallimard, 2013.

Díaz Quiñonez, Arcadio. *Sobre los principios: Los intelectuales caribeños y la tradición*. Buenos Aires: Universidad Nacional de Quilmes, 2006.

Dussel, Enrique. *Historia de la filosofía latinoamericana y filosofía de la liberación*. Bogota: Editorial Nueva América, 1994.

Ellison, Fred P. *Alfonso Reyes e o Brasil: Um mexicano entre os cariocas*. Rio de Janeiro: Topbooks, 2002.

Escalante Gonzalbo, Fernando. *El crimen como realidad y representación*. Mexico City: El Colegio de México, 2012.

———. *Historia mínima del neoliberalismo*. Mexico City: El Colegio de México, 2015.

———. *In the Eyes of God: A Study on the Culture of Suffering*. Translated by Jessica C. Locke. Austin: University of Texas Press, 2006.

Escobar, Arturo. *Encountering Development: The Making and Unmaking of the Third World*. Princeton, NJ: Princeton University Press, 1995.

Espinosa, Aurelio M. *América española o hispano América: El término América latina es erróneo*. Translated by Felipe M. de Septién. Madrid: Comisaría Regia del Turismo, 1919.

———. *The Folklore of Spain in the American Southwest*. Edited by J. Manuel Espinosa. Norman: University of Oklahoma Press, 1985.

———. *The Spanish Language in New Mexico and Southern Colorado*. Santa Fe: New Mexican Printing Company, 1911.

Estrade, Paul. "Del invento de 'América Latina' en París por latinoamericanos (1856–1889)." In *París y el mundo ibérico e iberoamericano: Actas del XXVIII Congreso de la Sociedad de Hispanistas Franceses, París, 21, 22 y 23 de marzo de 1997*, edited by Jacques Maurice and Marie-Claire Zimmermann, 179–88. Paris: Université de Paris X, Nanterre, 1998.

Eyzaguirre, José Ignacio Víctor. *Los intereses católicos en América*. Paris: Librería de Garnier Hermanos, 1859, 1:iv–v.

Feres, João. *A história do conceito de "Latin America" nos Estados Unidos*. Bauru, Brazil: EDUSC, 2005.

Filippi, Fabio. *Una vita pagana: Enrico Corradini dal superomismo dannunziano a una politica di massa*. Florence: Vallecchi Editore, 1989.

Flores Galindo, Alberto. *Buscando un inca*. Lima: Instituto de Apoyo Agrario, 1987.

Flores, Ruben. *Backroads Pragmatists: Mexico's Melting Pot and Civil Rights in the United States*. Philadelphia: University of Pennsylvania Press, 2014.

Foley, Neil. *The White Scourge: Mexicans, Blacks, and Poor Whites in Texas Cotton Culture*. Berkeley: University of California Press, 1997.

Fonseca, Edson Nery da, and Gilberto Freyre. *Americanidade e latinidade da América Latina e outros textos afins*. Brasilia: Editora UnB; São Paulo, Imprensa Oficial, 2003.

Fradera, Josep María. *La nación imperial*. 2 vols. Barcelona: Edhasa, 2015.

Freyre, Gilberto. *O brasileiro entre os outros hispanos: Afinidades, contrastes e possíveis futuros nas suas interrelações*. Rio de Janeiro: Livraria José Olympio, 1975.

Frigessi, Delia. *Cesare Lombroso*. Torino: Giulio Einaudi Editore, 2003.

Fry, Peter. *A persistência da raça: Ensaios antropológicos sobre o Brasil e a Africa austral*. Rio de Janeiro: Civilização Brasileira, 2005.

Gaos, José. *Confesiones profesionales*. Mexico City: Fondo de Cultura Económica, 1958.

———. *Pensamiento de lengua española*. Mexico City: Editorial Stylo, 1945.

García Calderón, Francisco. *Les démocraties latines de l'Amérique*. Paris: Ernest Flammarion, 1912.

Gay, Daniel. *Les élites québécoises et l'Amérique latine*. Montreal: Nouvelle Optique, 1983.

Gerab Baggio, Kátia. "A 'outra' América: A América Latina na visão dos intelectuais brasileiros das primeiras décadas republicanas." PhD diss., Universidade de São Paulo, 1998.

Gilman, Nils. *Mandarins of the Future: Modernization Theory in Cold War America*. Baltimore, MD: John Hopkins University Press, 2003.

Gobat, Michel. "The Invention of Latin America: A Transnational History of Anti-Imperialism, Democracy, and Race." *American Historical Review* 118, no. 5 (2013): 1345–75.

Gobineau, Arthur, Comte de. *Œuvres*. Paris: Gallimard, 1983.

González, Alexandra Pita, and Carlos Marichal Salinas, eds. *Pensar el antiimperialismo: Ensayos de historia intelectual latinoamericana, 1900–1930*. Mexico City: El Colegio de México, Universidad de Colima, 2012.

González, Robert Alexander. *Designing Pan-America: U.S. Architectural Visions for the Western Hemisphere*. Austin: University of Texas Press, 2011.

Gracia, Jordi. *La resistencia silenciosa: Fascismo y cultura en España*. Barcelona: Anagrama, 2004.

Gracia, Jorge E., and Elizabeth Millan-Zaibert, eds. *Latin American Philosophy for the 21st Century*. New York: Prometheus Books, 2004.

Grandin, Greg. *Empire's Workshop*. New York: Metropolitan Books, 2006.

Grassi, Ernesto. *Viajar sin llegar: Un encuentro filosófico con Iberoamérica*. Translated from German by Joaquín Barceló. Rubí: Anthropos; Mexico City: Universidad Autónoma Metropolitana-Iztapalapa, 2008.

Guerra, François-Xavier. *Modernidad e independencias: Ensayos sobre las revoluciones hispánicas*. Madrid: Mapfre, 1992.

Gutiérrez, Ramón A. "What's in a Name? The History and Politics of Hispanic and Latino

Panethnic Identities." In *The Contours of Latino Studies*, edited by Tomás Almaguer and Ramón A. Gutiérrez. Berkeley: University of California Press, forthcoming.

———, and Genaro Padilla, eds. *Recovering the U. S. Hispanic Literary Heritage*. Vol. 3. Houston: Arte Público Press, 2000.

Hale, Charles A. "Political and Social Ideas in Latin America, 1970–1930." In *The Cambridge History of Latin America*, edited by Leslie Bethell, 367–442. Vol. 4. Cambridge: Cambridge University Press, 1986.

Hanks, William F. *Converting Words: Maya in the Age of the Cross*. Berkeley: University of California Press, 2010.

Harcourt, Bernard E. *The Illusion of Free Markets*. Cambridge, MA: Harvard University Press, 2011.

Hartz, Louis, ed. *The Founding of New Societies. Studies in the History of the United States, Latin America, South Africa, Canada, and Australia*. New York: Harcourt, Brace & World, 1964.

Hespanha, António Manuel. *As vésperas do Leviathan: Instituções e poder político, Portugal século XVII*. Coimbra: Livraia Almedina, 1994.

Hollinger, David. *Postethnic America: Beyond Multiculturalism*. New York: Basic Books, 1995.

Ianni, Octavio. *O laberinto latinoamericano*. São Paulo: Voces, 1993.

Iber, Patrick. *Neither Peace nor Freedom: The Cultural Cold War in Latin America*. Cambridge, MA: Harvard University Press, 2015.

International Center for the Arts of the Americas at the Museum of Fine Arts, Houston. Documents of 20th-Century Latin American and Latino Art, A Digital Archive, http://icaadocs.mfah.org/icaadocs/en-us/about/theproject/whatistheicaadocumentsprojeet.aspx.

Irby, James A. *Backdoor at Bagdad: The Civil War on the Rio Grande*. El Paso: Texas Western Press, University of Texas at El Paso, 1977.

Jaksić, Iván. *Ven conmigo a la España lejana: Los intelectuales norteamericanos ante el mundo hispano, 1820–1880*. Santiago: Fondo de Cultura Económica, 2007.

Kagan, Richard, ed. *Spain in America: The Origins of Hispanism in the United States*. Chicago: University of Illinois Press, 2002.

Kaplowitz, Craig. *LULAC, Mexican Americans and National Policy*. College Station: Texas A&M University Press, 2005.

Kohn, Hans. *Pan-Slavism, Its History and Ideology*. Notre Dame, IN: University of Notre Dame Press, 1953.

Lallemand, Claude-François. *Le hachych*. Paris: Paulin, 1843.

Larsen, Neil. "Latin America as a Historico-Philosophical Relation." *CR: The New Centennial Review* 3, no 1 (2003): 55–66.

———. "Latin-Americanism without Latin America: 'Theory' as Surrogate Periphery in the Metropolitan University." *A Contracorriente* 3, no 3 (2006): 37–46.

Lasso, Marixa. *Myths of Harmony: Race and Republicanism during the Age of Revolution, Colombia, 1795–1831*. Pittsburgh, PA: University of Pittsburgh Press, 2007.

Lastarria, José Victorino, Álvaro Covarrubias, Domingo Santa María, and Benjamín Vicuña Mackenna. *Colección de ensayos i documentos relativos a la unión i confederación de los pueblos hispano-americanos. Publicada a espensas de la "Sociedad de la unión americana de Santiago de Chile," por una comisión nombrada por la misma i compuesta de los señores don José Victorino Lastarria, don Álvaro Covarrubias, don Domingo Santa María i don Benjamín Vicuña Mackenna*. Santiago: Imprenta Chilena, 1862.

Levallois, Michel. *Ismaÿl Urbain (1812–1884): Une autre conquête de l'Algérie*. Paris: Maisonneuve et Larose, 2001.

MacCormack, Sabine. *On the Wings of Time: Rome, the Incas, Spain, and Peru.* Princeton, NJ: Princeton University Press, 2007.

Marfany, Joan-Lluís. *La cultura del catalanisme: El nacionalisme en els seus inicis.* Barcelona: Biblioteca Universal Empúries, 1995.

———. *La llengua maltractada: El castellà i el català a Catalunya del segle XVI al segle XIX.* Barcelona: Editorial Empúries, 2001.

Mariátegui, José Carlos. *Temas de nuestra América.* Vol. 12 of *Obras completas de Mariátegui.* Lima: Biblioteca Amauta, 1960.

Martí, José. *Guatemala.* Guatemala City: Universidad de San Carlos de Guatemala, 1998.

———. *Los Estados Unidos.* Madrid: Sociedad Española de Librerías, 1915.

Martínez, María Elena. *Genealogical Fictions: Limpieza de Sangre, Religion, and Gender in Colonial Mexico.* Stanford, CA: Stanford University Press, 2008.

Martínez Estrada, Ezequiel. *Diferencias y semejanzas entre los países de América Latina.* Mexico City: Universidad Nacional Autónoma de México, 1962.

McGuinness, Aims. "Searching for 'Latin America': Race and Sovereignty in the Americas in the 1850s." In *Race and Nation in Modern Latin America,* edited by Nancy P. Appelbaum, Anne S. Macpherson, and Karin Alejandra Rosemblatt, 87–107. Chapel Hill: University of North Carolina Press, 2003.

Medina Ascensio, Luis. *Historia del Colegio Pío Latino Americano (Roma: 1858–1978).* Mexico City: Jus, 1979.

Meireles Pereira, Maria da Conceição. *A questão ibérica: Imprensa e Opinião (1850–1870).* 2 vols. PhD diss., Universidade do Porto, 1995.

Mignolo, Walter D. "The Global South and World Dis/Order." *Journal of Anthropological Research* 67, no. 2 (2011): 165–88.

———. *The Idea of Latin America.* Malden, MA: Blackwell, 2005.

Mires, Fernando. *El discurso de la miseria, o la crisis de la sociología en América Latina.* Caracas: Nueva Sociedad, 1993.

Momigliano, Arnaldo. *Essays in Ancient and Modern Historiography.* Chicago: University of Chicago Press, 2012.

Mora, G. Cristina. *Making Hispanics: How Activists, Bureaucrats, and Media Constructed a New American.* Chicago: University of Chicago Press, 2014.

Moraña, Mabel, Enrique Dussel, and Carlos A. Jáuregui, eds. *Coloniality at Large: Latin America and the Postcolonial Debate.* Durham, NC: Duke University Press, 2008.

Moreira, Paulo. *Literary and Cultural Relations between Brazil and Mexico: Deep Undercurrents.* New York: Palgrave Macmillan, 2013.

Moreno Luzón, Javier, and José M. Núñez Seixas. *Ser españoles, imaginarios nacionales en el siglo XX.* Barcelona: RBA, 2013.

Morgan, Edmund S. *Inventing the People: The Rise of Popular Sovereignty in England and America.* New York: W. W. Norton, 1988.

Morrison, Michael A. *Slavery and the American West: The Eclipse of Manifest Destiny and the Coming of the Civil War.* Chapel Hill: University of North Carolina Press, 1997.

Morse, Richard M. *El espejo de Próspero.* Translated by Stella Mastrangelo. Mexico City: Siglo XXI, 1986.

———. *New World Soundings: Culture and Ideology in the Americas.* Baltimore, MD: John Hopkins University Press, 1989.

Mosquera, Gerardo. "Good-bye identidad, welcome diferencia. Del arte latinoamericano al arte desde América Latina: Transitos globales" (2000), available online at www.fba.unlp.edu.ar/visuales4/Mosquera.doc.

Moya, José, ed. *The Oxford Handbook of Latin American History*. New York: Oxford University Press, 2010.

Moyn, Samuel, and Andrew Sartori, eds. *Global Intellectual History*. New York: Columbia University Press, 2013.

Narloch, Leandro, and Duda Teixeira. *Guia politicamente incorreto da América Latina*. São Paulo: Leya, 2011.

Newcomb, Robert P. *Nossa and Nuestra América: Inter-American Dialogues*. West Lafayette, IN: Purdue University Press, 2012.

Nietzsche, Friedrich, "On the Uses and Disadvantages of History in Life," in *Untimely Meditations*, trans. R. J. Hollingdale, 57–124. Cambridge: Cambridge University Press, 1997.

O'Gorman, Edmundo. *Conciencia de la historia: Ensayos escogidos*. Mexico City: Consejo Nacional para la Cultura y las Artes, 2011.

———. *La invención de América: Investigación acerca de la estructura histórica del Nuevo Mundo y del sentido de su devenir*. 3rd ed. Mexico City: Fondo de Cultura Económica, 2001.

Oliveira Lima, Manuel de. *América latina e America ingleza: A evolução brazileira comparada com a hispano-americana e com a anglo-americana*. Rio de Janeiro: Livraria Garnier, 1913.

Packenham, Robert. *The Dependency Movement: Scholarship and Politics in Development Studies*. Cambridge, MA: Harvard University Press, 1992.

Pakkasvirta, Jussi. *Nationalism and Continentalism in Latin American History*. Institute of Development Studies, University of Helsinki, Working Papers (14/96), online at http://www.helsinki.fi/aluejakulttuurintutkimus/tutkimus/xaman/articulos/9701/ 9701_jup.html.

Palomino, Pablo. "Nationalist, Hemispheric, and Global: 'Latin American Music' and the Music Division of the Pan American Union, 1939–1947." *Nouveaux mondes, mondes nouveaux—Novo Mundo, Mundos Novos—New World, New Worlds* (2015), online at http://nuevomundo.revues.org/68062.

Palti, Elías José, ed. *Mito y realidad de la cultura política latinoamericana*. Buenos Aires: Prometeo, 2010.

Panick, Käthe. *La race latine: Politischer Romanismus im Frankreich des 19. Jahrhunderts*. Bonn: Röhrscheid, 1978.

Pascoe, Peggy. *What Comes Naturally: Miscegenation Law and the Making of Race in America*. New York: Oxford University Press, 2009.

Patriarca, Silvana. *Italian Vices: Nation and Character from the Risorgimento to the Republic*. Cambridge: Cambridge University Press, 2010.

Phelan, John L. "Pan-Latinism, French Intervention in Mexico (1861–1867) and the Genesis of the Idea of Latin America." In *Conciencia y autenticidad histórica*, edited by José Ortega y Medina, 123–77. Mexico City: Universidad Nacional Autónoma de México, 1968.

Piñero, Gabriela A. "Políticas de representación/políticas de inclusión: La actualización del debate de lo latinoamericano en el arte durante la primera etapa de la globalización (1980–1990)." *Anales del Instituto de Investigaciones Estéticas* 36, no. 104 (2014): 157–86.

Pollock, Sheldon. *The Language of the Gods in the World of Men: Sanskrit, Culture, and Power in Premodern India*. Berkeley: University of California Press, 2006.

Portillo Valdés, José María. *Crisis atlántica: Autonomía e independencia en la crisis de la monarquía hispana*. Madrid: Marcial Pons, 2006.

———. *Monarquia y gobierno provincial: Poder y constitución en las provincias vascas (1760–1808)*. Madrid: Centro de Estudios Constitucionales, 1991.

Prat de la Riba, Enric. *La nacionalitat catalana*. Barcelona: L'Anuari de la Exportació, 1906.

Preuss, Ori. *Bridging the Island: Brazilians' Views of Spanish America and Themselves, 1865–1912*. Frankfurt: Iberoamericana Vervuert, 2011.

———. *Transnational South America: Experiences, Ideas, and Identities, 1860–1920*. New York: Routledge, 2016.

Quijada, Mónica. "Latinos y anglosajones: El 98 en el fin de siglo sudamericano." *Hispania* 57, no. 196 (1997): 589–609.

———. "Sobre el orígen y difusión del nombre 'América Latina': O una variación heterodoxa en torno al tema de la construcción social de la verdad." *Revista de Indias* 58, no. 214 (1998): 595–616.

Quijano, Aníbal. *Modernidad, identidad y utopía en América Latina*. Lima: Ediciones Sociedad Política, 1988.

Rafanell, August. *La il·lusió occitana*. 2 vols. Barcelona: Quaderns Crema, 2006.

Ranke, Leopold von. *History of the Latin and Teutonic Nations (1491 to 1514)*. Translated by Philip A. Ashworth. London: George Bell and Sons, 1887.

Reséndez, Andrés. *Changing National Identities at the Frontier: Texas and New Mexico, 1800–1850*. New York: Cambridge University Press, 2004.

Resina, Joan R. *Del hispanismo a los estudios ibéricos: Una propuesta federativa para el ámbito cultural*. Madrid: Editorial Biblioteca Nueva, 2009.

———, ed. *Iberian Modalities: A Relational Approach to the Study of Culture in the Iberian Peninsula*. Liverpool: Liverpool University Press, 2013.

Ribeiro, Darcy. *A América latina existe?* São Paulo: Fundação Darcy Ribeiro, 2010.

Rippy, J. Fred. "Literary Yankeephobia in Hispanic America." *Journal of International Relations* 12, no. 3 (1922): 350–71.

———. "Literary Yankeephobia in Hispanic America (Concluded)." *Journal of International Relations* 12, no. 4 (1922): 524–38.

Rist, Gilbert. *Le développement: Histoire d'une croyance occidentale*. Paris: Presses de Sciences Po, 1996.

Rivera, Salvador. *Latin American Unification: A History of Political and Economic Integration Efforts*. London: McFarland, 2014.

Robb, John Donald. *Hispanic Folk Music of New Mexico and the Southwest*. Albuquerque: University of New Mexico Press, 2014.

Roche, Alphonse V. *Provençal Regionalism: A Study of the Movement in the Revue Félibréenne, Le feu, and Other Reviews of Southern France*. Evanston, IL: Northwestern University Press, 1954.

Rodgers, Daniel. *Age of Fracture*. Cambridge, MA: Harvard University Press, 2011.

Rojas, Rafael. *Las repúblicas de aire: Utopía y desencanto en la revolución de Hispanoamérica*. Madrid: Taurus, 2009.

———. "Plumas que matan: El duelo intelectual entre Gabriel García Moreno y Juan Montalvo en el XIX ecuatoriano." *Istor* 12, no. 50 (2012): 7–37.

Rojas Mix, Miguel. *Los cien nombres de América, eso que descubrió Colón*. Barcelona: Lumen, 1991.

Rubió i Tudurí, Nicolau María. *Llatins en servitud, París 1940–1944*. Translated from French by J. M. Quintana. Barcelona: Leonard Muntaner Editor, 2006.

———. *La patrie latine: De la Méditerranée à l'Amérique*. Paris: La Nouvelle Édition, 1945.

Sagalen, Victor. *Essai sur l'exotisme: Une esthétique du divers*. Paris: Fata Morgana, 1978.

Sainlaude, Stève. *Le gouvernement impérial et la guerre de Sécession (1861–1965): L'action diplomatique.* Paris: l'Harmattan, 2011.

Salles, Arleen L. F., and Elizabeth Millán-Zaibert, eds. *The Role of History in Latin American Philosophy: Contemporary Perspectives.* New York: State University of New York Press, 2005.

Salles, Ricardo. *Nostalgia imperial.* 2nd ed. Rio de Janeiro: Ponteio, 2013.

Sánchez, George I. *Forgotten People: A Study of New Mexicans.* Albuquerque: University of New Mexico Press, 1940.

Sánchez, Luis Alberto. *¿Existe América Latina?* Mexico City: Fondo de Cultura Económica, 1945.

Sanders, James E. *The Vanguard of the Atlantic World: Creating Modernity, Nation, and Democracy in Nineteenth-Century Latin America.* Durham, NC: Duke University Press, 2014.

Santiago, Silviano. *As raízes e o labirinto da América Latina.* Rio de Janeiro: Rocco, 2006.

Santos, Luís Cláudio Viliafañe G. *O Brasil entre a América e a Europa: O Império e o interamericanismo, do Congress do Panamá à Conferência de Washington.* São Paulo: Editora Unesp, 2004.

———. *O império e as repúblicas do Pacífico: As relações do Brasil com Chile, Bolívia, Peru, Equador e Colômbia.* Curitiba: Editora UFPR, 2002.

Sardinha, António. *A questão ibérica.* Lisbon: Almeida, Miranda & Sousa, 1916.

Sheffer, Jolie A. *The Romance of Race: Incest, Miscegenation, and Multiculturalism in the United States, 1880–1930.* New Brunswick, NJ: Rutgers University Press, 2012.

Sibley, Henry Hopkins. *The Civil War in West Texas and New Mexico.* El Paso: Texas Western Press, 2001.

Speranza, Graciela. *Atlas portátil de América Latina.* Barcelona: Anagrama, 2012.

Stavans, Ilan, ed. *The Norton Anthology of Latino Literature.* New York: W. W. Norton, 2011.

Streckert, Jens. *Die Hauptstadt Lateinamerikas: Eine Geschichte der Lateinamerikaner im Paris der Dritten Republik (1870–1940).* Cologne: Böhlau Verlag, 2013.

Subrahmanyam, Sanjay. *Aux origines de l'histoire globale.* Leçons Inaugurals du Collège de France, Paris: Collège de France, Fayard, 2015.

———. "Historicizing the Global, or Laboring for Invention." *History Workshop Journal* 64, no. 1 (2007): 329–34.

Thompson, Jerry. *Civil War in the Southwest: Recollections of the Sibley Brigade.* College Station: Texas A&M University Press, 2001.

Torchia Estrada, Juan Carlos. "'América Latina': Origen de un nombre y una idea." *Inter-American Review of Bibliography* 32, no. 1 (1982): 47–53.

Torres Caicedo, José María. *Unión latino-americana pensamiento de Bolívar para formar una liga americana. Su origen y sus desarrollos y estudio sobre la gran cuestión que tanto interesa a lo estados débiles, a saber, ¿un gobierno legitimo es responsable por los daños y perjuicios ocasionados a los extranjeros por las facciones?* Paris: Librería de Rosa y Bouret, 1865.

Ucelay-Da Cal, Enric. *El imperialismo catalán.* Barcelona: Edhasa, 2003.

Ugarte, Manuel. *El porvenir de la América latina; la raza—la integridad territorial y moral; la organización interior.* Valencia: F. Sempere, 1911.

Valero Pie, Aurelia. *José Gaos en México: Una biografía intelectual, 1938–1969.* Mexico City: El Colegio de México, 2015.

Vallerange, Prosper. *Le panlatinisme, confédération Gallo-Latine et Celto-Gauloise contre-testament de Pierre le Grand et contre-Panslavisme ou . . . .* Paris: Passard, Libraire-Éditeur, 1860.

Varela, Javier. *La novela de España.* Madrid: Taurus, 1999.

Várvaro, Alberto. *Storia, problemi e metodi della linguistica romanza*. Naples: Liguari, 1968.

Vasconcelos, José. *Indología: Una interpretación de la cultura ibero-americana*. Barcelona: Agencia Mundial de Librería, 1927.

———. *La raza cósmica: Misión de la raza iberoamericana. Notas de viajes a la América de Sur*. Paris: Agencia Mundial de Librería, 1925.

Vaz Ferreira, Carlos. *Fermentario*. Montivedeo: Cámara de Representantes de la República Oriental del Uruguay, 1957.

Ventura, Roberto. *Estilo tropical*. São Paulo: Companhia das Letras, 1991.

Villoro, Juan. *Efectos personales*. Mexico City: Era, 2000.

Villoro, Luis. *Los grandes momentos del indigenismo en México*. Mexico City: El Colegio de México, 1996.

Volpi, Jorge. *El insomnio de Bolívar*. Barcelona: Random House Mondadori, 2009.

Vrbata, Aleš. "Between Latinité and Aliança Peninsular: Mediterranean Thought in Search of Renewal." *Studia Historica Nitriensia* 17, no. 1 (2013): 93–111.

Walch, Jean. *Michel Chevalier, économiste saint-simonien, 1806–1879*. Paris: J. Vrin, 1975.

Wallen, Henry Davies. *New Mexico Territory during the Civil War*. Albuquerque: University of New Mexico Press, 2008.

Werneck Vianna, Luiz. *A revolução passive: Iberismo e americanismo no Brasil*. Rio de Janeiro: Editora Revan, 1997.

Wink, Georg. *Die Idee von Brasilien: Eine kulturwissenschaftliche Untersuchung der Erzählung Brasiliens als vorgestellte Gemeinschaft im Kontrast zu Hispanoamerika*. Frankfurt: Peter Lang, 2009.

Wolff, Larry. *Inventing Eastern Europe: The Map of Civilization on the Mind of the Enlightenment*. Stanford, CA: Stanford University Press, 1994.

Wong, Aliza S. *Race and the Nation in Liberal Italy, 1861–1911: Meridionalism, Empire, and Diaspora*. New York: Palgrave, 2006.

Zambrano, María. *Hacia un saber sobre el alma*. Madrid: Alianza, 1987.

Zea, Leopoldo. *América como conciencia*. Mexico City: Fondo de Cultura Económica, Universidad Nacional Autónoma de México, Centro de Estudios Filosóficos, 1957.

———. *Filosofía de la historia americana*. Mexico City: Fondo de Cultura Económica, 1978.

———, ed. *Fuentes de la cultura latinoamericana*. 2 vols. Mexico City: Fondo de Cultura Económica, 1993.

INDEX